D0138869

# Teaching Language Arts to English Language Learners

Today's language arts classrooms increasingly include students for whom English is a second language. *Teaching Language Arts to English Language Learners* provides readers with the comprehensive understanding of both the challenges that face ELLs and the ways in which educators might address them in the language arts classroom. The authors offer proven techniques that teachers can readily use to teach reading, writing, grammar, and vocabulary, as well as speaking, listening, and viewing skills. A complete section is also devoted to ways that teachers can integrate all five strands of the language arts curriculum into a comprehensive unit of study with meaningful accommodations for ELLs. An annotated list of web and print resources completes the volume, making this a valuable reference for language arts teachers to meet the challenges of including all learners in effective instruction.

Special features:

- Over a dozen learning activities for each of the main areas of the language arts curriculum
- Engaging vignettes vividly illustrate real-life interactions of teachers and ELLs in the classroom
- Graphs, tables, and illustrations provide additional access points to the text in clear, meaningful ways

**Anete Vásquez** is an Instructor of English Education in the Department of Secondary Education at the University of South Florida.

**Angela L. Hansen** is Assistant Professor of English Education at Northern Arizona University.

**Philip C. Smith** is the Foreign Language/ESOL Education program coordinator in the College of Education at the University of South Florida.

**Teaching English Language Learners Across the Curriculum**
Series Editors: Tony Erben, Bárbara C. Cruz, Stephen J. Thornton

**Teaching Mathematics to English Language Learners**
*Gladis Kersaint, Denisse R. Thompson, Mariana Petkova*

**Teaching English Language Learners in Career and Technical Education Programs**
*Victor M. Hernández-Gantes and William Blank*

**Teaching English Language Learners through Technology**
*Tony Erben, Ruth Ban, Martha Castañeda*

**Teaching Social Studies to English Language Learners**
*Bárbara C. Cruz and Stephen J. Thornton*

**Teaching Language Arts to English Language Learners**
*Anete Vásquez, Angela L. Hansen, Philip C. Smith*

# Teaching Language Arts to English Language Learners

Nyack College - Bailey Library
One South Blvd.
Nyack, NY 10960

ANETE VÁSQUEZ

ANGELA L. HANSEN

PHILIP C. SMITH

428.24
V44

Nyack College Library

Routledge
Taylor & Francis Group

NEW YORK AND LONDON

First published 2010
by Routledge
270 Madison Avenue, New York, NY 10016

Simultaneously published in the UK
by Routledge
2 Park Square, Milton Park, Abingdon, Oxon OX14 4RN

*Routledge is an imprint of the Taylor & Francis Group, an informa business*

© 2010 Taylor & Francis

Typeset in MinionPro and Helvetica Neue by Prepress Projects Ltd, Perth, UK
Printed and bound in the United States of America on acid-free paper by Edwards
Brothers, Inc.

All rights reserved. No part of this book may be reprinted or reproduced or utilised
in any form or by any electronic, mechanical, or other means, now known or here-
after invented, including photocopying and recording, or in any information storage
or retrieval system, without permission in writing from the publishers.

**Trademark Notice**: Product or corporate names may be trademarks or registered
trademarks, and are used only for identification and explanation without intent to
infringe.

*Library of Congress Cataloging in Publication Data*
Vásquez, Anete.
Teaching language arts to English language learners / Anete Vásquez, Angela L.
Hansen, Philip C. Smith.
p. cm.—(Teaching English language learners across the curriculum)
Includes bibliographical references and index.
1. English language—Study and teaching—United States—Foreign speakers. 2.
Language arts—Study and teaching—United States. 3. Second language acquisi-
tion—United States. I. Hansen, Angela L. II. Smith, Philip C. III. Title.
PE1128.A2V38 2010
428.2′4—dc22
2009050809

ISBN10: 0-415-99531-0 (hbk)
ISBN10: 0-415-99532-9 (pbk)
ISBN10: 0-203-85648-1 (ebk)

ISBN13: 978-0-415-99531-3 (hbk)
ISBN13: 978-0-415-99532-0 (pbk)
ISBN13: 978-0-203-85648-2 (ebk)

#298781451

We dedicate this book to our families and to our students; without them, this book could not have been written.

# Contents

# Figures

# Tables

# Series Introduction

No educational issue has proven more controversial than how to teach linguistically diverse students. Intertwined issues of ethnic and cultural differences are often compounded. What is more, at the time of writing, December 2007, how immigrants and their heritages *ought* to fit with the dominant culture is the subject of rancorous debate in the United States and a number of other nations.

However thorny these issues may be to some, both legally and ethically, schools need to accommodate the millions of English language learners (ELLs) who need to be educated. Although the number of ELLs in the United States has burgeoned in recent decades, school programs generally remain organized via traditional subjects, which are delivered in English. Many ELLs are insufficiently fluent in academic English, however, to succeed in these programs. Since policymakers have increasingly insisted that ELLs, regardless of their fluency in English, be mainstreamed into standard courses with all other students, both classroom enactment of the curriculum and teacher education need considerable rethinking.

Language scholars have generally taken the lead in this rethinking. As is evident in Part 1 of the volumes in this series, language scholars have developed a substantial body of research to inform the mainstreaming of ELLs. The primary interest of these language scholars, however, is almost by definition the processes and principles of second language acquisition. Until recently, subject matter has typically been a secondary consideration, used to illustrate language concerns. Perhaps not surprisingly, content-area teachers sometimes have seen this as reducing their subjects to little more than isolated bits of information, such as a list of explorers and dates in history or sundry geological formations in science.

In contrast, secondary school teachers see their charge as effectively conveying a principled understanding of, and interest in, a subject. They look for relationships, seek to develop concepts, search for powerful examples and analogies, and try to explicate principles. By the same token, they strive to make meaningful connections among the subject matter, students' experience, and life outside of school. In our observations, teacher education programs bifurcate courses on content-area methods and (if there are any) courses designed to instill principles of teaching ELLs. One result of this bifurcation seems to be that prospective and in-service teachers are daunted by the challenge of using language principles to inform their teaching of subject matter.

For example, Gloria Ladson-Billings (2001) has experimented with how to prepare new teachers for diverse classrooms through a teacher education program focused on "diversity, equity, and social justice" (p. xiii). Teachers in her program are expected, for instance, to confront rather than become resigned to low academic expectations for children in urban schools. From Ladson-Billings's perspective, "no matter what else the schools find themselves doing, promoting students' academic achievement is among their primary functions" (p. 56).

The authors in this series extend this perspective to teaching ELLs in the content areas. For example, how might ELLs be included in a literature lesson on Hardy's use of landscape imagery in *The Mayor of Casterbridge*, or an economics lesson on the principle of comparative advantage, or a biology lesson on the ecosystem of a pond? Such topics, experienced educators quickly recognize, are often difficult for native speakers of English. How can teachers break down these subjects into topics in a way that is educationally significant for ELLs?

The purpose of this series is to assist current and prospective educators to plan and implement lessons that do justice to the goals of the curriculum and make sense to and interest ELLs. If the needs of diverse learners are to be met, Ladson-Billings (2001) underscores that innovation is demanded, not that teachers merely pine for how things once were. The most obvious innovation in this series is to bring language scholars and specialists in the methods of teaching particular school subjects together. Although this approach is scarcely unique, it remains relatively uncommon. Combining the two groups brings more to addressing the problems of instruction than could be obtained by the two groups working separately. Even so, these volumes hardly tell the reader "everything there is to know" about the problems addressed. But we do know that our teacher education students report that even modest training to teach ELLs can make a significant difference in the classroom. We hope this series extends those successes to all the content areas of the curriculum.

# Acknowledgements

The authors would like to acknowledge the efforts and contributions of the following individuals who helped bring this project to fruition:

Kris Harris, Dr. Allen Woodman, and Beverly Cleland, who provided help and support.

Asja Vásquez, Bryan Williams, and the Critical Friends Writing Group of Kathryn Boney, Dr. Patricia Daniel, Christi Edge and Dr. Cheryl Ellerbrock, who assisted with revisions.

Dr. Joan Kaywell, who shared young adolescent literature compliments to the classics, and Dr. Jean Boreen, who shared the Author's Pomise Activity.

Marinés Uscategui, who allowed us to adapt her writing activity.

Elizabeth Visedo, who contributed using humor in language arts.

Dr. Stephen Thornton and Dr. Bárbara Cruz, who gave us the opportunity to write this book.

# Introduction

I first met Andre Ferreira, a quiet 14-year-old eighth grader, on the first day of the new school year when he was placed in my third period language arts class. His father was a teacher and his mother was a nurse. He had moved to the United States from a city in Brazil's northeast coastal area six months earlier with his parents, an older sister, and two younger brothers. His father had come to the United States to complete graduate studies.

Andre came from a learning environment where books and magazines in both English and Portuguese were available in abundance. Andre had also studied English for several years in his home country of Brazil prior to his arrival. His family spoke Portuguese at home, but he appeared to be very fluent in English. Andre loved sports, and all he could talk about was soccer, but he wasn't able to play much since our school did not have a soccer team. At school he kept mostly to himself and would go home to play soccer with his younger brothers at the end of the day.

Whenever I spoke to him outside of class, he always responded quite easily; in class it was a different story. I had the impression that he was not focused on class; he never finished his work, and what he did complete seemed sloppy. On several occasions, I told him to pay more attention and try harder, but most of the time I did not really notice him because he was so well behaved.

Things started to change when the first report card was issued. Andre got a D– in Language Arts, and I got a visit from Andre's father, who was quite surprised with his son's low grade. He told me his son had always done well in school. He asked to see his son's work. When I showed him what appeared to me to be careless work, his father saw something else. He saw someone who fully understood neither the questions being asked nor what answers were expected of him in homework assignments.

As a teacher who had never had any English as a second language (ESL) training, I didn't understand that there were two kinds of language, conversational (basic interpersonal communication skills, or BICS) and academic (cognitive/academic language proficiency, or CALP). Andre was perfectly functional in conversational English but not in academic English.

After that day, I started on a quest to learn ways I could help Andre develop his academic English ability. I started to simplify instructions, raise the contextual support when teaching, provide examples of what was expected and use a lot more modeling. I also started to consciously find and take advantage of the language-teaching opportunities present in every lesson. At the same time, I began to notice how many students like Andre were being overlooked. I also realized that there were a lot of students in the school that were interested in soccer, so I began to provide after-school academic help, and formed a club for soccer players that included both native and non-native speakers. The combination of the after-school tutoring and the bonds formed on the soccer field among players boosted language fluency for English language learners (ELLs). The Andres in our school are no longer invisible to me.

There has been a significant increase in the percentage of teachers who encounter students like Andre in their mainstream classrooms. In 1991–1992, only 15 percent of teachers instructed ELLs; in 2001–2002, this percentage rose to 42.6 percent (August & Shanahan, 2006). The population of immigrant children is the fastest-growing student population (Kindler, 2002) and federal mandates have been moving ELLs out of ESL classrooms and into mainstream classrooms (Rance-Roney, 2008).

Research indicates that it takes ELLs five to seven years to develop CALP (Cummins, 2000), yet, at the time of this writing in 2009, No Child Left Behind (NCLB) mandates that ELLs who have been enrolled in school in the United States for more than one year must meet the same grade level expectations as native English speakers in order to graduate from high school. According to the 2005 National Assessment of Education Progress (NAEP), 74 percent of non-ELL twelfth-grade students score at or above the basic reading level, but only 31 percent of ELLs score at or above the basic reading level (NAEP, 2005). Data from the 2007 NAEP indicate that this gap exists at the middle school level as well, where ELL eighth graders scored 42 points below non-ELLs in reading (Lee, Grigg, & Donahue, 2007).

School districts place a heavy burden on English language arts (ELA) teachers to bring ELL students to the proficient level yet our conversations with many ELA teachers indicate that they feel underprepared to work with ELLs. The goal of this book is to provide ELA teachers with background knowledge about ELL students, summaries of research-based best practices and examples of teaching activities that will work in a mainstream ELA classroom to boost the language proficiency of ELL students and integrate them into the social milieu of the classroom.

## Who Can Benefit from this Book?

Although there are many excellent generic ELL books, they are often more appropriate for English teachers of other languages (ESOL) than for secondary ELA teachers who have ELLs in their classrooms. This book focuses on the instructional issues inherent to ELA and is specifically useful for:

- *Pre-service ELA teachers* who want to become better prepared to meet the challenges of their future classrooms.
- *Practicing ELA teachers* who would like a "refresher" or perhaps never received ELL training in their teacher preparation program.
- *ESOL aides and support staff* who would like to learn more about issues, strategies, and content related to ELA education.
- *English language arts teacher educators* who would like to address ELL instruction in their methods courses.
- *ESOL teacher educators* who would like to infuse their methods courses with content-specific information and strategies.
- *District curriculum supervisors* who are responsible for curriculum development, modification, and teacher training.
- *Administrators* such as school principals and assistant principals who would like to improve the quality of instruction for ELLs in their schools and offer support for teachers.

## How to Use this Book

The central purpose of this book is to provide ELA teachers with practical, teacher-friendly methods that should be effective not only with ELLs, but with all students. The book is intended for grades 6–12 (middle and high school).

Part I of this book, by the language scholar Tony Erben, presents an overview of theory and research on ESOL teaching and learning. Part I reviews research with an eye to providing guidance for the design and teaching of school programs. It is written for a general audience—that is, not for ELA teachers in particular—although much of what is said will echo throughout the ELA-specific parts of this book.

Prior to discussing the creation or modification of learning activities to suit the needs of ELLs, it is important to outline the main principles that guide our recommendations for instruction and the underlying beliefs upon which we center the activities. Part II summarizes the limited research base of ELA-focused ESOL research and creates a transition between the general information of Part I and the ELA activities of Part III.

Part III contains sections with learning activities in the main areas of the ELA curriculum. Sections 2 and 3 concentrate on reading instruction. Section 2 introduces before-, during- and after-reading strategies that are effective in supporting ELLs literacy development, and Section 3 offers suggestions for teaching the district-mandated literature curriculum to ELLs, a task that ELA teachers tell us they find the most daunting. Sections 4–8 focus on other common aspects of the ELA curriculum: writing, grammar, vocabulary, speaking, listening, and viewing. Although we separate the various facets of ELA instruction as if they are discrete entities, we know that, in practice, the classroom is a much more complex realm; in literacy learning, these aspects of instruction are and should be interrelated and interdependent. One of the challenges of teaching is the seamless integration of all of these parts into one whole. We offer recommendations for how to do this whenever appropriate throughout the sections and provide specific suggestions in

Section 9 about developing a unit of study for a complete work that honors the goal of promoting ELLs literacy skills. Section 9 also models how to adapt the activities in the previous sections to the teaching of other works.

The three sections in Resources provide direction to print and internet resources for teachers and for teachers to recommend to their ELL students. We include the Resources sections because we know that our book cannot possibly answer all of your questions about teaching your particular curriculum to ELL students. But, if you are reading this book, we know that you, like us, are seeking better ways to include ELLs as legitimate and authentic participants in constructing classroom knowledge and to help ELLs develop academic language proficiency while at the same time fostering their love of language, literature, and learning. It is our hope that this book will facilitate your quest and enable you to capitalize on the language and cultural diversity in your classroom to enrich the learning of all students.

# Part 1
# Your English Language Learner

**Tony Erben**
**University of Tampa**

# 1.1
# Orientation

English language learners (ELLs) represent the fastest growing group throughout all levels of schooling in the United States. For example, between the 1990–1991 school year and the 2000–2001 school year, the ELL population grew approximately 105 percent nationally, while the general school population grew only 12 percent (Kindler, 2002). In several states (including Texas, California, New Mexico, Florida, Arizona, North Carolina, and New York), the percentage of ELLs within school districts ranges anywhere between 10 and 50 percent of the school population. In sum, there are over 10 million ELLs in U.S. schools today. According to the U.S. Department of Education, one out of seven students in our nation's classrooms speaks a language other than English at home. Although many of these students are heritage language learners and are proficient in English, many others are recent immigrants with barely a working knowledge of the language let alone a command of academic English. Meeting the needs of such students can be particularly challenging for all teachers given the often text-dependent nature of content areas. The language of the curriculum is often abstract and includes complex concepts calling for higher-order thinking skills. Additionally, many ELLs do not have a working knowledge of American culture that can serve as a schema for new learning.

But let's now look at these English language learners. Who are they and how do they come to be in our classrooms?

ELL is the term used for any student in an American school setting whose native language is not English. Their English ability lies anywhere on a continuum from knowing only a few words to being able to get by using everyday English, but still in need of acquiring more English so that they can succeed educationally at school. All students enrolled in an American school, including ELLs, have the right to an equitable and quality education. Traditionally, many ELLs are placed in stand-alone English to speakers of other languages (ESOL) classes and learn English until they are deemed capable of following the regular curriculum in English. However, with the introduction of federal and state legislation such as *No Child Left Behind* (2002), Proposition 227 in California, and other English-only legislation in other states, many school systems now require ELLs to receive their English instruction not through stand-alone ESOL classes, but directly through their curriculum content classes.[1] Today "mainstreaming" is the most frequently used method of language instruction for ELL students in U.S. schools. Mainstreaming involves placing ELLs in content-area classrooms where the curriculum is delivered through English; curricula and instruction are typically not modified in these classrooms for non-native English speakers (Carrasquillo & Rodriguez, 2002). According to Meltzer and Hamann (2005), placement of ELLs in mainstream classes occurs for a number of reasons including assumptions by non-educators about what ELLs need, the scarcity of ESOL-trained teachers relative to demand, the growth of ELL populations, the dispersal of ELLs into more districts across the country, and restrictions in a growing number of states regarding the time ELLs can stay in ESOL programs. They predict that, unless these conditions change, ELLs will spend their time in school (1) with teachers not adequately trained to work with ELLs, (2) with teachers who do not see it as a priority to meet the needs of their ELLs, and (3) with curricula and classroom practices that are not designed to target ELL needs (Coady et al., 2003). As we shall later see, of all possible instructional options to help ELLs learn English, placing an ELL in a mainstreamed English-medium classroom where no accommodations are made by the teacher is the least effective approach. It may even be detrimental to the educational progress of ELLs.

This then raises the question of whether or not the thousands of curriculum content teachers across the United States, who now have the collective lion's share of responsibility in providing English language instruction to ELLs, have had preservice or in-service education to modify, adapt, and make the appropriate pedagogical accommodations within their lessons for this special group of students. This is important: ELLs should remain included in the cycle of everyday learning and make academic progress commensurate with grade-level expectations. It is also important that teachers feel competent and effective in their professional duties.

The aim of Part 1 of this book is to provide you the reader with an overview of the linguistic mechanics of second language development. Specifically, as teachers you will learn what to expect in the language abilities of ELLs as their proficiency in English develops over time. Although the rate of language development among ELLs depends on the particular instructional and social circumstances of each ELL, general patterns and expectations will be discussed. We will also outline for teachers the learning outcomes that ELLs typically accomplish in differing ESOL programs and the importance of the maintenance of first language development. School systems differ across the United States in the ways in which they try to deal with ELL populations. Therefore, we describe the pedagogical pros and cons of an array of ESOL programs as well as clarify terminology used in the field. Part 1 will also profile various ELL populations that enter U.S. schools (e.g. refugees vs. migrants, special needs) and share how teachers can make their pedagogy more culturally responsive. Finally, we will also survey what teachers can expect from the cultural practices that ELLs may engage in in the classroom as well as present a myriad of ways in which both school systems and teachers can better foster home–school communication links.

# 1.2
# The Process of English Language Learning and What to Expect

It is generally accepted that anybody who endeavors to learn a second language will go through specific stages of language development. According to some second language acquisition theorists (e.g. Pienemann, 2007), the way in which language is produced under natural time constraints is very regular and systematic. For example, just as a baby needs to learn how to crawl before it can walk, so too a second language learner will produce language structures only in a predetermined psychological order of complexity. What this means is that an ELL will utter "homework do" before being able to utter "tonight I homework do" before ultimately being able to produce a target-like structure such as "I will do my homework tonight." Of course, with regard to being communicatively effective, the first example is as successful as the last example. The main difference is that one is less English-like than the other. Pienemann's work has centered on one subsystem of language, namely morphosyntactic structures. It gives us an interesting glimpse into how an ELL's language may progress (see Table 1.1).

Researchers such as Pienemann (1989; 2007) and Krashen (1981) assert that there is an immutable language acquisition order and, regardless of what the teacher tries to teach to the ELL in terms of English skills, the learner will acquire new language structures only when (s)he is cognitively and psychologically ready to do so.

What can a teacher do if an ELL will only learn English in a set path? Much research has been conducted over the past 20 years on this very question and the upshot is that, although teachers cannot change the route of development for ELLs, they *can* very much affect the rate of development. The way in which teachers can stimulate the language development of ELLs is by providing what is known as an acquisition-rich classroom. Ellis (2005), among others, provides useful research generalizations that constitute a broad basis for "evidence-based practice." Rather

**TABLE 1.1.** Generalized patterns of ESOL development stages

| Stage | Main features | Example |
|-------|--------------|---------|
| 1 | Single words; formulas | My name is_____. How are you |
| 2 | Subject–Verb object word order; plural marking | I see school I buy books |
| 3 | "Do"-fronting; adverb preposing; negation + verb | Do you understand me? Yesterday I go to school. She no coming today. |
| 4 | Pseudo-inversion; yes/no inversion; verb + to + verb | Where is my purse? Have you a car? I want to go. |
| 5 | 3rd person –s; do-2nd position | He works in a factory. He did not understand. |
| 6 | Question-tag; adverb–verb phrase | He's Polish, isn't he? I can always go. |

*Source: Pienemann (1988).*

than repeat them verbatim here, we have synthesized them into *five principles for creating effective second language learning environments*. They are presented and summarized below.

## Principle 1: Give ELLs Many Opportunities to Read, to Write, to Listen to, and to Discuss Oral and Written English Texts Expressed in a Variety of Ways

> Camilla had only recently arrived at the school. She was a good student and was making steady progress. She had learned some English in Argentina and used every opportunity to learn new words at school. Just before Thanksgiving her science teacher commenced a new unit of work on the periodic table and elements. During the introductory lesson, the teacher projected a periodic table on the whiteboard. She began asking the students some probing questions about the table. One of her first questions was directed to Camilla. The teacher asked, "Camilla, tell me what you see on the right hand side of the table." Camilla answered, "I see books, Bunsen burner, also pencils."
>
> Of course the teacher was referring not to the table standing in front of the whiteboard, but to the table projected onto the whiteboard. Though a simple mistake, the example above is illustrative of the fact that Camilla has yet to develop academic literacy.

In 2001, Meltzer defined academic literacy as the ability of a person to "use reading, writing, speaking, listening and thinking to learn what they want/need to learn AND [to] communicate/demonstrate that learning to others who need/want to know" (p. 16). The definition is useful in that it rejects literacy as something static and implies agency on the part of a learner who develops an ability to successfully put her/his knowledge and skills to use in new situations. Being proficient in academic literacy requires knowledge of a type of language used predominantly in classrooms and tied very much to learning. However, even though it is extremely important for ELLs to master, not many content teachers take the time to provide explicit instruction in it. Moreover, many content teachers do not necessarily know the discipline-specific discourse features or text structures of their own subject areas.

Currently, there is much research to suggest that both the discussion of texts and the production of texts are important practices in the development of content-area literacy and learning. For ELLs this means that opportunities to create, discuss, share, revise, and edit a variety of texts will help them develop content-area understanding and also recognition and familiarity with the types of texts found in particular content areas (Boscolo & Mason, 2001). Classroom practices that are found to improve academic literacy development include teachers improving reading comprehension through modeling, explicit strategy instruction in context, spending more time giving reading and writing instruction as well as having students spend more time with reading and writing assignments, providing more time for ELLs to talk explicitly about texts as they are trying to process and/or create them, and helping to develop critical thinking skills as well as being responsive to individual learner needs (Meltzer & Hamann, 2005).

The importance of classroom talk in conjunction with learning from and creating texts cannot be underestimated in the development of academic literacy in ELLs. In the case above, rather than smiling at the error and moving on with the lesson, the teacher could have further developed Camilla's vocabulary knowledge by easily taking a two-minute digression from the lesson to brainstorm with the class all the ways the word *table* can be used at school—in math, social studies, language arts, etc.

## Principle 2: Draw Attention to Patterns of English Language Structure

In order to ride a bike well, a child needs to actually practice riding the bike. Sometimes, training wheels are fitted to the back of the bike to help the younger child maintain his/her balance. In time, the training wheels are taken away as the child gains more confidence. As this process unfolds, parents also teach kids the rules of the road: how to read road signs, to be attentive to cars, to ride defensively, etc. Although knowing the rules of the road won't help a child learn to ride the bike better in a physical sense, it will help the child avoid being involved in a road accident. Knowing the rules of the road—when and where to ride a bike, etc.—will make the child a more accomplished bike rider. Why use this example? Well, it is a good metaphor to explain that language learning needs to unfold in the same way. An ELL, without much formal schooling, will develop the means to communicate in English. However, it will most likely be only very basic English. Unfortunately, tens of thousands of adult ELLs across this country never progress past this stage. School-age ELLs have an opportunity to move beyond a basic command of English—to become accomplished communicators in English. However, this won't happen on its own. To do so requires the ELL to get actively involved in classroom activities, ones in which an ELL is required to practice speaking.

As mentioned above, early research into naturalistic second language acquisition has evidenced that learners follow a "natural" order and sequence of acquisition. What this means is that grammatical structures emerge in the communicative utterances of second language learners in a relatively fixed, regular, systematic, and universal order. The ways in which teachers can take advantage of this "built-in syllabus" are to implement an activity-centered approach that sets out to provide ELLs with language-rich instructional opportunities and offer ELLs explicit exposure and instruction related to language structures that they are trying to utter but with which they still have trouble.

## Principle 3: Give ELLs Classroom Time to Use their English Productively

A theoretical approach within the field of second language acquisition (SLA) called the interaction hypothesis and developed primarily by Long (1996; 2006) posits that acquisition is facilitated through interaction when second language learners are engaged in negotiating for meaning. What this means is that, when ELLs are engaged in talk, they make communication modifications that help language become more comprehensible, they more readily solicit corrective feedback, and they adjust their own use of English.

The discrepancy in the rate of acquisition shown by ELLs can be attributed to the amount and the quality of input they receive as well as the opportunities they have for output. Output means having opportunities to use language. Second language acquisition researchers agree that the opportunity for output plays an important part in facilitating second language development. Skehan (1998) drawing on Swain (1995) summarizes the contributions that output can make: (1) by using language with others, ELLs will obtain a richer language contribution from those around them, (2) ELLs will be forced to pay attention to the structure of language they listen to, (3) ELLs will be able to test out their language assumptions and confirm them through the types of language input they receive, (4) ELLs can better internalize their current language knowledge, (5) by engaging in interaction, ELLs can work towards better discourse fluency, and (6) ELLs will be able to find space to develop their own linguistic style and voice.

It behooves teachers to plan for and incorporate ELLs in all language activities in the classroom. Of course an ELL will engage with an activity based on the level of proficiency (s)he has at any given time and the teacher should take this into account when planning for instruction. Under no circumstances should ELLs be left at the "back of the classroom" to linguistically or pedagogically fend for themselves.

## Principle 4: Give ELLs Opportunities to Notice their Errors and to Correct their English

Throughout the day, teachers prepare activities for students that have the sole intent of getting them to learn subject matter. Less often do teachers think about the language learning potential that the same activity may generate. This can be applied to ELLs: Teachers encourage them to notice their errors, to reflect on how they use English, and to think about how English works, which plays a very important role in their language development. In a series of seminal studies, Lyster and his colleagues (Lyster, 1998; 2001; 2004; 2007; Lyster & Ranta, 1997; Lyster & Mori, 2006) outline six feedback moves that teachers can use to direct ELLs' attention to their language output and in doing so help them correct their English.

### Example 1

*Student:* "The heart hits blood to se body. . ."
*Teacher:* "The heart pumps blood to the body."

In the above example, an ELL's utterance is incorrect, and the teacher provides the correct form. Often teachers gloss over explicitly correcting an ELL's language for fear of singling out the student in class. However, *explicit correction* is a very easy way to help ELLs notice the way they use language.

## Example 2

*Student:* "I can experimenting with Bunsen burner."
*Teacher:* "What? Can you say that again?"

By using phrases such as "Excuse me?", "I don't understand," or "Can you repeat that?", the teacher shows that the communication has not been understood or that the ELL's utterance contained some kind of error. *Requesting clarification* indicates to the ELL that a repetition or reformulation of the utterance is required.

## Example 3

*Student:* "After today I go to sport."
*Teacher:* "So, tomorrow you are going to play sports?"
*Student:* "Yes, tomorrow I am going to play sport."

Without directly showing that the student's utterance was incorrect, the teacher implicitly *recasts* the ELL's error, or provides the correction.

## Example 4

*Teacher:* "Is that how it is said?" or "Is that English?" or "Does that sound right to you?"

*Without* providing the correct form, the teacher provides a *metalinguistic clue*. This may take the form of asking a question or making a comment related to the formation of the ELL's utterance.

## Example 5

*Teacher:* "So, then it will be a . . ." (with long stress on "a")

The teacher directly gets the correct form from the ELL by pausing to allow the student to complete the teacher's utterance. *Elicitation* questions differ from questions that are defined as metalinguistic clues in that they require more than a yes/no response.

## Example 6

*Student:* "The two boy go to town tomorrow."
*Teacher:* "The two boys go to town tomorrow." (with teacher making a prolonged stress on "boy"

*Repetitions* are probably one of the most frequent forms of error correction carried out by teachers. Here a teacher repeats the ELL's error and adjusts intonation to draw an ELL's attention to it.

Using these corrective feedback strategies helps to raise an ELL's awareness and understanding of language conventions used in and across content areas.

## Principle 5: Construct Activities that Maximize Opportunities for ELLs to Interact with Others in English

One day, when we had visitors from up north, our daughter came home very excited and said that the teacher had announced that the class would be learning Spanish from the beginning of the month. Our friend, ever the pessimist, said, "I learned Spanish for four years at high school, and look at me now, I can't even string a sentence together in Spanish." What comes to mind is the old saying, "use it or lose it." Of course, my friend and I remember our foreign language learning days being spent listening to the teacher, usually in English. We were lucky if we even got the chance to say anything in Spanish. Since we never used Spanish in class, our hopes of retaining any Spanish diminished with each passing year since graduation. My daughter's 20-year-old brother, on the other hand, had the same Spanish teacher that my daughter will have. He remembers a lot of his Spanish, but also that his Spanish classes were very engaging. A lesson would never pass in which he didn't speak, listen to, read, and write in Spanish. He was always involved in some learning activity and he always expressed how great it was to converse during the class with his friends in Spanish by way of the activities that the teacher had planned.

I use this analogy as it applies to ELLs as well. In order for ELLs to progress with their English language development, a teacher needs to vary the types of instructional tasks that the ELL will engage in. Student involvement during instruction is the key to academic success whereas constant passive learning, mostly through lecture-driven lessons, will greatly impede any language learning efforts by an ELL.

Our five principles provide a framework with which to construct a curriculum that is sensitive to the language developmental needs of ELLs. However, to further solidify our understanding of an ELL's language progress, it is necessary to have a clear picture of what ELLs can do with their language at different levels of proficiency and what implications this has for instruction. Although many taxonomies exist that seek to categorize the developmental stages of second language learners, many education systems throughout the United States have adopted a four-tier description.

The four stages are called Preproduction, Early Production, Speech Emergence, and Intermediate Fluency (Krashen & Terrell, 1983).

The **preproduction stage** applies to ELLs who are unfamiliar with English. They may have had anything from one day to three months of exposure to English. ELLs at this level are trying to absorb the language, and they can find this process overwhelming. In a school context, they are often linguistically overloaded, and get tired quickly because of the need for constant and intense concentration. An ELL's language skills are at the receptive level, and they enter a "silent period" of listening. ELLs at this stage are able to comprehend more English than they can produce. Their attention is focused on developing everyday social English. At the preproduction stage, an ELL can engage in nonverbal responses; follow simple commands; point and respond with movement; and utter simple formulaic structures in English such as "yes," "no," "thank you," or use names. ELLs may develop a receptive vocabulary of up to 500 words.

By the time an ELL enters the **early production stage**, (s)he will have had many opportunities to encounter meaningful and comprehensible English. They will begin to respond with one- or two-word answers or short utterances. ELLs may now have internalized up to 1,000 words in their receptive vocabulary and anything from 100 to 500 words in their active vocabulary. In order for ELLs to begin to speak, teachers should create a low-anxiety environment in their classrooms.

At this stage, ELLs are experimenting and taking risks with English. Errors in grammar and pronunciation are to be expected. Pragmatic errors are also common. Teachers need to model/demonstrate with correct language responses in context. Redundancies, repetitions, circumlocutions, and language enhancement strategies are important for teachers to use when interacting with ELLs at this level.

At the **speech emergence stage**, an ELL will begin to use the language to interact more freely. At this stage, ELLs have a 7,000-word receptive vocabulary. They may have an active vocabulary of up to 2,000 words. By this time, ELLs may have had between one and three years' exposure to English. It is possible that they have a receptive understanding of academic English; however, in order to make content-area subject matter comprehensible, teachers are advised to make great use of advance organizers. Teachers should make explicit attempts to modify the delivery of subject matter, to model language use, and to teach metacognitive strategies in order to help ELLs predict, describe, demonstrate, and problem solve. Because awareness of English is growing, it is also important for teachers to provide ELLs at this stage with opportunities to work in structured small groups so that they can reflect and experiment with their language output.

At the stage of **intermediate fluency**, ELLs may demonstrate near-native or native-like fluency in everyday social English, but not in academic English. Often teachers become acutely aware that, even though an ELL can speak English fluently in social settings (the playground, at sport functions, etc.), they will experience difficulties in understanding and verbalizing cognitively demanding, abstract concepts taught and discussed in the classroom. At this stage ELLs may have developed up to a 12,000-word receptive vocabulary and a 4,000-word active vocabulary. Teachers of ELLs at the intermediate fluency level need to proactively provide relevant content-based literacy experiences such as brainstorming, clustering, synthesizing, categorizing, charting, evaluating, journaling, or log writing, including essay writing and peer critiquing, in order to foster academic proficiency in English.

At the University of South Florida, we have developed online ELL databases that have been created to provide pre- and in-service teachers with annotated audio and video samples of language use by ELLs who are at each of the four different levels of language proficiency. The video and audio files act as instructional tools that allow teachers to familiarize themselves with the language ability (speaking, reading, writing) of ELLs who are at different stages of development. For example, teachers may have ELLs in classes and not be sure of their level of English language development, nor be sure what to expect the ELL to be able to do with English in terms of production and comprehension. This naturally impacts how a teacher may plan for instruction. By looking through the databases, a teacher can listen to and watch representations of ELL language production abilities at all four levels (preproduction, early production, speech emergence, and intermediate fluency). In addition, the databases feature interviews with expert ESOL teachers, examples of tests used to evaluate the proficiency levels of ELLs, and selected readings and lesson plans written for ELLs at different levels of proficiency. Lastly, they provide case studies that troubleshoot pedagogical problem areas when teaching ELLs.

There are three databases: one that features ELLs at the elementary school level, one featuring ELLs at the middle school level, and one featuring ELLs at high school.

The three ELL databases can be found at:

- http://esol.coedu.usf.edu/elementary/index.htm (elementary school language samples);
- http://esol.coedu.usf.edu/middleschool/index.htm (middle school language samples);
- http://esol.coedu.usf.edu/highschool/index.htm (high school language samples).

It is important to remember that a lack of language ability does not mean a lack of concept development or a lack of ability to learn. Teachers should continue to ask inferential and higher-order questions (questions requiring reasoning ability, hypothesizing, inferring, analyzing, justifying, and predicting) that challenge an ELL to think.

---

**Teaching Help**

For two good websites that outline ways to enhance questioning using Bloom's taxonomy see www.teachers.ash.org.au/researchskills/dalton.htm (Dalton & Smith, 1986) and www.nwlink.com/~donclark/hrd/bloom.html (Clark, 1999). The latter gives a further detailed breakdown of Bloom's Learning Domains in terms of cognitive, affective, and psychomotor key words and how these can be used to foster an ELL's language learning.

---

Zehler (1994) provides a list of further strategies that teachers can use to engage ELLs at every stage. These include:

- asking questions that require new or extended responses;
- creating opportunities for sustained dialogue and substantive language use;
- providing opportunities for language use in multiple settings;
- restating complex sentences as a sequence of simple sentences;
- avoiding or explaining use of idiomatic expressions;
- restating at a slower rate when needed, but making sure that the pace is not so slow that normal intonation and stress patterns become distorted;
- pausing often to allow students to process what they hear;
- providing specific explanations of key words and special or technical vocabulary, using examples and non-linguistic props when possible;
- using everyday language;
- providing explanations for the indirect use of language (for example, an ELL student may understand the statement, "I like the way Mary is sitting" merely as a simple statement rather than as a reference to an example of good behavior).

# 1.3
# Deciding on the Best ESOL Program

This section outlines the learning outcomes that ELLs typically accomplish in differing ESOL programs and the importance of the maintenance of first language development. Although school systems differ across America in the ways in which they try to deal with ELL populations, this section describes the pedagogical pros and cons of an array of ESOL programs and clarifies terminology used in the field.

There are several factors that influence the design of an effective ELL program. These include considerations regarding the nature of the ELL student demographics to be served, district resources, and individual student characteristics. The MLA Language Map at www.mla.org/map_main provides an interactive look into the distribution of languages spoken in the United States. The online maps are able to show numbers as well as percentages by state, district, and zip code. Over 30 languages may be geographically represented and compared. The MLA Language Map shows graphically that not all districts are the same. ELL populations differ across the country. Some areas may have an overwhelming majority of Spanish speaking ELLs whereas other districts may have an equally large numbers of ELL students but speaking 50–100 different languages. On the other hand, some districts may have very few ELLs while other districts experience an influx of ELLs of whose language and culture the area's schools have little knowledge (for example, Hmong in Marathon County in Wisconsin, Haitian Creole in Palm Beach, Broward, and Dade counties in Florida, and Somali/Ethiopian in Hennepin and Ramsey counties in Minnesota). Cultural and linguistic differences, as well as factors such as size, age, and mobility of community members, very much influence the types of ESOL instructional programs that school districts choose to develop. Refer to *English Language Learner Programs at the Secondary Level in Relation to Student Performance* (www.nwrel.org/re-eng/products/ELLSynthesis.pdf) for a wonderful research-based yet easy-to-read outline of how the implementation of different ELL programs in schools affects the language learning gains of ELLs.

As mentioned above, not all ELLs are the same. ELLs may enter a school with vastly different educational backgrounds. Some enter U.S. schools with a strong foundational knowledge in their first language. This means that they may have had schooling in their first language, have literacy skills in their first language, and/or have developed social everyday language competency as well as academic proficiency in their first language. Other ELLs may have had less or even no academic schooling in their first language. Many ELLs, especially refugees, may have attended school in their homeland only for it to have been interrupted by famine or war, or for other socioeconomic or political reasons. Some ELLs arrive in the United States with their families at a very young age and, although they speak their first language at home, they may have never developed reading or writing proficiency in it. As will be discussed in the next chapter, it is of great importance to uncover the nature of an ELL's first language development since this has a profound bearing on how an ELL manages to acquire English.

A third factor, according to the Center for Applied Linguistics (CAL, 1987, at www.cal.org), is the resources that a district has at its disposal. Some districts may have a cadre of qualified ESOL specialists working in schools, whereas other districts may only be able to use paraprofessionals and yet others draw on the surrounding community for help. Based on these constraints, one can classify different ESOL programs into what Baker (2001) terms strong and weak forms of bilingual education. Table 1.2 provides an overview of the merits of the many types of ESOL programs operating across the United States.

According to a report submitted to the San Diego County Office of Education (Gold, 2006), "there is no widely accepted definition of a bilingual school in published research in this country" (p. 37). As a rule of thumb, they are widely understood to be schools that promote bilingualism and literacy in two or more languages as goals for students (Baker, 2001; Crawford, 2004).

**TABLE 1.2.** Types of ESOL programs in the United States

| Type of program | Target ELLs and expectations | Program description | What research says |
|---|---|---|---|
| Submersion | All ELLs regardless of proficiency level or length of time since arrival. No accommodations are made. The goal is to reach full English proficiency and assimilation | ELLs remain in their home classroom and learn with native speakers of English. The teacher makes no modifications or accommodations for the ELL in terms of the curriculum content or in teaching English | States such as Florida have in the past faced potential litigation because of not training teachers to work with ELLs or modifying curriculum and/or establishing ELL programs. In order to avoid submersion models, Florida has established specific ELL instructional guidelines (Consent Decree, 1990) |
| ESL class period | As above, though usually in school districts with higher concentrations of ELLs | Groups ELLs together, to teach English skills and instruct them in a manner similar to that used in foreign language classes. The focus is primarily linguistic and ELLs visit these classes typically 2 or 3 times per week | This model does not necessarily help ELLs with academic content. The effect is that these programs can tend to create "ESL ghettos." Being placed in such programs can preclude ELLs from gaining college-entrance applicable credits (Diaz-Rico & Weed, 2006) |
| ESL-plus (sometimes called submersion with primary language) | ELLs who are usually at speech emergence and/or intermediate fluency stage. The aim is to hasten ELL's ability to integrate and follow content classroom instruction | Includes instruction in English (similar to ESL class period and pull-out) but generally goes beyond the language to focus on content-area instruction. This may be given in the ELL's native language or in English. Often these programs may incorporate the ELL for the majority or all of the school day | According to Ovando & Collier (1998) the most effective ESL-plus and content-based ESL instruction is where the ESL teacher collaborates closely with the content teacher |
| Content-based ESL | As above | ELLs are still separated from mainstream content classes, but content is organized around an academic curriculum with grade-level objectives. There is no explicit English instruction | See above |

*continued overleaf*

**TABLE 1.2.** *(continued)* Types of ESOL programs in the United States

| Type of program | Target ELLs and expectations | Program description | What research says |
|---|---|---|---|
| Pull-out ESL | Early arrival ELLs. Usually in school districts with limited resources. Achieving proficiency in English fast is a priority so that the ELL can follow the regular curriculum | ELLs leave their home room for specific instruction in English: grammar, vocabulary, spelling, oral communication, etc. ELLs are not taught the curriculum when they are removed from their classrooms, which may be anything from 30 minutes to 1 hour every day | This model has been the most implemented though the least effective program for the instruction of ELLs (Collier & Thomas, 1997) |
| Sheltered instruction or SAIDE (specifically designed academic instruction in English). Sometimes called structured immersion | Targets all ELLs regardless of proficiency level or age. ELLs remain in their classrooms | This is an approach used in multilinguistic classrooms to provide principled language support to ELLs while they are learning content. Has same curriculum objectives as mainstream classroom in addition to specific language and learning strategy objectives | ELLs are able to improve their English language skills while learning content. Exposure to higher-level language through content materials and explicit focus on language fosters successful language acquisition (Brinton, 2003) |
| Transitional bilingual | Usually present in communities with a single large ELL population. Geared towards grades K–3. Initial instruction in home language and then switching to English by grade 2 or 3 | ELLs enter school in kindergarten and the medium of instruction is in the home language. The reasoning behind this is to allow the ELL to develop full proficiency in the home language so that the benefits of this solid linguistic foundation may transfer over to and aid in the acquisition of English. Intended to move ELL students along relatively quickly (2–3 years) | Of all forms of traditional bilingual programs, the transitional model entails the least benefit to the ELL in terms of maintaining and building CALP in their home language |

**TABLE 1.2.** *(continued)* Types of ESOL programs in the Unites States

| Type of program | Target ELLs and expectations | Program description | What research says |
|---|---|---|---|
| Maintenance bilingual | As above, but the ELL continues to receive language and content instruction in the home language along with English | As above, but are geared to the more gradual mastering of English and native language skills (5–7 years) | ELLs compare favorably on state standardized tests when measured against achievement grades of ELLs in transitional bilingual programs or ESL pull-out, ESL class period and ESL-plus programs (Hakuta et al., 2000) |
| Dual language/ Two-way immersion | This model targets native speakers of English as well as native speakers of other languages, depending which group predominates in the community | The aim of this program is for both English native speakers and ELLs to maintain their home language as well as acquire another language. Curriculum is delivered in English as well as in the ELL's language. Instructional time is usually split between the two languages, depending on the subject area and the expertise of the teachers | Dual language programs have shown the most promise in terms of first and second language proficiency attainment. Research results from standardized assessments across the United States indicated that ELLs can outperform monolingual English children in English literacy, mathematics, and other content curriculum areas. Has also many positive social and individual affective benefits for the ELL (Genesee, 1999) |
| Heritage language | Targets communities with high native population numbers, e.g. Hawai'i, Native Americans in New Mexico. Community heritage language maintenance is the goal | In heritage language programs, the aim can be to help revitalize the language of a community. Sometimes English is offered as the medium of instruction in only a few courses. Usually the majority of the curriculum is delivered in the home language | Language diversity can be seen as a problem, as a right, or as a resource. Heritage language programs are operationalized through local, state, and federal language policies as emancipatory (Cummins, 2001) |

# 1.4
# Teaching for English Language Development

This section explains the very practical implications of research in the phenomenon of bilingualism for classroom teachers as it relates to a context where many ELLs are learning English as their second, third, or even fourth language. One very important objective of this section is to help teachers understand how they can positively and purposefully mediate an ELL's language development in English.

A very prevalent concept of academic English that has been advanced and refined over the years is based on the work of Jim Cummins (1979; 1980; 1986; 1992; 2001). Cummins analyzed the characteristics of children growing up in two language environments. He found that the level of language proficiency attained in both languages, regardless of what they may be, has an enormous influence on and implications for an ELL's educational success. One situation that teachers often discover about their ELLs is that they arrived in the United States at an early age or were born in the United States but did not learn English until commencing school. Once they begin attending school, their chances for developing their home language are limited, and this home language is eventually superseded by English. This phenomenon is often referred to as limited bilingualism or subtractive bilingualism. Very often ELLs in this situation do not develop high levels of proficiency in either language. Cummins has found that ELLs with limited bilingual ability are overwhelmingly disadvantaged cognitively and academically from this linguistic condition. However, ELLs who develop language proficiency in at least one of the two languages derive neither benefit nor detriment. Only in ELLs who are able to develop high levels of proficiency in both languages did Cummins find positive cognitive outcomes.

The upshot of this line of research in bilingualism seems counterintuitive for the lay person, but it does conclusively show that, rather than providing ELLs with more English instruction, it is important to provide ELLs with instruction in their home language. By reaching higher levels of proficiency in their first language, an ELL will be able to transfer the cognitive benefits to learn English more effectively.

Of course, we don't live in a perfect world, and it is not always feasible to provide instruction in an ELL's home language, so it behooves all teachers to be cognizant of the types of language development processes that ELLs undergo. Cummins (1981) also posited two different types of English language skills. These he called BICS and CALP. The former, basic interpersonal communication skills (BICS), correspond to the social, everyday language and skills that an ELL develops. BICS is very much context-embedded in that it is always used in real-life situations that have real-world connections for the ELL, for example in the playground, at home, shopping, playing sports, and interacting with friends. Cognitive academic language proficiency (CALP), by contrast, is very different from BICS in that it is abstract, decontextualized, and scholarly in nature. This is the type of language required to succeed at school or in a professional setting. CALP, however, is the type of language that most ELLs have the hardest time mastering exactly because it is not everyday language.

Even after being in the United States for years, an ELL may appear fluent in English but still have significant gaps in their CALP. Teachers can be easily fooled by this phenomenon. What is needed is for teachers in all content areas to pay particular attention to an ELL's development in the subject-specific language of a school discipline. Many researchers (Hakuta et al., 2000) agree that an ELL may easily achieve native-like conversational proficiency within two years, but it may take anywhere between five and ten years for an ELL to reach native-like proficiency in CALP.

Since Cummins's groundbreaking research, there has been a lot of work carried out in the area of academic literacy. An alternative view of what constitutes literacy is provided by Valdez (2000), who supports the notion of *multiple literacies*. Scholars holding this perspective suggest that efforts to teach academic language to ELLs are counterproductive since it comprises multiple dynamic and ever-evolving literacies. In their view, school systems should accept multiple ways of communicating and not marginalize students when they use a variety of English that is not accepted in academic contexts (Zamel & Spack, 1998).

However, one very important fact remains. As it stands now, in order to be successful in a school, all students need to become proficient in academic literacy.

A third view is one that sees academic literacy as a dynamic interrelated process (Scarcella, 2003), one in which cultural, social, and psychological factors play an equally important role. She provides a description of academic English that includes a phonological, lexical (vocabulary), grammatical (syntax, morphology), sociolinguistic, and discourse (rhetorical) component.

Regardless of how one defines academic literacy, many have criticized teacher education programs for failing to train content-area teachers to recognize the language specificity of their own discipline and thus being unable to help their students recognize it and adequately acquire proficiency in it (Bailey et al., 2002; Kern, 2000).

Ragan (2005) provides a simple framework to help teachers better understand the academic language of their content area. He proposes that teachers ask themselves three questions:

- What do you expect ELLs to know after reading a text?
- What language in the text may be difficult for ELLs to understand?
- What specific academic language should be taught?

Another very useful instructional heuristic to consider when creating materials to help ELLs acquire academic literacy was developed by Cummins and is called Cummins' Quadrants. In the Quadrants, Cummins (2001) successfully aligns the pedagogical imperative with an ELL's linguistic requirements. The four quadrants represent a sequence of instructional choices that teachers can make based on the degree of contextual support given to an ELL and the degree of cognitive demand placed on an ELL during any given instructional activity. The resulting quadrants are illustrated in Table 1.3.

**TABLE 1.3. Cummins' Quadrants**

| | |
|---|---|
| Quadrant I:<br>High context embeddedness, and<br>Low cognitive demand (easiest) | Quadrant III:<br>High context embeddedness, and<br>High cognitive demand |
| Quadrant II:<br>Low context embeddedness, and<br>Low cognitive demand | Quadrant IV:<br>Low context embeddedness, and<br>High cognitive demand (most difficult) |

Quadrant I corresponds to pedagogic activities that require an ELL to use language that is easy to acquire. This may involve everyday social English and strategies that have a high degree of contextual support (i.e. lots of scaffolding, visual clues, and manipulatives to aid understanding, language redundancies, repetitions, and reinforcements) or this may include experiential learning techniques, task-based learning, and already familiarized computer programs. Activities in this quadrant also have a low degree of cognitive demand (i.e. are context embedded). In other words, they are centered on topics that are familiar to the ELL or that the ELL has already mastered and do not require abstract thought in and of themselves.

Quadrant IV corresponds to pedagogic activities that require the ELL to use language that is highly decontextualized, abstract, subject-specific, and/or technical/specialized. Examples of these include lectures, subject-specific texts, and how-to manuals. The topics within this quadrant may be unfamiliar to the ELL and impose a greater cognitive demand on the ELL. Academic language associated with Quadrant IV is difficult for ELLs to internalize because it is usually supported by a very low ratio of context-embedded clues to meaning (low contextual support). At the same time, it is often centered on difficult topics that require abstract thought (high cognitive demand). It is important for the teacher to (1) elaborate language, as well as (2) provide opportunities for the ELL to reflect on, talk through, discuss, and engage with decontextualized oral or written texts. By doing this the teacher provides linguistic scaffolds for the ELL to grasp academically.

Quadrants II and III are pedagogic "go-between" categories. In Quadrant II, the amount of context embeddedness is lessened, and so related development increases the complexity of the language while maintaining a focus on topics that are easy and familiar for the ELL. In Quadrant III, language is again made easier through the escalation of the level of context embeddedness to support and facilitate comprehension. However, Quadrant III instruction allows the teacher to introduce more difficult content-area topics.

When a teacher develops lesson plans and activities that are situated within the framework of Quadrant I and II, the ELL engages in work that is not usually overwhelming. In low-anxiety classrooms, ELLs feel more comfortable to experiment with their language to learn more content. As an ELL moves from level 1 of English language development (preproduction) to level 3 (speech emergence), a teacher may feel that the time is right to progress to creating lesson plans and activities that fit pedagogically into Quadrants III and IV. A gradual progression to Quadrant III reinforces language learning and promotes comprehension of academic content. According to Collier (1995):

> A major problem arising from the failure of educators to understand the implications of these continuums is that ELLs are frequently moved from ESOL classrooms and activities represented by Quadrant I to classrooms represented by Quadrant IV, with little opportunity for transitional language experiences characterized by Quadrants II and III.

Such a move may well set the stage for school failure. By attending to both language dimensions (level of contextual support and degree of cognitive demand) and planning accordingly, schools and teachers can provide more effective instruction and sounder assistance to second-language learners. (p. 35).

The degree of cognitive demand for any given activity will differ for each ELL, depending on the ELL's prior knowledge of the topic.

# 1.5
# Not All ELLs are the Same

The United States continues to be enriched by immigrants from countries the world over. Many cities have ethnic enclaves of language minority and immigrant groups and these populations are reflected in school classrooms. This section outlines the background characteristics of ELLs that teachers need to be aware of when planning or delivering instruction. Certainly, ELLs bring their own strengths to the task of learning but they also face many challenges. Equally, these diverse backgrounds impact classroom practices culturally in terms of how ELLs behave in classrooms, how they come to understand curriculum content, and how their interactions with others are affected (Zehler, 1994). The following affords a glimpse of their diversity:

María is seven years old and is a well-adjusted girl in second grade. She was born in Colombia, but came to the United States when she was four. Spanish is the medium of communication at home. When she entered kindergarten, she knew only a smattering of English. By grade 2 she had developed good basic interpersonal communication skills (BICS). These are the language skills needed to get by in social situations. María sounded proficient in English; she had the day-to-day communication skills to interact socially with other people on the playground, in the lunchroom, and on the school bus. Of course, all these situations are very much context-embedded and not cognitively demanding. In the classroom, however, María had problems with her cognitive academic language proficiency (CALP). This included speaking, reading, and writing about subject-area content material. It was obvious to her teacher that Maria needed extra time and support to become proficient in academic areas but, because she had come to the United States as a four-year-old and had already been three years in the school, she was not eligible for direct ESOL support. Collier and Thomas (1997) have shown that, if young ELLs have no prior schooling or have no support in native language development, it may take seven to ten years for them to catch up to their peers.

Ismael Abudullahi Adan is from Somalia. He is 13 and was resettled in Florida as a refugee through the Office of the United Nations High Commissioner for Refugees (UNHCR; see www.unhcr.org/home.html). As is the case with all refugees in the USA, Ismael's family was matched with an American resettlement organization (see www.refugees.org/). No one in his family knew any English. They were subsistence farmers in Somalia and, because of the civil war in Somalia, Ismael had never attended school. The resettlement organization helped the family find a place to live, but financial aid was forthcoming for only six months. While all members of the family were suffering degrees of war-related trauma, culture shock, and emotional upheaval, as well as the stress and anxiety of forced migration, Ismael had to attend the local school. Everything was foreign to him. He had no idea how to act as a student and all the rules of the school made no sense to him. All Ismael wanted to do was work and help his family financially; he knew that at the end of six months financial aid from the government would stop and he worried about how his family was going to feed itself. He is currently placed in a sheltered English instruction class at school.

José came to the United States from Honduras with his parents two years ago. He is now 14. His parents work as farm laborers and throughout the year move interstate depending where crops are being harvested. This usually involves spending the beginning of the calendar year in Florida for strawberry picking, late spring in Georgia for the peach harvest, early fall in North Carolina for the cotton harvest, and then late fall in Illinois for the pumpkin harvest. When the family first came to the United States from Honduras as undocumented immigrants, José followed his parents around the country. His itinerancy did not afford him any consistency with schooling. Last year, his parents decided to leave José with his uncle and aunt in North Carolina so that he would have more chances at school. Now he doesn't see his parents for eight months out of the year. He misses them very much. At school José has low grades and has been retained in grade 8 because he did not pass the North Carolina High School Comprehensive Test. He goes to an ESOL pull-out class once a day at his school.

Andrzej is 17 years old. He arrived with his father, mother, and 12-year-old sister from Poland. They live in Baltimore where his father is a civil engineer. The family immigrated the year before so that Andrzej's mother could be closer to her sister (who had married an American and had been living in the United States for the past 10 years). Andrzej always wanted to be an engineer like has father, but now he isn't sure what he wants to do. His grades at school have slipped since leaving Poland. He suspects that this is because of his English. Even though he studied English at school in Poland, he never became proficient at writing. Because he has been in the United States for more than a year, he no longer receives ESOL support at school. His parents, however, pay for an English tutor to come to his house once a week.

The above cases reflect the very wide differences in the ELL population in schools today. One cannot assume that every ELL speaks Spanish or that all ELLs entered the country illegally. The ELL population in a school may include permanent residents, naturalized citizens, legal immigrants, undocumented immigrants, refugees, and asylees. Of this foreign-born population, 4.8 million originate from Europe, 9.5 million from Asia, 19 million from Latin America, 1.2 million from Africa, and 1 million from other areas including Oceania and the Caribbean (U.S. Census Bureau, 2005).

## Stages of Cultural Adjustment

What the above cases of María, Ismael, José, and Andrzej also identify is that since the nation's founding immigrants have come to the United States for a wide variety of reasons. These may include one or any combination of economic, political, religious, and family reunification reasons. Depending on the reason for coming to the United States, an ELL might be very eager to learn English since they might see having English proficiency as the single best means to "get ahead" economically in their new life, or they might resist learning English because they see this as an erosion of their cultural and linguistic identity. A teacher may find an ELL swaying between these two extremes simply because they are displaying the characteristics and stages of *cultural adjustment*.

The notion of cultural adjustment or, as it is sometimes called, "culture shock" was first introduced by anthropologist Kalvero Oberg in 1954. The emotional and behavioral symptoms of each stage of this process can manifest themselves constantly or only appear at disparate times.

### Honeymoon Stage

The first stage is called the "honeymoon" stage and is marked by enthusiasm and excitement by the ELL. At this stage, ELLs may be very positive about the culture and express being overwhelmed with their impressions particularly because they find American culture exotic and are fascinated by it. Conversely, an ELL may be largely passive and not confront the culture even though (s)he finds everything in the new culture wonderful, exciting, and novel. After a few days, weeks, or months, ELLs typically enter the second stage.

### Hostility Stage

At this stage, differences between the ELL's old and new cultures become aggravatingly stark. An ELL may begin to find anything and everything in the new culture annoying and/or tiresome. An ELL will most likely find the behavior of those around him/her unusual and unpredictable and thus begin to dislike American culture as well as Americans. They may begin to stereotype Americans and idealize their own culture. They may experience cultural confusion and communication difficulties. At this stage, feelings of boredom, lethargy, restlessness, irritation, antagonism, depression, and feelings of ineptitude are very common. This occurs when an ELL is trying to acclimatize to the new culture, which may be very dissimilar to the culture of origin. Shifting between former cultural discourse practices and those of the new country is a problematic process and can take a very long time to overcome. If it is prolonged, an ELL may withdraw because of feelings of loneliness and anxiety.

### Home Stage

The third stage is typified by the ELL achieving a sense of understanding of the new culture. The ELL may feel more comfortable living in the new country and experiencing the new culture. They may regain their sense of humor. In psychological terms, an ELL may start to feel a certain emotional balance. Although feelings of isolation may persist, the ELL may stop feeling lost and even begin to have a feeling of direction. The ELL re-emerges more culturally stable, being more familiar with the environment and wanting to belong. For the ELL, this period of new adjustment could initiate an evaluation of old cultural practices versus new ones.

## Assimilation Stage

In the fourth stage, the ELL realizes that the new culture has positives as well as negatives to offer. Integration patterns and practices displayed by the ELL become apparent. It is accompanied by a more solid feeling of belonging. The ELL enjoys being in the new culture, functions easily in the new environment (even though they might already have been in the new culture for a few years) and may even adopt cultural practices of the new culture. This stage may be seen as one of amalgamation and assimilation.

## Re-Entry Shock Stage

This happens when an ELL returns to the old culture for a visit and notices how many things have changed in the country as well as how they themselves have changed. Upon returning from the home country, an ELL will have developed a new sense of appreciation and of belonging to the new culture.

Worthy of note is the fact that the length of time an ELL spends in each of these stages varies considerably. The stages are neither discrete nor sequential and some ELLs may completely skip stages. They may even exhibit affective behaviors characteristic of more than one stage.

## Cultural Practices at School

Whenever an ELL steps into a new school environment, the ELL will be sure to go through a process of cultural adjustment. For an ELL, the countless arrays of unspoken rules acquired in his/her culture of origin may not be suitable in the new school and a new set of practices needs to be discovered and internalized. These include, but are of course not limited to, school rules, what it means to be a "good" student, how to interact with fellow students and teachers, eating practices, bathroom practices, and even ways of learning. It would be fairly easy to learn new rules for living if such were made explicit and one were provided with lists of things to learn. However, most cultural rules operate at a level below conscious awareness and are not easily relayed to students.

Often ELLs find themselves in the position of having to discover these rules on their own. Shared cultural discourse practices can be seen as the oil that lubricates social interaction; however, what a community's cultural practices are, as well as the meanings that group members attach to their shared repertoire of cultural practices, are not always made explicit. Unfamiliarity with these cultural rules on the part of an ELL can cause a great deal of stress.

Many definitions regarding what culture is or is not abound. Diaz-Rico and Weed (2006) provide a very nice overview of the characteristics of culture. For them, culture is an adaptive mechanism, culture is learned, cultures change, culture is universal, culture provides a set of rules for living and a range of permissible behavior patterns, culture is a process of deep conditioning, culture is demonstrated in values, people usually are not aware of their culture, people do not know all of their own culture, culture is expressed verbally and non-verbally, culture no longer exists in isolation, and, last but very poignantly, culture affects people's attitudes toward schooling and it governs the way they learn. It can affect how they come to understand curriculum content and how they interact with fellow students.

Diaz-Rico and Weed (2006) offer a number of strategies to promote cultural pluralism and assuage potential exclusionary practices such as stereotyping, prejudice, and racism in the classroom. Ways to acknowledge different values, beliefs, and practices include accommodating different concepts of time and work rhythms, as well as different concepts of work space. Being open to culturally sensitive dress codes and inclusive of culture in school rituals are effective ways of promoting cultural pluralism. Considering different notions about work and play and maintaining an inclusive understanding of different health and hygiene practices as well as being tolerant of different religious practices and food and eating practices are critical in teaching acceptance. Most important to remember in relation to your ELL students are culturally based educational expectations (roles, status, gender), different discourse patterns, and your need to foster cultural pride and home–school communication.

One way to ease your ELL's cultural adjustment while demonstrating inclusiveness is to get to know where your ELLs come from and then incorporate aspects of their culture into your lessons. You could overtly ask your ELL about their home country, but this tactic may not provide you with the type of information you want since your ELL may not have the language proficiency in English to express abstract cultural concepts. Therefore, you should observe your ELL and how they behave, interview people from the same country, conduct a home visit, or visit the community in which the ELL lives. Of course, teachers are often constrained by time, so an alternative is to conduct internet research or buy appropriate books.

# 1.6
# Culturally Responsive Pedagogy

As more and more students from diverse backgrounds populate 21st century class-rooms, and efforts mount to identify effective methods to teach these students, the need for pedagogical approaches that are culturally responsive intensifies. Today's classrooms require teachers to educate students varying in culture, language, abilities, and many other characteristics.

(Gollnick & Chinn, 2002 p. 21)

The question is: How does a teacher adequately respond to the multicultural classroom?

In 2000 Gay wrote that culturally responsive pedagogy is validating, comprehensive, multidimensional, empowering, transformative, and emancipatory. In other words, culturally responsive pedagogy necessitates that teachers tread outside their comfort circles. It is only natural for humans to see, understand, judge, make sense of, and canonize the world around them through their own discursive norms of practice. What this means in the context of education is that teachers make choices every day about what they will and will not teach. More importantly, teachers make choices as to how they will present and frame their curriculum choices. Of course this sends a subtle message to students: What curriculum matter is taught and how it is framed tends to legitimatize, validate, and endorse it over other potential curricular perspectives, which by default are marginalized.

Thus, teachers instruct in ways and about things that are familiar to them. They usually adopt and transmit the dominant voice in society, namely that of white middle-class America. The problem is, if a student is an ELL, (s)he is usually not white, middle-class, or American. This is where the practice of culturally responsive pedagogy can help. Look at the reflection vignette below. It shows how the media can tend to reinforce dominant societal perspectives, perspectives that are reinforced and repeated in school curricula and textbooks across the country.

**Reflection Vignette**

I was driving my 12-year-old son to school in the fall of 2003 when over the radio we heard a commercial for the movie *Alamo*. Coincidently, the previous day we had been to the movies and one of the trailers was for the same movie. Kevin Costner was one of the Texan heroes in the movie, and every time the movie trailer showed the Texans the screen was bright and full of smiling people. The music was light and they were obviously the "good guys." However, when the screen shot showed the Mexican antagonists, the screen was dark, with hues of blue and red, the background images were full of cannon sounds, and the faces were "mean-looking."

Back in the car, I asked my son, who at the time was focused on playing his Gameboy, "You're doing American history now in your social studies class, right?"

My son, recognizing that another of dad's teachable moments was upon him, just rolled his eyes and disgruntledly put down his Gameboy.

"Yes, why?" he said.

"What aspect of U.S. history are you learning about now?" I asked.

"We're learning about the westward colonization of North America."

"Did you hear that ad?" I asked.

"Sure."

"Let me ask you something. What do you think would happen if a bunch of Cubans came into the middle of Florida, bought up a cluster of farms, and then told the government they were not going to pay taxes?"

"I suppose the government would fine them," he said.

"Well, what would happen if those same Cubans then told the government that they were going to create their own country?"

"The government would send in the army and kick 'em all out and probably send them back to Cuba."

At that point, I could see a flash of realization cross my son's face. "Oh, I get it," he said, "the Cubans are the Texans."

In the United States the Alamo is usually constructed as part of a righteous war of independence against an autocratic foreign government, namely Mexico. Yet in Mexican schools the war surrounding the Alamo is constructed as an aggressive grab for land by non-Spanish speaking settlers. Who is right? Perhaps the question should be: Am I teaching curriculum matter in a way that alienates and inadvertently marginalizes my students? How would a Mexican ELL feel in your classroom if you taught a unit on the Alamo, or on the westward European settlement of North America, and Mexico and the Mexicans were portrayed as the baddies? At the very least it marginalizes an ELL's voice in the classroom and indirectly discredits his/her potential contribution of another perspective for the class to think about.

Using Gay's (2000) principles of culturally responsive pedagogy, how does a teacher make the curriculum more validating, comprehensive, multidimensional, empowering, transformative, and emancipatory?

The first step is to be conscious of our choice of language. Language is never neutral. What and how we say things in the classroom affects the way our students perceive curriculum matter. The second step is to be conscious of the images we present to the students. The third step is to engage in critical and reflexive thinking and writing tasks. By getting teachers to reflect critically on the language, images, and content of their teaching, we begin to open the door on *other* ways to think about teaching that are less ethnocentric. The fourth step is to learn the history and culture of the ELL groups in your classroom. The fifth step is to try and visit teachers who are successful at implementing culturally responsive pedagogy and, last, become an advocate in your own educational institution to reform ethnocentric discursive practices so that it becomes more inclusive. Richards, Brown, and Forde (2004) suggest the following activities to become more culturally responsive:

1. acknowledge students' differences as well as their commonalities;
2. validate students' cultural identity in classroom practices and instructional materials;
3. educate students about the diversity of the world around them;
4. promote equity and mutual respect among students;
5. assess students' ability and achievement validly;
6. foster a positive interrelationship among students, their families, the community, and school;
7. motivate students to become active participants in their learning;
8. encourage students to think critically;
9. challenge students to strive for excellence as defined by their potential;
10. assist students in becoming socially and politically conscious.

# 1.7
# Not All Parents are the Same
## Home–School Communication

Any school administrator and teacher will readily admit that the key to a school's success and indeed the key to a child's learning success is the active involvement of parents in the learning process. In the case of ELLs, parents are often at a loss because of barriers that prevent them from fully participating in the school community. Parents' hesitancy to involve themselves in their child's school arises from barriers such as the frustration they feel because of their own limited knowledge of English, their own possible lack of schooling, perceptions about power and status roles, or the anxiety they have because of different cultural norms such that they do not readily understand American school cultures or the cultural expectations, rights, roles, and responsibilities of teachers, parents, and students.

Schools can greatly enhance the effectiveness of ELL home–school communication and involvement by taking active steps to reduce these barriers. Careful planning is required to meet these challenges, though it can be done.

1. *Knowledge is King!* Get as much background information as is possible. Information useful to schools and teachers includes home language, home cultural/ethnic values, parental attitudes towards education, work schedules of parents, English proficiency, and the circumstances under which they have come to be in the United States (e.g. are they refugees, itinerant migrants, political asylees, second or third generation heritage speakers?). Depending on the information a school receives, a classroom teacher may make informed decisions about bilingual aide support, translation support, and changing school cultural practices that raise rather than bring down barriers to ELL home–school communication and parental involvement.

2. *Communicate as if it is going out of style!* The importance of fostering ELL parental involvement centers foremost on fostering and maintaining good lines of communication between the

school/teacher and the home/parents. An important facet that frames parents' participation in schools is their perceptions of school personnel. Is the school inviting and welcoming? Are teachers and the administration approachable? Are teachers empathetic to ELL parental concerns, wishes, contributions, values, and cultural practices? How often are they invited to attend school functions? Do teachers follow through on their communications? Do teachers make an effort to talk directly and in person with parents? Are parents allowed to visit often and learn what goes on in the classroom? Do teachers take the time to explain the whats, whys, and hows of their teaching and the ELL child's learning?

3. *It's not just about educating the ELL!* If schools want to enlist the support and help of ELL parents, then both the administration of a school and its teachers need to be prepared to extend their instruction beyond the ELL student to the ELL parent—beyond the classroom and into the ELL home. In other words, in order to break down the types of barriers that inhibit ELL parents from school involvement, steps need to be taken to educate the parents in matters concerning English language, as well as U.S. school customs. What would such steps look like? In an article published in *Essential Teacher* (2004), Bassoff says it centers solely on *access, approachability,* and *follow-through.*

## Ideas: On Fostering Access

- Create, endorse, and implement an ELL parent–school participation program/policy.
- Have an ELL parent representative on school committees.
- Make the school a place to foster ELL community events.
- Provide access to the school library to aid ELL parents' learning of English.
- Translate all school communications into the home language.
- Make sure all written communication reaches the ELL parent.
- Foster in-school support groups for ELL parents.
- Advocate that your school district establish an "Intake Center" for new arrivals that will help ELL newcomers with school registrations, placement, testing, and information services.
- Allow ELL parents to come to school professional development opportunities.
- Provide ELL parent education workshops and orientation opportunities.
- Advertise the contact information of bilingual school staff.

## Ideas: On Fostering Approachability

- Use ELL parents as sources of information.
- Invite ELL parents to school.
- Use parents to raise multicultural awareness in the school and classroom; multiculturalism is a two-way street—foster inclusion through the provision of multicultural workshops, presentations, and events to mainstream monolingual school personnel and students.
- Multicultural appreciation events could include ethnic music and dance performances, art displays, drama shows, science fairs, and festival evenings, all accompanied by talks from ELL parents or ELL community leaders.
- Be amenable and open to different ways about thinking about education—show this through inclusive classroom practices, activities, realia, and visuals.
- Embed multicultural routines in everything and all the time.
- Foster ELL literacy family evenings.
- Establish native language parent groups.

## Ideas: On Achieving Good Follow-Through

- Give mainstream students service-learning opportunities to help ELL parents/families adjust to U.S. life.
- Foster ELL parent network circles.
- Provide classes that help ELL parents to meet their children's education needs.
- Have the school library purchase a wide range of fiction and non-fiction bilingual books.
- Take the time to learn about the culture, language, and education system of the ELLs' home countries and apply what you learn in your classroom.
- Create virtual spaces to post ongoing information for ELL parents as well as WWW links to useful websites.[1]

# 1.8
# English Language Learners with Special Needs

We want to highlight an important subset of the ELL population that is often disadvantaged because its members fall simultaneously into two underrepresented groups: special needs and ELL. They are underprivileged because many teachers within these separate discipline areas have not been trained to work with this population of students—ESOL teachers with special needs students, or special needs teachers with ELLs.

In 1984 the National Office for Educational Statistics reported that 500,000 students in the United States were English language learners with exceptionalities. Today, more than 20 years later, it is projected that there are more than 1 million ELLs with special needs in the United States (Baca & Cervantes, 2004).

Despite an abundance of legislative initiatives (*Civil Rights Act—Title VI* in 1963, *Title VII of the Elementary and Secondary Education Act* (ESEA) reauthorized in 1974, 1978, 1984, and 1998, *Lau v. Nichols* in 1974, and the *Equal Educational Opportunity Act*, extending the Lau decision to all schools, *President's Committee on Mental Retardation* in 1970, the *Education for All Handicapped Children Act* in 1975, the *Bilingual Education Act* in 1984, reauthorization of the ESEA in 1994 coupled with a Presidential Executive Order in 2000, the *Individuals with Disability Education Act* (IDEA) of 1997 and *Title II* of the *No Child Left Behind* (NCLB) *Act* 2002), inappropriate referrals, assessments, and the institutionalization of inappropriate instructional processes remain crucial issues in the education of ELL special needs children.

A colleague of ours once told the story of when he first came to the United States. His son was seven years old and at the end of the summer in 2005 was ready to be placed in grade 2. In Florida, the parents of every newly enrolled student are obliged to fill out a home language survey form. Our colleague was raising his children bilingually and both his children were equally fluent in English and German. When asked on the form what languages were spoken at home, he wrote German and English. A week later, his son innocuously said at the dinner table that he enjoyed being pulled out of the classroom, whereupon both parents asked the son what he meant. "Why I love being in the ESOL class with all the kids who speak other languages." Little did my colleague know that, because he had written German on the home language survey, the school was legally bound to place his son in ESOL classes. The upshot of the story was that our colleague went to the school and explained to the administration that his son was a balanced bilingual speaker and having him in ESOL classes was unnecessary. The administration told him that there was nothing they could do because the home survey was filled out as it was. Ultimately, my colleague had to disenroll his son, re-enroll him in the same school, and fill out the home survey again (this time just putting English as the home language) to finally have him pulled from the ESOL classes. The reason this story is related is because parents and teachers are all too familiar with the fact that, within education environments, rule-driven practices, acronyms, and terminologies abound that more often than not pigeon-hole students into predetermined roles and assign these students to inevitable and predictable expectations. Unfortunately, ELLs with special needs have fallen prey to this stereotyping. There is, however, an ever-increasing but incomplete body of research that spotlights instructional strategies for ELLs with special needs that teachers may draw upon to help them in their efforts to identify, instruct, and assess. The following section summarizes some of the more important aspects of this research. The following two points may act as instructional guides:

- Students with mild to severe disability levels benefit from native language instruction (de Valenzuela & Niccolai, 2004).
- Instruction needs to be enriching and not remedial, empower language learners, recognize the learners' culture and background, provide learners with authentic and meaningful activities, connect students to real-life experiences, begin with context-embedded material that leads to the use of context-reduced material, and provide a literacy/language-rich environment (Echeverria & McDonough, 1993).

But how can we translate the above into effective classroom practice?

There are various pedagogic models that have been developed based on theoretical frameworks, research findings, and recommended practices appropriate for ELLs with special needs (Ruiz, 1995a,b). Ortiz (1984) describes four basic types of pedagogic models that offer structured institutional support for ELLs with special needs to achieve more accomplished social and academic skill levels. These models are:

1. *Coordinated services model*—assists the ELL with special needs with a monolingual English speaking special education teacher and a bilingual educator.
2. *Bilingual support model*—bilingual paraprofessionals are teamed with monolingual English speaking special educators and assist with the individualized education plans of ELLs with special needs. Wherever noted on the individualized education program (IEP), the bilingual paraprofessional provides home language instruction concurrently with the teacher providing content expertise.
3. *Integrated bilingual special education model*—consists of one teacher who is certified in both bilingual education and special education, where the teacher is able to assist with level-appropriate English language instruction as the learner develops in proficiency.
4. *Bilingual special education model*—in this model all professionals interacting with the ELL special needs student have received bilingual special education training and are qualified to provide services that meet the goals outlined in any IEP.

Another model, the Optimal Learning Environment (OLE) Project (Ruiz, 1989), is based on a constructivist philosophy and works within a holistic–constructivist paradigm, focusing on the extensive use of interactive journals, writers' workshops, shared reading practices, literature conversations, response journals, patterned writing, as well as the provision of extended assessment time. The aim of the strategies is to build on a student's schema and interest.

The benefits of such models highlight the individualized and diverse needs of language learning students with special needs. As yet, guaranteeing unambiguous benefits across the board is not possible precisely because of the dearth of empirical research on instructional planning and curriculum design in this area. A very real consequence of this situation is the paucity of curricular materials available specifically geared to bilingual special education. Both fields of education have propagated methods on preparing either English language learners or special needs students. The main point to be internalized here is that materials must be integrated and specifically designed for English language learners *with* special needs. It is not enough that they receive "half of each curriculum" (Collier, 1995). Lack of curricular materials and trained personnel is still cited as the greatest barrier to providing services to English language learners with special needs.

So, what can teachers do to facilitate language learning for ELL students with a special need?

Of course, implementing well-informed instructional practices is one thing, but awareness raising, understanding of difficulties, and knowledge of differences and disorders are also an integral part of assisting the English language learner with disabilities.

In conclusion, we offer Hoover and Collier's (1989) recommendations as a point of departure to think about teaching ELLs with special needs:

1. Know the specific language abilities of each student.
2. Include appropriate cultural experiences in material adapted or developed.
3. Ensure that material progresses at a rate commensurate with student needs and abilities.
4. Document the success of selected materials.
5. Adapt only specific materials requiring modifications, and do not attempt to change too much at one time.
6. Try out different materials and adaptations until an appropriate education for each student is achieved.
7. Strategically implement materials adaptations to ensure smooth transitions into the new materials.
8. Follow some consistent format or guide when evaluating materials.
9. Be knowledgeable about particular cultures and heritages and their compatibility with selected materials.
10. Follow a well-developed process for evaluating the success of adapted or developed materials as the individual language and cultural needs of students are addressed. (Hoover & Collier, 1989: 253)

## Conclusion

Understanding your English language learners can be daunting. They are different; they probably come from very different home environments from you, their teachers. Some of your students may be third-generation American and yet others may be newly arrived undocumented immigrants.

After reading Part 1, we don't expect you to now know everything there is to know about ELLs. We did not set out to provide you in these few short pages with an all-inclusive research-informed, all-encompassing treatise on ELLs in education. We have been circumspect, to be sure, in trying to introduce you to ELLs. There are plenty of ELL-specific books for that. It *was* our intent, however, to raise your awareness about the educational implications of having ELLs in your classroom. Our goal with this is to start drawing a picture of who an English language learner is and from this position help you think about the educational possibilities for your class.

Parts 2, 3, and 4 of this book are devoted exclusively to completing this picture. Not in a global sense, but finely etched within the parameters of your own content area.

What will be introduced to you in the pages to come will undoubtedly refer back to some of the points raised in Part 1. We have no intention of offering you static teaching recipes; instead we offer something akin to ideas, understandings, and skills that you can transfer to your own classrooms. Last, we refer you to Part 4 of this book, which offers you avenues for future professional development.

# Part 2
# Principles of English/Language Arts Teaching and Learning

# 2.1
# English/Language Arts-Focused ESOL Research

In *Made in America: Immigrant Students in our Public Schools*, Olsen (1997) writes:

> The point from which newcomer students observe, learn about, and begin to interact with "America" is always from the sideline . . . Their view of other students and of the life of the school is truly a view from afar, a view from the margins of the life of the school. (p. 44)

One of the goals of ELA teachers who work with linguistically diverse students is to get students off of the sidelines and into the action of active learning in the classroom. There exists a synergy among the strands of ELA instruction: reading, writing, speaking, listening, and viewing; and, when ELLs listen to others and engage in academic conversations themselves, the vocabulary and syntax of academic English are internalized and automated. In addition to uncovering this synergy, researchers have discovered that oral language and aural comprehension play a large role in fostering reading comprehension skills and that co-constructing knowledge and investigating deep questions increase comprehension and motivation for deeper inquiry (Meltzer & Hamann, 2005). It is our hope that this review of the literature on teaching ELLs in the ELA classroom will provide guidance to you when working with the diverse learners in your classroom.

In his review of research on teaching ELLs, Goldenberg (2008) states, "What we know about good instruction and curriculum in general holds true for ELLs" (p. 17). With this in mind, ELA teachers can feel confident that, when they are using best practices for all of their students, they are also supporting ELLs. However, there are strategies and techniques that have been proven to be effective in helping ELL students improve their reading, writing, listening, and speaking skills. The following is a review of ELA-focused ESOL research, which includes supporting students' home languages, encouraging talk and interaction between ELLs and English-proficient students, including and using students' backgrounds and experiences in the curriculum, selecting appropriate texts including multicultural literature, promoting effective classroom discussions through instructional conversations, using literature study groups, modeling explicit cognitive strategies, using effective teaching strategies and techniques for ELLs, incorporating effective writing instruction into the curriculum, and using appropriate assessment procedures.

## Students' Native Language

Research in both general instruction for ELLs and instruction specific to the teaching of ELA strongly supports the inclusion of students' native language in the classroom and curriculum. The National Council of Teachers of English (NCTE) and the International Reading Association (IRA) Standards for the ELA state: "Students whose first language is not English [should be able to] make use of their first language to develop competency in the English language arts and to develop understanding of content across the curriculum" (NCTE & IRA, 1996). Supporting students' native language in the classroom is important for many reasons. First, teachers need to promote respect for the diversity of their students' cultural backgrounds; when a student's language is forbidden or denigrated in the classroom, opportunities for learning are hindered for all students. Groenke, Scherff, and Rodriguez (2008) state: "The strength of our students lies in their home languages, so we must ensure that students have the opportunity to share their linguistic and cultural wealth in our classrooms" (p. 1).

Research also suggests that, when students' native language is used and supported in the curriculum, students are better able to transfer language skills from one language to the next. In a review of research on teaching ELLs, Goldenberg (2008) notes:

> With respect to English language learners, a substantial body of research reviewed by both CREDE [Center for Research on Education, Diversity, and Excellence] and NLP [National Literacy Panel] researchers suggests that literacy and other skills and knowledge transfer across languages. That is, if you learn something in one language—such as decoding, comprehension strategies, or a concept as democracy—you either already know it in (i.e., transfer it to) another language or can more easily learn it in another language. (p. 15)

Specifically, Goldenberg cites several studies that focus on reading instruction, where findings indicate that teaching students to read in their first language promotes reading achievement in English.

In addition to the correlation between reading achievement in students' native language and in English, research also indicates that using their native language as a scaffold to ELA instruction can improve students' literacy skills. In a study conducted by Rubin and Patterson (2002), teachers used the concept of a bilingual Reading Detective Club to help students develop their use of reading strategies in their native language and in English. Students worked in small groups or clubs to solve mysteries by using their reading abilities; teachers used scenarios in both Spanish and English and asked them to compare the reading strategies they used to solve the mysteries. Students discovered similarities between the reading strategies they used to read in both Spanish and English and their awareness of their own strategy use increased. Many texts such as poems, short stories, and novels used in ELA classrooms are also available in other languages. Research in teaching ELA also encourages teachers to allow students to use their native language in writing assignments such as reading logs, journals, interactive writing assignments between peers, personal history books, vocabulary activities, and expressive and expository writing (Anstrom & DiCerbo, 1998; Young, 1996).

NCTE's *Position Paper on the Role of English Teachers in Educating English Language Learners* (2006) suggests several strategies for incorporating students' native language into classroom instructional practices such as:

- recognizing that second language acquisition is a gradual developmental process and is built on students' knowledge and skill in their native language;
- providing authentic opportunities to use language in a nonthreatening environment;
- asking families to read with students a version in the heritage language;
- providing opportunities for silent reading in either the student's first language or in English.

Although ELA teachers may find the concept of creating classroom materials that support student learning in their native language daunting, low-stakes informal activities such as journaling, sharing personal histories, and working in small groups can recognize and support students' native language while helping them acquire academic English.

## Talk and Interaction

Research in teaching ELLs emphasizes the importance of frequent and varied opportunities for students to speak and interact with other students, especially those who have a greater proficiency in English. Ernst-Slavit, Moore, and Maloney (2002) state that speaking and listening are integral to language development, especially in language arts classrooms:

> Talk and interaction not only help students understand new concepts but also provide a scaffold for learning through the other language modes of reading and writing. Through talking and listening to one another (not only the teacher) and working on activities involving reading and writing (not only their own), learners are able to both develop increasing facility in all language modes and increasing control over social interaction, thinking, and learning. (p. 119)

When discussing the development of students' oral language proficiencies, Young (1996) states that students need open time to talk to one another and that collaborative learning strategies promoted in a trusting environment can lead to better success for ELLs.

When ELLs have opportunities to work with other students who are more proficient in English, they can expand their academic vocabulary, acquire new learning strategies, construct and negotiate meaning with their peers, and have an authentic audience with which to share ideas and written work. Allowing time for students to work together is a best practice for teaching ELA but can be even more critical for ELLs as they need time and practice to learn new language skills as well as new content skills.

## Emphasis on Students' Experiences

Another important aspect of instruction for ELLs is to value and develop students' background knowledge of subject matter as well as to recognize and utilize students' experiences in the curriculum. Ernst-Slavit, Moore, and Maloney (2002) encourage educators not to focus on what students lack but rather to focus on what students have. Activities designed to activate background knowledge can occur in many places in a lesson or unit. For example, teachers can use pre-reading strategies such as anticipation guides, simulation activities, and eliciting predictions from students to help them access what they already know about a topic (Anstrom & DiCerbo, 1998). Teachers can also use supplemental materials to establish background knowledge when students do not have the requisite prior knowledge such as showing films and using informational texts such as newspaper articles and informational picture books (Rubinstein-Avila, 2003). Strategies designed to help students generate ideas such as brainstorming, semantic mapping, structured overviews of a topic, and KWL organizers (in which students write what they Know, Want to know, and have Learned about a topic) can also help students connect what they already know to new knowledge (Young, 1996).

In addition, lessons that begin with students' experiences, which then are scaffolded to include more complex concepts and skills, can be very successful for ELLs. For example, in her article "Can English Language Learners Acquire Academic English?" MaryCarmen Cruz (2004) begins with a controversial topic and solicits students' opinions as to what they would do in a specific situation. After they have shared their opinions as a group and discussed facts surrounding the issues, students pair up and try to resolve the dilemma. Next, Cruz asks students to consider the topic from different viewpoints, which are more removed from the students' experiences. At this point students will typically have to conduct more research into the topic, thus adding to their background knowledge. Next, students break into groups of pro and con and work together to analyze informative and persuasive articles and practice skills such as summarizing, taking notes, and asking questions. Finally, Cruz models how to prepare arguments and provides students with sample sentence patterns for arguments and models preliminary and counter speeches. Eventually students are ready to defend their ideas in persuasive essays. Cruz's model for scaffolding lessons begins with students' own experiences and opinions and incorporates several research-based techniques including activating background knowledge, promoting talk and interaction, cooperative learning, modeling, and strategic instruction.

## Text Selection

Another aspect of curriculum development for ELA teachers of ELL students that often corresponds to considering students' experiences is choosing appropriate texts:

> Research into reading indicates that students use past experiences and background knowledge to make sense out of unfamiliar texts. For this reason, English language learners may have difficulty with texts that are culturally unknown to them, contain difficult vocabulary and complex themes, or use academic or archaic syntax. Literature that is relevant to the life experiences and cultures of ELL students, including folktales or myths from their first culture, can facilitate cognitive and language development. (Anstrom & DiCerbo, 1998: 4)

The use of multicultural literature in ELA classrooms has long been considered a best practice for ELA teachers, and students from all cultural backgrounds can benefit from its integration into the curriculum. Multicultural literature is available in a variety of forms including picture books, poetry, drama, short stories, novels, nonfiction, and personal essays.

In its position paper on educating ELLs (2006), NCTE makes the following recommendations for selecting materials in the ELA classroom:

- Choose a variety of texts around a theme.
- Choose texts at different levels of difficulty.

- Choose reading and writing materials that represent the cultures of the students in the class.
- When possible, include texts in the native languages of the ELLs in the class. The following considerations should be used as a guide for choosing texts that support bilingual learners:

    - Materials should include both literature and informational texts.
    - Materials should include culturally relevant texts.
    - Authentic materials should be written to inform or entertain, not to teach a grammar point or a letter–sound correspondence.
    - The language of the text should be natural.
    - If translated, the translation should be good.
    - Materials should include predictable text for emergent readers.
    - Materials should include texts with nonlinguistic cues that support comprehension.

Of course, simply including multicultural and high interest texts may not improve students' literacy skills; strategies for accessing these texts need to be employed.

The role of determining appropriate culturally relevant texts to use in the English language arts classroom does not have to fall solely upon the teacher. Supporting the belief that ELL readers are better able to construct meaning through texts that utilize their background knowledge, Freeman and Freeman (2004) offer research-based questions that teachers and students can use together to guide students' selection of culturally relevant texts:

- Have you ever had an experience like one described in this story?
- Have you lived in or visited places like those in the story?
- Could this story take place this year?
- How close do you think the main characters are to you in age?
- Are the main characters in the story boys or girls?
- Do the characters talk like you and your family do?
- How often do you read stories like these?

Encouraging students to find texts that they can relate to not only helps them develop their reading fluency through utilizing background knowledge but also validates students' experiences and makes the ELA curriculum more relevant.

## Instructional Conversations

Research has shown that students, especially ELLs, need frequent opportunities to construct meaning with other students through discussion. When researching what constituted good classroom discussions, Goldenberg (1992) developed a list of elements that make up effective instructional conversations, which he divided into two groups: instructional and conversational. The instructional elements for effective discussions include having a thematic focus to the discussion, activating and using students' background knowledge in discussion, direct teaching of skills and concepts when necessary, the promotion of more complex language and expression including follow-up questions, asking for elaboration and extended contributions, and asking students for the basis for their statements and opinions (in ELA this is often done by asking students for evidence from the text). The conversational elements of effective discussion include asking fewer known-answer questions, responding to student contributions, connection discourse where comments build upon and extend previous ones, providing a challenging, but nonthreatening, atmosphere, and generally participating, including self-selected turns (p. 319).

The role of the teacher in developing effective instructional conversations is critical. Goldenberg uses the metaphor of weaving to describe what the teacher must do: the teacher must weave together the students' comments with the concepts and ideas from the lesson, weave students' prior knowledge with new knowledge being presented, and weave together the elements of instructional conversations. Instructional conversations can be especially useful in ELA classrooms. Goldenberg (1992) provides the following suggestions for teachers when planning for instructional conversations around a story or a book:

1. Select a story or a book that is appropriate for your students.
2. Read the story (or book) several times until you feel you understand it thoroughly.
3. Select a theme to focus the discussion, at least initially.
4. Identify and provide, as needed, background knowledge students must have in order to make sense of what they will be reading.
5. Decide on a starting point for discussion to provide an initial focus.
6. Plan and think through the lesson mentally.
7. Finally, consider some suitable follow-up activities, particularly ones that will help you gauge what the students have learned from the IC [instructional conversation]. (pp. 322–323)

Saunders and Goldenberg (1999) extended the research on instructional conversations in a study examining their effects, along with those of literature logs in which students were given prompts relating a story to their own experiences, on students' story comprehension and thematic understanding. The results of the study indicated that the combined use of instructional conversations and literature logs improved factual and interpretive comprehension for all students, regardless of language proficiency. In addition, for limited English-proficient students, the use of instructional conversations and literature logs improved their understanding of story theme. Although Saunders and Goldenberg's study focused on fourth- and fifth-grade students, the influence of instructional conversations using focused thematic topics, using scaffolded questions, activating background knowledge, and encouraging student participation, along with the use of literature logs, are effective practices in the secondary ELA classroom.

## Literature Study Groups

Whereas instructional conversations are often used for whole group instruction, studies have also shown the importance of using small group literary discussions to improve ELLs' reading comprehension. Wolfe (2004) examined the effects of literature studies, small group meetings of teachers and students in which particular novels are studied in depth, on student understanding of abstract literary concepts. As in instructional conversations, the role of the teacher is to direct the discussion of a text to a more complex and critical understanding and interpretation. In Wolfe's study, ELL students read the novel *Bless Me, Ultima* (Anaya, 1972) in sections, meeting with their teacher for literature study sessions as they were reading the text. During these sessions, the teacher used several strategies to scaffold student discussion to move from more concrete to abstract understandings of the text: (1) he validated student contributions; (2) he restated student comments in more "adult-like ways" while still attributing the remarks to the students; (3) he connected "complex ideas of symbolism and theme to more concrete examples" and made connections to other events in the texts, across texts, and to students' lives; and (4) he gave repeated examples of literary interpretations (Wolfe, 2004: 411). These strategies were designed to help students develop their understanding of abstract literary concepts and resulted in students' improved ability to understand the concepts of symbolism and theme in a novel. According to Wolfe (2004), the implications for teachers of ELLs include providing extended and multiple opportunities for students to discuss a text and "the need for quality literature that lends itself to discussion of more abstract concepts such as symbolism and theme" (p. 412).

Kooy and Chiu (1998) emphasize the importance of small group discussions of literature for ELLs. Nonnative speakers who may be reluctant to participate in whole group discussions can use small groups to rehearse what they would like to say in a less intimidating environment. In their research, Kooy and Chiu (1998) found that small group discussions centering around "hot" issues arising from the readings could become highly animated and informative. Placing ELLs in small group discussions of literature is beneficial for all students: ELLs get to share their insights and views of the world, which enriches all students' literary understanding.

## Cognitive Strategies

Explicit strategy instruction is an important component of ELA-based ESOL research. Olson and Land (2007) examined the effectiveness of cognitive strategies instruction on the reading and writing abilities of ELLs and found significant gains on assessments of academic writing. The cognitive strategies approach was developed by the University of California Irvine (UCI) Writing Project and emphasizes the importance of teachers making visible what effective readers and writers do by modeling explicit learning strategies and developing students' metacognitive awareness of those strategies. Teachers were exposed to cognitive strategy instruction through a professional development program called the Pathway Project, in which students began the program in the sixth grade in a class that prepared ELLs to enter mainstream ELA classes. Teachers were exposed to a wide range of cognitive strategies and curricular approaches to strategy use. The program emphasized three kinds of knowledge for students: declarative knowledge, whereby students were exposed to specific and explicit cognitive strategies; procedural knowledge, whereby students learned how to use the cognitive strategies in their reading and writing processes; and conditional knowledge, whereby students learned when and why to use cognitive strategies and how to monitor and regulate their use (Olson & Land, 2007). They introduced teachers to a "readers and writers tool kit," which included the following strategies:

- Planning and Goal Setting
- Tapping Prior Knowledge
- Asking Questions and Making Predictions
- Constructing the Gist
- Monitoring
- Revising Meaning: Reconstructing the Draft
- Reflecting and Relating
- Evaluating. (p. 277)

Teachers modeled the strategies for their students through such practices as guided reading, using sentence starters to help students talk about their reading and writing; metacognitive reflection, using think-alouds and written reflections of students' meaning-making processes; scaffolding strategy instruction by beginning with students' own knowledge and moving to more complex knowledge and processes; and color-coding texts to improve analytical thinking. ELL students trained in cognitive strategy instruction showed significant gains on writing assessments calling for literary interpretation. Students need to know what strategies to use, how to use them, and when and why to use them. Explicit modeling of what good readers and writers do benefits all students in ELA classrooms.

## Teaching Strategies

Although cognitive strategy instruction is specific to the program developed by the UCI Writing Project, many researchers emphasize the importance of teaching literacy strategies to ELLs. Young (1996) identified a number of strategies and techniques that English language art teachers can use in their classrooms to help ELL students. To foster students' oral language development Young emphasizes cooperative learning in which students can orally practice their language skills, especially in pairs. In addition, Young recommends sheltered instruction, which includes "a thematic approach; objectives for both content and language; and experiential and trial-and-error guided practice" (1996: 21). To develop ELL students' reading achievement, Young recommends graphic organizers to help students activate background knowledge such as semantic maps, brainstorming, and structured overviews; teachers should also help students identify purposes for reading, examine text layouts, and skim, scan, and read for main ideas. Finally, to develop ELLs' writing competence, Young recommends using journals such as buddy journals, interactive writing experiences such as pen-pals, and using pictures and student drawings in journals, learning vocabulary, and sharing their personal histories (1996: 22–23). Rubinstein-Avila (2003) also provides ELA teachers with several research-based strategies for instruction when integrating ELLs into mainstream English classes:

- Slowing down one's verbal output
- Displaying lessons on the board or overhead
- Using cooperative activities to promote talk including peer-led discussions and reading circles
- Activating prior knowledge
- Providing supplemental resources such as visual aids
- Using picture books to provide background knowledge
- Explicit modeling of the processes of tasks
- Identifying unfamiliar words and working with peers to determine their meaning
- Identifying text structure
- Providing explicit feedback on ELL's written language
- Incorporating curriculum which includes students' experiences
- Demonstrating caring, with Empathy and Understanding. (pp. 129–133)

Teachers can keep these strategies and techniques in mind as they plan their curriculum for their ELA classes.

## Writing Instruction

In its position statement on educating ELLs, NCTE (2006) states that writing well in English is often the most difficult skill for ELLs to master. Many aspects of writing instruction may be unfamiliar to ELLs such as terminology, the writing process (drafting, revising, editing), and other aspects of writing such as audience, purpose, and genre. In addition, students from different cultural backgrounds may not be familiar with, or comfortable with, certain rhetorical strategies and levels of discourse. NCTE provides several recommendations for teachers to support ELLs in their writing by:

- Providing a nurturing environment for writing;
- Introducing cooperative, collaborative writing activities which promote discussion;
- Encouraging contributions from all students, and promoting peer interaction to support learning;
- Replacing drills and single-response exercises with time for writing practice;
- Providing frequent meaningful opportunities for students to generate their own texts;
- Designing writing assignments for a variety of audiences, purposes, and genres, and scaffolding the writing instruction;
- Providing models of well-organized papers for the class. Teachers should consider glossing sample papers with comments that point to the specific aspects of the paper that make it well written;
- Offering comments on the strength of the paper, in order to indicate areas where the student is meeting expectations;
- Making comments explicit and clear (both in written response and oral response). Teachers should consider beginning feedback with global comments (content and ideas, organization, thesis) and then moving on to more local concerns (or mechanical errors) when student writers are more confident with the content of their draft;
- Giving more than one suggestion for change—so that students maintain control of their writing;
- Not assuming that every learner understands how to cite sources or what plagiarism is. (NCTE, 2006)

Carroll, Blake, Camalo, and Messer (1996) recommend that teachers utilize students' personal experiences in writing, such as having students write personal narratives and autobiographical pieces that include information about their literacy experiences in their home languages. Similarly, Brisk (1998) recommended the use of critical autobiographies in helping students develop their literacy skills. Students wrote narratives about their literacy experiences while simultaneously engaging in discussions about external factors influencing their lives. Students were able to improve their writing skills while also engaging in a climate which supported their cultures and experiences. Engaging students in metacognitive activities that call attention to students' writing processes and literacy experiences as well as providing meaningful writing assignments are excellent practices for all learners in ELA classrooms.

## Assessment

Little research has been conducted on effective assessment practices that are specific to ELLs in English classrooms. However, in their research entitled *Attributes of Effective Programs and Classrooms Serving English Language Learners*, August and Pease-Alvarez (1996) identify several successful assessment practices that can be applied to ELA classrooms. One attribute of successful programs and classrooms is that "students are assessed for content knowledge and language proficiency" (p. 31). It is very important for ELA teachers to remember that they will have both content and language objectives in their lesson plans and that their assessments evaluate both types of objectives. Another attribute is that "assessment entails the use of multiple measures (e.g. observations, conferencing, samples of student work, tests. Knowledge and skills are evaluated in multiple contexts)" (p. 32).

It is especially important for ELA teachers to use a variety of methods to determine ELLs' abilities in reading, writing, listening, speaking, and viewing. Alternative assessments such as portfolios can inform teachers and students of academic progress. English language arts classrooms lend themselves to a variety of performance assessments such as presentations, dramatic activities, projects, and writing samples. August and Pease-Alvarez noted that in successful classrooms teachers were aware of the purpose of the assessment and communicated that to their students; this is a characteristic of best practice in all ELA classrooms. Finally, they state that, "In order to interpret assessment information, teachers know and understand the background of students" (p. 32). English language arts teachers can use activities to get to know students such as using reading and writing surveys and questionnaires, interviews with family members, and cultural heritage projects. English language arts teachers must consider what ELL students are able to do and provide support and encouragement for what they bring to the classroom.

## Conclusion

Although these practices have been discussed separately, there is tremendous overlap. Best practice in ELA instruction emphasizes the integration of reading, writing, listening, speaking, and viewing into the curriculum on a daily basis. What is apparent from this research is the importance of getting to know the ELLs in our classrooms. Understanding and validating our students' backgrounds and experiences, and their home languages, can foster a positive classroom climate, benefit all students in the classroom, and scaffold students' ELA learning. In addition, explicit modeling of learning processes and strategies will make visible the cognitive processes that are necessary for successful academic progress in English classrooms. Teachers need to provide a balance of direct teaching methods with cooperative and collaborative activities that will promote students' language learning in authentic and meaningful ways. Finally, although Chapter 1.6 of this book addresses culturally responsive teaching in general, we would like to direct ELA teachers' attention to the NCTE's position statement entitled *Supporting Linguistically and Culturally Diverse Learners in English Education* (2005), which outlines eight principles of culturally responsive teaching specific to the ELA classroom. The website (www.ncte.org/cee/positions/diverselearnersinee) outlines the philosophical base and provides practical suggestions for erasing inequalities in our classrooms.

# Part 3
# Teaching English/ Language Arts

# 3.1
# Introduction

Dear Professor,

I am now in my second semester teaching at the same middle school where I interned. I love it, and I think I am doing alright in most regards. Last semester, I found that I was a bit overwhelmed with classroom management issues, but I have been able to establish some systems and procedures that are really making class run much more smoothly. This semester, I have been able to turn my focus on student learning, and that is why I am writing you.

I feel as if I am not doing enough to reach my English language learner students. As you know, my county did away with pure ESOL classes two years ago; now, all of our ELL students are mainstreamed into regular classrooms immediately upon entering our school. I feel that I am not doing enough to differentiate learning for them. I am ashamed to admit it, but when I disaggregate my grades, my ELL students are not achieving at the same level as my native English speakers. I have sought help from my colleagues, but it seems that they are feeling underprepared to assist these students, too.

I find my biggest struggles come because of the fact that we are expected to teach the same curriculum to ELLs as we do to our native English-speaking students. One of my students, Joanna, who reads and writes on a second grade level, has struggled all year because the vocabulary and literature are simply not on her level. Although I create note cards for her, put her with peer tutors, and handwrite summaries for her, she still has major gaps in her knowledge. She is such a hard-working student and a delightful girl. What else can I do to help her? How can I teach Dickens' *Great Expectations* to someone who reads on a second-grade level?

I also have some specific questions:

1. How do I account for linguistic differences when teaching writing and grammar? For instance, Spanish-speaking students use Spanish word-order in their writing, which is grammatically incorrect in our language. To an extent, this is permissible for the culturally sensitive teacher, but where does one draw the line?
2. How do I modify grammar and spelling curriculum to benefit the student? Sometimes I worry that my modifications may inhibit my ELLs' ability to master English. Am I making too many modifications? Am I making the right kind?
3. As a slightly bilingual teacher, I sometimes give instructions in Spanish, which my students respond to. Is this ok?
4. I am not sure how much of the curriculum I should attempt to teach my ELL students; should I focus solely on listening and speaking skills or can I introduce them to reading literature?

On a positive note, let me tell you about a pleasant experience. One of my students invited me to her Quince Años last month; I wasn't going to go because it was on a Saturday, but a colleague of mine, Bárbara—who is Latina—told me I should go because, culturally, it is a huge honor to have "la maestra" attend the party. I am glad she told me, and I am glad I attended. I really enjoyed getting to know my student's family, and they were so welcoming!

I hope to hear from you soon.

Sincerely,

Shannon Faith Taylor (a graduate of Spring 2008)

"Shannon Faith Taylor" is not a real person; rather, she is a composite of many ELA teachers we have met and experiences we ourselves have had. Although English teachers want ELL students to learn the fundamentals of the English language in their classrooms, they also have an obligation, and a strong desire, to teach the content of their curriculum. In addition, ELA teachers will have a wide variety of students with diverse backgrounds and abilities; how can they change their curriculum and teaching methods to include ELLs while meeting the needs of all students in their classroom and embracing all the aspects of ELA?

Part III (Chapters 3.2–3.8) is our effort to answer this question by describing learning activities for middle and high school students. We have taken activities from the various aspects of teaching in the ELA classroom—teaching reading, teaching writing, teaching grammar and vocabulary, and teaching listening and speaking—and to each of these we have applied the principles discussed in the first two parts of this book. Chapter 3.9 demonstrates how each of these aspects of the ELA can be integrated to design a complete unit of study. We realize ELA teachers face a unique challenge when designing their curriculum: the choice of texts that can be chosen to promote these skills is seemingly endless. We have chosen examples from commonly taught works but have written the examples in a way that we hope will make adapting them to your particular curriculum or text uncomplicated.

Most of the learning activities have been aligned with the "natural approach" to second language acquisition (see Part I for the theory underlying the approach). The four levels are pre-production, early production, speech emergence, and intermediate fluency. Although there is overlap in the teaching strategies used at each level, we largely employ these levels in the learning exercises as shown in Table 3.1. This approach helps teachers choose effective teaching strategies for ELL students.

At all of these levels ELA instruction can be meaningful, but we realize that the greater challenges come at the lower levels. However, by immersing students in a language-rich environment where reading, writing, listening, and speaking are valued and celebrated, we believe all students can participate at some level. Whereas reading and writing activities will be more appropriate for the higher levels of ELLs, teachers can read aloud to their students, involve students in role play, use picture books, and incorporate visuals into their lessons, which will benefit all language learners. Whenever possible, we have endeavored to demonstrate how the more challenging activities that take place in the typical ELA classroom can be modified to reach all levels of ELLs.

To facilitate your use of the book and easily locate learning activities that correlate to levels of language ability, we have indicated at the top of each lesson which levels of language acquisition can be met by each lesson or exercise. In some cases, all four levels are included because modifications have been made for all levels of language acquisition. In other cases, fewer icons are included because the exercise was developed with only certain levels of language ability in mind. That is not to say, however, that the lesson couldn't be modified for other levels; we leave that to the discretion of the teacher and, in fact, invite readers to take this opportunity to adapt the learning activities for the specific needs of their students. You will also find "Teaching Tips" sprinkled throughout each of the content chapters. These tips are additional teaching ideas to consider or ELL modifications to keep in mind as you implement the learning activities in your classroom.

**TABLE 3.1.** Four levels of speech emergence

| | Preproduction | Early production | Speech emergence | Intermediate fluency |
|---|---|---|---|---|
| ELL linguistic ability | "Silent" period Point Respond with movement Follow command Receptive vocabulary up to 500 words | One- or two-word responses Labeling Listing Receptive vocabulary up to 1,000 words Expressive vocabulary 100–500 words | Short phrases and sentences Comparing and contrasting Descriptions Receptive vocabulary up to 7,000 words Expressive vocabulary 2,000 words | Dialogue Reading academic texts Writing Receptive vocabulary up to 12,000 words Expressive vocabulary 4,000 words |
| Teaching strategies | Yes/no questions Simplified speech Gestures Visuals Picture books Word walls KWL charts Simple cloze activities Realia TPR | Questions that require: yes/no; either/or; two-word response Lists of words Definitions Describing Reader's theater Drama Graphic organizers | How and why questions Modeling Demonstrating Cooperative learning Comprehension checks Alternative assessments Simulations | Brainstorming Journal writing Literary analysis Problem solving Role playing Monologues Story telling Oral reports Interviewing and applications |

TPR, Total Physical Response.

If you've not read Part I, we encourage you to do so now, so that you have a solid understanding and frame of reference for the different levels of language acquisition. Another excellent overview of second language acquisition theory can be found on the website of the Northwest Regional Educational Laboratory (www.nwrel.org/request/2003may/overview.html). You can also view and hear the four different stages of English language development by accessing the University of South Florida's online database of video samples. These video clips feature students representing each of the language levels and include annotated audio that further assist users in understanding second language acquisition theory. The online database also includes speaking, reading, and writing samples of ELLs from different backgrounds, different ages, and grade levels along with a number of case studies for further study. The online databases for elementary, middle, and high school levels can be found at:

- http://esol.coedu.usf.edu/elementary/index.htm
- http://esol.coedu.usf.edu/middleschool/index.htm
- http://esol.coedu.usf.edu/highschool/index.htm

In addition to reviewing the levels of language acquisition, we would like to remind you that the learning activities presented in the following chapters are based on the five principles for creating effective learning environments, which are highlighted in Part I of this text.

Finally, we hope that the activities and strategies in Chapters 3.2–3.8 show how the principles in Parts I and II can be applied to the teaching methods and curriculum of mainstream ELA classrooms. Because we realize ELA teachers do not teach reading, writing, grammar, vocabulary, listening, and speaking in separate, isolated lessons, Chapter 3.9 demonstrates how each of these aspects can be integrated into a unit of study. We consider these activities and strategies not as complete lesson plans but rather as building blocks you can use to create your own lessons. Chapter 3.9 contains a chart that will help you create ELA lesson plans that contain modifications for ELL students. We realize the tremendous challenges ELA teachers face as their classrooms become more diverse and the expectations for all students increase.

# 3.2
# Reading Strategies

Adolescent literacy is a growing concern for policymakers and educators. The literacy expectations and demands on students continue to grow, and, in the past two decades, greater attention has been paid to the needs of adolescents in reading instruction. The reading skills adolescents need to handle the more complex texts and reading tasks they are expected to master in middle and high school have been identified and teachers across content areas are expected to provide instruction not only in their content areas but also in reading strategy instruction. English language arts teachers must prepare students for federally mandated testing, and the majority of these tests require students to answer reading comprehension questions about nonfiction texts.

Because of the increased understanding of the needs of adolescents with respect to literacy, ELA instruction has grown to include and encompass reading strategies. English language arts teachers no longer assign a text and then begin instruction. Instead, they help students access texts before, during, and after reading and teach students explicit strategies to handle the complex reading tasks expected of them. ELLs are especially in need of this type of instruction, and this chapter will discuss specific reading strategies that can help ELLs access texts, both fiction and nonfiction, through frontloading activities such as activating and building prior knowledge, developing specific reading skills through the explicit modeling of reading strategies, becoming active and engaged readers, and promoting further thinking and reflection through postreading activities. By considering the characteristics of effective readers, ELA teachers can teach explicit reading strategies to the ELLs in their classrooms and give these students the tools to become more aware of, and develop, their reading skills.

**ACTIVITY 3.1. Strategies and processes of effective readers**

| | |
|---|---|
| Before reading | Set a purpose for reading |
| | Set goals for reading |
| | Determine a plan for reading |
| | Activate background knowledge |
| | Make predictions |
| During reading | Ask questions |
| | Summarize |
| | Identify main ideas |
| | Make connections |
| | Make inferences |
| | Visualize |
| | Monitor comprehension |
| | Use fix-up strategies when they don't understand |
| | Use text features to assist comprehension |
| | Use strategies to understand new vocabulary |
| | Create interpretations of literature |
| After reading | Reflect on what they have read |
| | Revise interpretations |
| | Summarize main ideas |
| | Draw conclusions |
| | Seek additional information |
| | Evaluate what they have read |

English language learners can benefit from explicit strategy instruction in which reading strategies are introduced and reinforced over time. It is important to note that simply introducing a reading strategy and expecting students to adopt it and make it a part of their reading toolbox is unlikely to work.

Strategies should be used in a variety of lessons and students should be asked to reflect on their use of a strategy and its effectiveness. Many teachers who effectively use reading strategies choose only one or two to focus on at a time (in a semester or even in a school year) and continually reinforce their use in the classroom. If reading strategies are introduced explicitly and in a familiar manner to students, learning and using strategies can become a routine. The following is a series of steps that can be used to introduce and teach reading strategies to your ELLs; you may not always have time to go through all of the steps but they are designed to maximize student learning through scaffolding.

## Steps to Introduce Reading Strategies:

Step 1:   Identify the strategy.
Example: Today we will be learning a reading strategy called Talking to the Text.

Step 2:   Identify the purpose of the strategy.
Example: Talking to the Text helps us slow down and be sure we understand what we have read. It will help us remember important information from our reading. There are a lot of important details in this story which require us to use a variety of strategies to practice being good readers.

Step 3:   Identify the steps of the reading strategy. It is important to have clear and explicit instructions for each strategy. These steps should be displayed visually and preferably posted in the classroom so that students can refer to them when necessary.

Example directions for steps for Talking to the Text:

    a.   Stop at designated points.
    b.   Reflect on what you have read using the prompts for Talking to the Text (see reading strategy in this chapter).
    c.   Write down your responses.
    d.   Continue reading until next stopping point.

Step 4:   Model the reading strategy. Modeling is a critical component of effectively teaching learning strategies. Modeling will especially help level 2 and 3 students learn specific academic language involved with reading.

Step 5:   Have students practice the strategy with a short piece of text while you assist. Breaking the text into smaller bits helps the level 3 and 4 fluency ELLs. Depending upon the level of the language learner, you can modify the reading strategy activities to best suit their needs.

**ACTIVITY 3.2.** Activities for practicing reading strategies by level

| Level | Sample activities for practicing reading strategies |
|---|---|
| Preproduction (level 1) | Read the text aloud to the students or have a partner read to them. Use pictures to help students comprehend the passage. Have students match pictures with words. Have students retell a passage from the text aloud after listening to it in English. Use sentence completion activities after reading. |
| Early production (level 2) | Read the text aloud to the students or have a partner read to them. Have the students create pictures/illustrations of what is happening in the text and then have students label them. Create yes or no questions that students can answer as responses to the text. Create guiding questions such as who, what, where, how, and why questions in response to a text. Use role playing and dramatizing texts. |
| Speech emergence (level 3) | Use advanced graphic organizers to help students comprehend text. Have the students participate in literature response groups. Have the students write sentences and paragraphs in response to texts. Create how and why questions in response to texts. |
| Intermediate fluency (level 4) | Encourage students to participate in class discussions. Engage students in literary analysis. Have students create and perform in skits and role play. Have students paraphrase and retell texts. Engage students in writing projects using different genres and for varied purposes based on reading activities. |

Step 6:    Have students share their results in small groups. Make sure that ELL students of all language proficiencies are mixed in with fluent students. For example, with the strategy Talking to the Text students can share their sticky notes and talk about the different responses they came up with.

Step 7:    Have students share their results as a whole class. It is useful to post class results visually on an overhead or on the board.

Step 8:    Have students reflect on their strategy use. This reinforces the purpose and process of the strategy and should aid in metacognition. For example, have students write a brief description of the reading strategy on a three-by-five card and evaluate its success. ELL students can be presented with these strategies as options to choose from.

The purpose of teaching reading strategies is to help students create a toolkit of approaches to reading tasks. Not all students will want to use a particular strategy, so it helps to give them alternatives; ultimately the goal is to teach them to select and implement appropriate strategies and monitor and regulate their use (Olson and Land, 2007).

---

**Teaching Tip**

While you are teaching and modeling reading strategies, talk to students about your own reading processes and experiences. For example, you could state that sometimes you have trouble remembering what you have read and using the Talking to the Text strategy really helps you retain information.

---

## Before Reading

Traditionally, in many ELA classrooms, the format for teaching reading was to begin with the reading assignment itself: teachers assigned a particular text to be read, and then students read independently; the majority of classroom activities occurred after reading. However, struggling readers, especially ELLs, will need assistance approaching reading tasks. Activating background knowledge is especially important for ELLs who may not have the familiarity with the topic or structure of an assigned text. In addition, prior to creating reading assignments, it is important for teachers to get to know their students' reading abilities and backgrounds.

## Reading Surveys (Levels 1, 2, 3, and 4)

One way to get to know your students' literacy backgrounds and reading interests is through the use of a reading survey. Reading surveys can tell you about your students' attitudes toward reading, their likes and dislikes, and their reading processes and habits. The following is an example of a reading survey that can be used not only for you to get to know your students but also for students to get to know one another. Level 1 and level 2 students can participate in the reading survey by listening to the more English-proficient students share their answers to the questions. The responses of their peers can be transformed into questions that elicit yes/no and choice responses that level 1 and 2 students can respond to. In addition, teachers can modify the survey to have the questions require yes or no answers or provide lists of possible answers for students to choose from.

## ACTIVITY 3.3. Reading survey and activities

### Activity one

Directions: Please answer the following questions about your reading likes and dislikes in your own words. These are prompts to help you think about your reading habits.

- If English isn't your first language, what is your first language? Do you like to read in your native language?
- What types of books do you like to read?
- What is your all-time favorite story, book, or poem? Why?
- What types of reading do you dislike? Why?
- What is your least favorite story, book, or poem? Why?
- Describe your early memories of learning to read. Did you have favorite books? Did you like to be read to? Did you go to the library? Did your parents have an influence on your reading experiences?
- Describe your experiences with reading in school.
- Describe your reading habits. Do you read often? When you read, do you have a particular place where you like to read or a best time to read?
- Describe your personal reading strategies. Do you highlight, underline, or take notes when you are reading? Do you have any other strategies to help you understand what you read?
- Who is your favorite character in literature? If you do not have one, who is your favorite character from TV, movies, or comic books?
- What types of reading would you like to do in this class?

### Activity two

Directions: Get with a partner and discuss your responses to the reading survey. Listen carefully, as you will be introducing your partner to others.

### Activity three

In groups of four, introduce your partner to the rest of the group. Once you have finished your introductions, consider the following questions, which you will share with the whole class.
What experiences do members of the group have in common?
What differences did you find in your reading habits and interests?
What important things did you learn about yourselves and each other?

### Activity four

Share your group findings with the whole class.

Adapted from *Activity Sheet: Literary Hunt* from *Conversations in Literature,* www.learner.org/envisioninglit-erature.

### Teaching Tips

■ In order to minimize confusion, consider assigning students to pairs and groups of four prior to beginning the activity. In addition, you could have students answer the questions from Activity 3.3 on chart paper so that, when they present their findings to the whole class, they stay on topic.

■ The reading survey can help you understand your students' literacy backgrounds and experiences as well as help you determine their reading habits and abilities. Getting to know your students' reading interests can help you choose whole class texts and texts for literature circles, and make recommendations for independent reading. Choosing appropriate, high-interest texts can be critical to helping ELLs develop their reading skills (Anstrom & DiCerbo, 1998).

---

**Extension Activity**

Consider using the reading survey as a prewriting activity. Level 3 and 4 students could turn their responses into a short literacy biography (the story of their reading and writing experiences) or a literacy narrative (a story about an influential reading experience). Encourage students to interview family members to provide them with more information about their early reading experiences.

---

## Prereading Activities

Activating students' prior knowledge is important for all learners but especially important for ELLs whose background and experiences may be different from those of native English speakers. Prereading activities are great warm-ups for students to get them thinking about what they already know and to allow them to share their knowledge with others. Frontloading, preparing students with knowledge and procedures necessary for the upcoming lesson, can help teachers determine what students already know and identify holes or misconceptions in students' learning. In addition, frontloading activities can expose students to the upcoming reading assignments by helping them understand text structure and an author's writing style, and identify new and difficult vocabulary. As with any reading strategy, it is very important for students to have time to think about what they know—wait time, time to brainstorm, and time to put ideas into writing are critical. It is also important for students to have time to share their knowledge and ideas with others—consider having students share responses with partners or in small groups prior to a whole group discussion. Finally, as mentioned in the steps to introducing reading strategies, students should be encouraged to reflect on the purpose, procedures, and usefulness of the prereading strategy.

## Understanding the Organizational Structure of a Text (Levels 3 and 4)

Reading nonfiction, expository text can be more challenging for ELLs than reading narrative text. Whereas narrative text has a basic story structure that remains fairly consistent, informational text can be written in a variety of structures. English language learners often do not bring the requisite background knowledge about text structures and features that is required to understand factual information presented in expository texts. By helping students identify different text structures and providing them with tools to analyze these structures, ELA teachers can better support ELLs' reading comprehension. Irvin, Buehl, and Klemp (2007) identify six of the most common organizational structures of informational text: cause and effect, problem and solution, compare and contrast, sequence or chronological order, description, and proposition and support. English language learners can be taught to look for cues and signal words to help them determine the organizational structure of a text.

**ACTIVITY 3.4.** Text structure and cues

| Structure | Cues/signal words |
| --- | --- |
| Cause and Effect: The pattern shows the relationship between two things when one thing makes the other happen. | Because<br>So/So that<br>If . . . then<br>Consequently<br>As a result of<br>Therefore<br>Due to<br>Reasons for<br>Was caused by |
| Problem–Solution: The pattern presents a problem, one or more solutions, and possibly discusses the outcomes of the solution. | Problem<br>Solution<br>Question<br>Answers |
| Compare and Contrast: The pattern demonstrates similarities and differences in ideas or concepts. | In contrast<br>On the other hand<br>However<br>Alike<br>Different |
| Sequence or Chronological Order: The pattern groups ideas based on the order in which they occur. | First<br>Last<br>Next<br>Then |
| Description: The pattern provides information about a topic and its attributes. | For instance<br>For example<br>Such as<br>Includes<br>Consists of |
| Proposition and Support: The pattern presents a viewpoint, argument, or hypothesis and then provides support through facts, data, examples, etc. | Look for . . .<br>facts<br>statistics<br>examples<br>citing experts, authorities |

Students should preview a text looking for signal words or cues that will help them predict what type of text structure the author is using. In addition, students should determine what the text structure will indicate about the content of the material; this can be in the form of yes or no questions.

- Is the author discussing the results of an event and discussing what made it happen?
- Is the author explaining a problem and suggesting a solution?
- Is the author comparing two or more concepts? Is the author discussing similarities and/or differences?
- Is the author discussing the order of events or steps to a process?
- Is the author explaining the characteristics of something or providing a description?
- Is the author presenting an argument or hypothesis and providing support for the ideas?

Once students become knowledgeable about text structure, they can outline, chart, or map the information in a manner that will help them better comprehend and retain the information.

## Using Graphic Organizers (Levels 1, 2, 3, and 4)

After students have identified the organizational structure of a text, they can then read the text and highlight or underline key details that support their prediction about the text structure. Students then choose an appropriate graphic organizer to fill out with the main ideas and details from the text. The great advantage of using graphic organizers is that they can convey ideas with less text. Level 1 and 2 students can use vocabulary words and illustrations rather than full sentences. Next, students should compare their results in partners and in groups. Peer writing is generally more comprehensible to ELLs than other forms of text. Finally, the whole class should discuss which graphic organizers were used and the reasons for students' decisions. As the ELL students become more sophisticated at determining text structure, they should be encouraged to create their own graphic organizers that better represent the relationship between ideas, especially since authors may not use only one text structure in their writing. Teachers can obtain many sample graphic organizers from the internet (such as www.readwritethink.org); in addition, a good source for reproducible graphic organizers for both narrative and expository texts can be obtained through the series of texts by Billmeyer and Barton (1998) *Teaching Reading in the Content Area: If Not Me Then Who?*

## Text Features (Levels 2, 3, and 4)

In addition to understanding how an author organizes his/her ideas in a text, the features of a text need to be made explicit to students in order to provide them with the tools to comprehend expository text. Unfortunately, teachers sometimes assume that students will be familiar with the aspects of a text that are designed to provide information to the reader. English language learners should be explicitly taught to identify and use the following features of a text:

- Headings: Students should examine headings, ask themselves what they know about the topic, and make predictions about possible text content.
- Reader aids such as bolded words and italics: Students should be shown that these are often vocabulary words or key ideas in the selection.
- Visuals: Students need to learn how to read graphs and charts and examine pictures.
- Glossaries and indexes: Students should practice looking up unknown words if they are unable to determine the meaning from the context. In addition, ELLs should have access to bilingual dictionaries at all times.

ELLs can be given advanced organizers that outline the text structure and features, which can then guide them as they read.

## Anticipation Guides (Levels 1, 2, 3, and 4)

The purpose of anticipation guides can vary. Anticipation guides can be used to determine discrepancies between what students know and what is in the text, which is especially useful when teaching informational texts. In addition, anticipation guides can be used to help students generate opinions about important topics and themes in literary texts. Anticipation guides allow students a preview of important issues they will encounter in a text and also help facilitate a prereading discussion. Fostering meaningful discussions is a challenge for all classroom teachers, and anticipation guides allow opportunities for focused discussion. In addition, ELLs may be reluctant to volunteer opinions in an unstructured, large group discussion but may be more likely to share when they have had time to form specific opinions.

**ACTIVITY 3.5.** Anticipation guide for *To Kill a Mockingbird* by Harper Lee

---

**Part 1**

---

Directions: Before you read the novel, read each statement in part 1. If you agree with the statement, place a check in the agree column, if you disagree with the statement place a check in the disagree column. Underneath the statement, write the explanation for your choice.

---

| Agree | Disagree | |
|---|---|---|
| | | 1. Your family's background and social status determine who you are as a person and how you behave. (Sample modification: Your family determines who you are. Yes or No?) |
| | | 2. You shouldn't judge someone unless you have been through the same experiences as they have. (Sample modification: You shouldn't judge people. Yes or No?) |
| | | 3. Girls should act "ladylike" and not take part in the same activities as boys. (Sample modification: Girls should act differently than boys. Yes or No?) |
| | | 4. Ultimately, people are more alike than they are different. (Sample modification: People are mostly the same. Yes or No?) |
| | | 5. Even though people say everyone should be treated equally, people don't always practice it. (Sample modification: People aren't always treated the same by others. Yes or No?) |
| | | 6. If a jury finds someone guilty, that means they are. (Sample modification: Yes or No?) |

**Part 2**

---

Now that you have read *To Kill a Mockingbird*, go back and look at the statements and your choices. Decide again if you agree or disagree with each statement as it relates to the story. Next to the number write your choice using SUPPORT from the text to justify your decision.

---

| Agree | Disagree | Evidence from the text |
|---|---|---|
| | | 1 |
| | | 2 |
| | | 3 |
| | | 4 |
| | | 5 |
| | | 6 |

## Steps to Creating an Anticipation Guide:

Step 1:   Identify major issues and themes from the text you plan to teach.

Step 2:   Determine ways students might react to these themes and issues.

Step 3:   Create statements that are relevant to the text and to students' lives, with which they can agree or disagree. Statements should be thought-provoking and meaningful to the students. For level 1 and level 2 students, statements may be modified to be more simplistic, yes or no statements.

Step 4:    Create a place for students to write a justification for their response.

Step 5:    Share the anticipation guide with your students. Allow them time to provide thoughtful responses.

Step 6:    Have students share their responses to the anticipation guide. Consider using small groups before having a large group discussion. Encourage students to justify their opinions.

Step 7:    Read the selection of the text. This may be a short text such as a poem or short story, or it may be a long text such as a book chapter or entire novel.

Step 8:    Return to the anticipation guide as a postreading activity. Encourage students to respond to the statements with evidence from the text.

Anticipation guides give students a preview of the major ideas of a text, activate students' prior knowledge, can challenge students' beliefs, and can require students to support their ideas with evidence. They are useful tools for promoting and fostering discussion and are excellent tools for motivating students to read. If students are invested in the content of a text and are able to see the relevance of a text, they will be more likely to engage in reading.

---

**Teaching Tip**

If issues are complex and do not lend themselves to a simple agree or disagree response, which is appropriate for level 1, 2, and 3 students, you could use a Likert-type scale, such as 1 being strongly agree and 5 being strongly disagree, for level 4 students.

---

**Extension Activity**

In part 2, in order to raise comprehensibility for ELLs, students could adopt the role of a particular character and respond to the statements. For example, students could take on the role of Scout or Aunt Alexandra.

---

## Concept Maps (Levels 1, 2, 3, and 4)

Concept maps are diagrams that help students understand how words or ideas are related to one another. Typically, the main topic of the lesson or issue is placed in the middle of the map and then lines are used to show relationships between words and ideas. Concept maps help students brainstorm different aspects of a topic and help them organize information about that topic. Concept maps can be very simple or detailed, and you can encourage students to use their creativity. Concept maps work well for ELLs because they provide a visual representation of a concept, and students do not always have to rely solely on verbal representations of concepts; they can also use pictures and illustrations to demonstrate their knowledge. As a prereading activity, concept maps help students activate their prior knowledge of a topic and set the stage for ideas they will encounter in a text. You can also provide students with key vocabulary from the text and have them include those words in their concept map.

## Steps to Creating a Concept Map:

Step 1:   Before reading a text, write the concept you want students to explore in the middle of the board or have students write the word in the middle of their paper.

Step 2:   Have students brainstorm different words, ideas, and topics that they associate with the concept. You can list them on the board or have students write them on a piece of paper.

Step 3:   Have students group the ideas and identify their relationship to the main concept. Have students map the relationships to the main concept on their paper.

Step 4:   Have students share their maps and discuss the different attributes and related ideas of the concept.

Step 5:   Introduce key vocabulary from the text and have students place the vocabulary words next to the appropriate topic or subtopic on the map.

Step 5:   After reading the text, ask students to return to their concept maps and revise them or add details from their reading. You can also have students add quotations from the text to support their ideas.

Modifications for level 1 and 2 students: Students can use heritage language dictionaries to help them understand the new words and concepts they come across. Students can be given time to

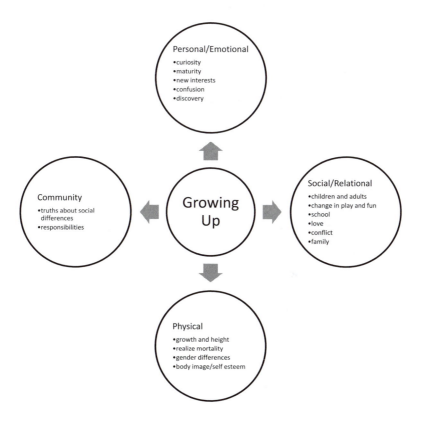

**FIGURE 3.1.**  Sample concept map for the unit theme "Growing Up."

translate the words and concepts that they have brainstormed into their native language; in addition, consider providing them with synonyms to words to help them increase their vocabulary knowledge.

---

**Extension Activity**

Concept maps can be used in a variety of ways in literature. They can be used as during-reading strategies in which students map relationships between characters or plot the events of a story. Students can map themes and symbols in a story and add quotations for support. Maps can also be used as cooperative learning activities. Concept maps make great study guides as well. In this way ELL students can show their understanding with a reduced amount of print.

---

## Author's Promise (Levels 1, 2, 3, and 4)

In order to introduce students to the writing style and key ideas of a novel, teachers can read aloud the first chapter or section of a novel to students. English language learners can benefit from read alouds as teachers can model effective reading techniques. According to Burke (2008), reading aloud to students not only helps them enjoy a good story and engage them in a text, it also assists struggling readers and ELL students by helping them understand what a text is supposed to sound like. This can be especially important when the author's writing style is unique or complex. Teachers can convey tone and mood, emphasize important passages, and make dialogue come to life through reading aloud. The Author's Promise is a prereading strategy that utilizes reading aloud.

### Steps to the Author's Promise Activity:

Step 1:  Read aloud the first chapter of a novel or first section of a longer text.

Step 2:  As you are reading aloud, ask students to jot down any questions they have about what is happening in the story. Student may jot down the following:

- questions about the characters in the story;
- questions about the setting of the story;
- questions about unfamiliar words or concepts;
- questions about particular events in the story;
- items that amused them;
- items that confused them;
- predictions about what they think will happen next.

although level 1 and level 2 students may not be able to create their own questions, they can benefit from listening to other students' questions and can be provided with the questions as a post-read aloud guide. The teacher can rephrase the responses of other students into yes/no and choice questions to ask these students. In addition, students could create visual representations of what is happening in the first chapter as you are reading aloud.

Step 3:    After reading the selection, have students share their questions and explain to students that the first chapter of a novel is very important. Authors establish expectations (make promises to the reader) in the first chapter that can help guide them throughout their reading of the novel.

Step 4:    Have students use the questions they generated as prompts and ideas to consider as they continue reading the novel. Students should keep these questions in their reading logs or journals and refer to them in large and small group discussions of the novel.

Adapted from an activity by Jean Boreen, Professor of English Education at Northern Arizona University.

## Sample Author's Promise Questions for *To Kill a Mockingbird* by Harper Lee (Chapter 1)

- What happened to Jem's arm?
- What were the "events leading to the accident?" (p. 1)
- Who is Boo Radley?
- Why won't he come out?
- Why does Scout call her father "Atticus" and not Dad?
- Why does Scout need to tell us the history of Maycomb and its inhabitants?
- What is Scout's family life like?
- How does Scout already know how to read?
- Where is Dill's father?
- What was the Battle of Hastings?
- Where is Maycomb on a map?
- How old is Scout when she is telling this story?

## Predicting and Confirming Activity (Levels 1, 2, 3, and 4)

Frequently used in social studies classrooms, the Predicting and Confirming Activity (PACA) can be used in the ELA classroom to help ELL students make predictions about a text and develop background and vocabulary knowledge. This strategy is especially useful if students have little first-hand experience about a topic and helps them set a purpose for reading. For example, an ELA teacher may teach a unit on the theme of "Overcoming Obstacles" and students will read novels set during the Great Depression. To enhance their understanding of the time period, as well as to develop their nonfiction reading comprehension skills, they would also be reading expository texts dealing with this time in U.S. history. Although students may have heard about the Great Depression, they may have misconceptions or gaps in their understanding, in which case the teacher may decide to use the PACA.

---

**Extension Activity**

The photographs from the American Memory Project are very powerful. Level 3 and 4 students could use them as visual prompts to help them write poems or short stories. For example, students could write a narrative poem about a character or scene in one of the photographs.

---

**ACTIVITY 3.6. Sample PACA using the Great Depression**

Step 1: The teacher poses a general question. For example: What was life like for people in the United States during the Great Depression?

Step 2: The teacher provides initial information. The teacher divides students into groups and gives groups a word list with terms associated with the topic. The teacher asks students, based on the list of terms, to determine what life was like for people during the Great Depression. Students discuss their answers to the question with their groups. Level 1 and level 2 students can be given time to translate the terms into their first language and can be provided with synonyms to help them improve their vocabulary.

| | | |
|---|---|---|
| stock market | Black Tuesday | The Dust Bowl |
| economy | lynching | Hoovervilles |
| foreclosure | The New Deal | panic |
| Okie migrations | radicals | endure |
| arduous | recovery | soup kitchens |
| segregation | drought | hobo |
| Federal Reserve | crash | speculation |

Step 3: Students write predictions. Based on their small group discussions, students predict what they think they will learn about life during the Great Depression. The teacher records these predictions (on an overhead or the chalkboard) and asks students to explain what words elicited their predictions. For example, students might predict that many people were poor during the Great Depression, that life was hard for people, that the government was responsible for the poverty, etc.

Step 4: The teacher provides new information: this could be through pictures, a film, a story, or an article. For example, the teacher could have students examine photographs from the American Memory Project, a collection available through the Library of Congress, which contains an extensive collection of photographs documenting American life during the Great Depression (http://memory.loc.gov/ammem/fsowhome.html). Level 1 and 2 students can be asked questions about what is happening in the pictures and be asked to provide words to describe them.

**FIGURE 3.2.** Dwellers in Circleville's "Hooverville," central Ohio, 1938.
Courtesy of the Library of Congress, LC-USF33-006580-M4.

**FIGURE 3.3.** Dwellers in Circleville's "Hooverville," central Ohio, 1938.
Courtesy of the Library of Congress, LC-USF33-006579-M2 .

Step 5: Students revise or modify their statements based on the new information. For example, students may have predicted that Hoovervilles were prosperous towns named to celebrate President Hoover, when in fact they were shanty towns for the homeless.

Step 6: Students actively read (or have a partner read to them) the assigned text selection, using their predictions as a guide.

Step 7: Students and the teacher work together to revise their predictions after reading.

Adapted from Irvin, Buehl, and Klemp (2007: 135–136).

## During-Reading Activities

In order to teach the processes and strategies of effective readers, it is important for students to engage in activities while they are reading. Simply giving a reading assignment and then questioning students about a text can be very problematic for ELLs; students need opportunities to practice becoming active readers. This may involve using guided reading activities in which the students and the teacher are reading together and stopping to practice a particular comprehension strategy such as making inferences, recognizing the main idea, or constructing meaning and interpretation. Other strategies include teaching students how to respond to a text independently as they are reading it. Sasser (1992) emphasizes the importance of helping students make literature more comprehensible through *during-reading activities* while actively teaching reading strategies.

## Talking to the Text (Levels 2, 3, and 4)

Effective readers actively engage in meaning making as they read literature. English language learners need opportunities to stop and reflect on what they have read. Students should be encouraged to respond directly to what they are reading; although writing on texts is not always feasible, teachers can use sticky notes to encourage students to interact with what they are reading. Sticky notes are popular with students because they can be small, and students may feel less intimidated to write. Also, sticky notes are not permanent, so they can appear informal and less threatening.

Teachers can model what good readers do by requiring that students record their thoughts about what they are reading on sticky notes and then use their responses to generate discussion about text content and reading processes. In the beginning, ELL students may need a lot of structure and directions for responding to what they are reading, and all students will need to be told explicitly what types of responses you are looking for.

## Steps to Talking to the Text:

Step 1: Preview the text and determine effective stopping places for students to respond to the reading selection. Texts can be divided into "chunks" based on length, transition points, difficult passages, important events, etc.

Step 2: Explain to students that they are going to record their thoughts about what they are reading and have them write their thoughts on a sticky note and place it next to the corresponding section of the text. English language learners may need prompts to help them get started recording their reader responses. If we go back to the strategies of effective readers, many of these can be turned into prompts or sentence starters that ELLs can use to talk to the text.

**ACTIVITY 3.7.  Prompts for Talking to the Text**

| | |
|---|---|
| Ask questions | I wonder . . . with the five W's and an H |
| Summarize | The author is saying . . . |
| Identify main ideas | This is important because . . . |
| Make connections | This reminds me of . . . |
| Make inferences | I think this . . . because . . . |
| Visualize | I imagine/picture/see (or simply create a drawing) |
| Monitor comprehension | I am confused because . . . |
| Use strategies to understand new vocabulary | I think this word means . . . because . . . |
| Create interpretations of literature | This sentence/passage means . . . |

Step 3: Model using sticky notes with a short selection such as a poem or passage from a short story. Then have students try it on their own. Level 2 students can create pictures or write one- to two-word responses on their sticky notes. Level 3 and 4 students can use the prompts provided.

Step 4: Once students have completed the reading, have them work in pairs or groups to share their responses. As students gain independence as active readers, the sticky notes can be turned in as accountability for active reading.

Step 5: Debrief the strategy with students. Ask them what kinds of questions this particular text created for them. What kinds of strategies/prompts did they find themselves using (for example, did they find themselves frequently making personal connections or did they find a number of unfamiliar words)?

### Extension Activities

- As students become more experienced with Talking to the Text, allow them to veer away from the prompts and simply record their thoughts. Then have students get into groups and cluster their responses and categorize them. Students can then generate a class set of prompts that may be more useful to them than the ones you created.

- Sticky notes can be expensive. Instead, create bookmarks on which students can record their responses and identify the page number or passage where they chose to respond.
- Annotating texts: For shorter texts, such as poems, you could photocopy the poem on one side of the page and on the other side indicate places for students to stop and respond. The same thing can be done for a section of a short story.

## Double Entry Journals (Levels 2, 3, and 4)

Like sticky notes, double entry journals promote active reading. Students must stop and reflect on what they are reading and pay closer attention to the content of the text. In *I Read It, but I Don't Get It*, Chris Tovani (2000) provides a number of recommendations for using "Double Entry Diaries (DEDS)" to help adolescents develop reading comprehension skills. The basic model for a double entry journal is to have students divide a piece of paper in half and then record items from the text on one side and their reading responses on the other. Depending upon the reading level of the student, teachers can provide prompts (such as those provided in the Talking to the Text section) or students can determine their own categories. Considering the needs of the language learner and the specific reading strategy you would like to teach, there can be numerous uses for double entry journals in the classroom. The following are just a few examples of what students may record in their journals.

**ACTIVITY 3.8.** Sample headings for double entry journals

| Left hand side | Right hand side | Reinforces |
|---|---|---|
| Quotations from the text | Questions (questioning the author, questions for discussion, I wonder . . . ) | Developing questioning strategies |
| Quotations from the text | Explanation of its significance Identification of literary devices | Literary interpretations |
| Quotations from the text | This reminds me of . . . <br> my experiences (text to self) <br> other things I have read (text to text) <br> important issues (text to world) | Making connections |
| Quotations from the text | This is important because | Identifying main ideas |
| What the text says | What it means | Summarizing |
| Quotations from the text | Drawings | Visualizing |
| Unfamiliar words and what I think they mean | Why I think that | Using context clues |
| What confused me about the text | How I figured it out | Using fix-up strategies |

**Teaching Tip**

Although double entry journals can be very useful for getting students to take a closer look at a text, for some students they can seem daunting. Students sometimes indicate that having to stop and copy quotations interrupts their flow during reading and results in a loss of comprehension. Again, chunking the text into sections is especially useful for ELLs. Teachers can determine appropriate stopping places and then students can go back and choose important or significant passages to record.

**Extension Activities**

- Reading logs: Level 3 and 4 students can be encouraged to write their own responses to literature in sentence and paragraph form in the style of journal entries.
- Dialogue journals: Students write their reading log responses as letters to a peer and students can trade reading log entries and respond to each other's letters.
- Additions of specific elements: Teachers can use reading logs to reinforce daily lessons, such as having students identify certain literary elements such as symbolism or theme, and as extensions of topics that come up during discussion.

## Literature Circles (Levels 2, 3, and 4)

Many of these strategies have emphasized the importance of providing ELLs with frequent and regular opportunities to speak and interact with other students, especially those who have a greater proficiency in English (Ernst-Slavit, Moore, & Maloney, 2002). When conducted properly, using literature circles can be a successful way to help ELLs improve their reading skills through collaboration with their peers while also engaging and motivating them to read. For an in-depth discussion of how to implement literature circles in the ELA classroom, see Harvey Daniels's (2002) *Literature Circles: Voice and Choice in Book Clubs and Reading Groups*. Modeled after adult book clubs, literature circles are designed to engage students in authentic and meaningful discussion of texts while providing students with the tools to become better readers. Although there are a great many ways to conduct literature circles, ranging from the very structured to the very casual, the following is a discussion of specific attributes of literature circles that can be beneficial to ELLs. Although literature circles are geared more toward level 3 and 4 students, level 2 students can practice literature circles with picture books and use graphic organizers such as the role sheets discussed below.

- Texts for literature circles are selected by the students. Texts should be of high interest and accessible to students. Multicultural literature and/or adolescent literature work well for ELLs. Allowing students ownership over their choice of text can help to motivate them to read and finding culturally relevant texts can help ELLs use their background knowledge to improve their reading comprehension.
- Literature circles consist of small heterogeneous groups of students based on book choice. This aspect is conducive to ELLs because it provides opportunities for students to work with

students who may be more proficient in English; of course, ELA teachers may need to help with choosing groups, as students' reading abilities will need to be considered.

- Students divide the text into chunks and meet regularly to discuss the reading. Breaking a text into smaller sections allows students the opportunity to discuss the text while they are reading, which can improve ELLs' reading comprehension.
- Students generate the discussion topics. This provides a more authentic opportunity for ELLs to engage in open-ended conversations with less pressure to provide a "right answer." English language learners can practice and develop their language skills in a low-stakes environment. In addition, ELLs can learn new reading strategies as they listen to their peers' experiences with the text.
- The teacher serves as a facilitator, not an instructor, and evaluation is through observation and student self-assessment. Students are encouraged to assess their own progress and participation in literature circles; this can improve their metacognitive skills while also providing intrinsic motivation to read. Because the teacher did not *teach* the text to the class, it should not be measured by a formal assessment such as an exam over its content, which may be problematic for ELLs in lower proficiency levels.
- When groups finish their text, they share it with the rest of the class and new groups are formed. The sharing of the literature circles text provides a multitude of opportunities for students to express their learning in alternative ways: Students can perform a section of the text dramatically; they could create a movie trailer advertising the book; they could use technology to create a slide show of possible book covers, etc. English language learners can benefit from more creative ways of expressing their knowledge of a text, and they can rely on their strengths and multiple intelligences.

Again, there are many ways to conduct literature circles in the ELA classroom; some teachers choose to use a more structured approach whereby students all study the same text and the teacher has more of a role in instruction. The decisions teachers make about using literature circles should depend on their knowledge of their students' needs and abilities.

Because students need to come to group meetings prepared to discuss what they have read, they should be encouraged to use an active reading tool. Any of the during-reading strategies discussed in this chapter can be used for literature circles: Talking to the Text with sticky notes, double entry journals, and reading logs. In addition, Daniels (2002) developed the concept of role sheets whereby students rotate responsibilities for generating group discussion based on specific reading skills and tasks. These roles mirror many of the practices of effective readers that teachers should make explicit to their ELLs. Students are provided with specific roles to use during reading, fill out their role sheets before group meetings, and then share what they have discovered with their group. Daniels (2002) divides the roles into two groups, basic and optional, depending upon the needs of the reader and the type of text being used:

- Basic roles:

  - "Connector": This person's job is to make connections to the text such as personal connections (text to self), connections across texts (text to text), and connections to events in society (texts to world).
  - "Questioner": This person's job is to generate questions for group discussion that can encourage students to develop their abilities to critically analyze a text.
  - "Literary luminary/passage master": This person's job is to find important passages in the text and bring them to the group for discussion.

- "Illustrator": This person creates a visual image of something from the reading selection such as illustrating a scene, a character, or more abstract concepts such as symbolism or theme. This role can be especially beneficial for ELLs who may not be completely confident in their writing ability.

- Optional roles:

  - "Summarizer": This person creates summaries of the text selection focusing on main ideas or events.
  - "Researcher": This person finds outside information related to topics from the text selection to provide background information or elaborate on ideas presented in the reading.
  - "Travel tracer/scene setter": This person keeps track of changes in the setting of the story.
    Adapted from Daniels (2002: 103).

Graphic organizers tailored to the activity help lower-level ELLs work through the linguistic aspects of their roles. As with any other reading strategy, teachers will need to model using literature circles effectively. Teachers can give students a short reading selection such as a book chapter or short story and have students practice using the role sheets. The whole class can meet to debrief the processes required in using the role sheets and talk about how to use them during group meetings. Teachers can also ask for groups to volunteer to model a group meeting for the rest of the class. Students, especially ELLs, may need additional help with reading skills and strategies such as creating good questions and choosing appropriate passages for group discussion. English language arts teachers can create mini-lessons that demonstrate these skills as well as more complex literary processes such as identifying themes and symbolism. Finally, Daniels points out that students may also need lessons on the social skills required for working in groups such as listening effectively, taking turns, and responding to others appropriately. Students should be encouraged to conduct self-evaluations, which include their preparedness for group meetings and their contributions to discussion. Teachers can have whole class debriefing sessions when they talk with students about what worked and what didn't during the day's meeting.

## Directed Reading Sequence: Summarizing, Identifying Main Ideas and Details (Levels 2, 3, and 4)

A cooperative learning strategy that can be adapted to help ELLs comprehend informational texts is the directed reading sequence. In this activity, students read together in small groups while the teacher facilitates. Working collaboratively helps ELLs practice their language skills in a low-stakes setting, helps them learn reading strategies from more proficient readers, and helps them develop specific reading skills including summarizing, elaborating, and retelling. Level 2 students can benefit from hearing a text read aloud and participating in the group activities. Like many reading strategies, directed reading sequence chunks the text into manageable pieces and has students stop and discuss the text while they are reading it. The following steps are an adaptation of the directed reading sequence discussed in *Reading and the High School Student* (Irvin, Buehl, & Klemp, 2007).

### Steps to Conducting a Directed Reading Sequence:

Step 1:    Choose an appropriate text and divide it into sections based on the needs and abilities of the ELL students as well as the text structure. Sections may be easy to establish based on section headings and subheadings, or teachers may have to preview the text looking for appropriate stopping points such as dividing up more challenging sections into manageable chunks.

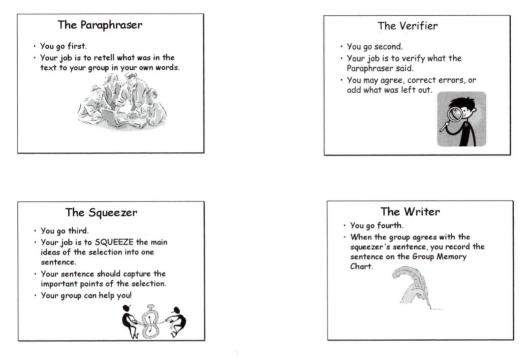

**The Paraphraser**

· You go first.
· Your job is to retell what was in the text to your group in your own words.

**The Verifier**

· You go second.
· Your job is to verify what the Paraphraser said.
· You may agree, correct errors, or add what was left out.

**The Squeezer**

· You go third.
· Your job is to SQUEEZE the main ideas of the selection into one sentence.
· Your sentence should capture the important points of the selection.
· Your group can help you!

**The Writer**

· You go fourth.
· When the group agrees with the squeezer's sentence, you record the sentence on the Group Memory Chart.

**FIGURE 3.4.** Sample directed reading sequence role cards.

Step 2:    Students are given specific reading roles, similar to literature circle roles, which they will rotate as they read a section. The difference between these roles is that they focus more on the strategies necessary for understanding informational text (summarizing and retelling). The roles can be put on cards with instructions and handed out to students. The first role is the "paraphraser," who summarizes what was in the selection; the next role is the "verifier"/illustrator, who clarifies and fills in any details that the paraphraser missed—if the verifier doesn't have anything to add, he/she can create an illustration that represents the gist of the selection; the third role is the "squeezer," who takes the summary and puts it into one sentence; and the fourth role is the "writer," who writes the sentence onto the "group memory chart."

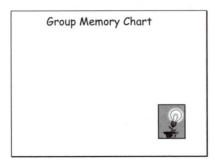

**Group Memory Chart**

Step 3:    The group memory chart acts as the record of the summaries of the reading and can be used as a study guide for the students. Once the groups have recorded their sentence onto the group memory chart, the teacher could ask for volunteers to share their sentences and record them on the board as models. In addition, the students could debrief the strategy and discuss the characteristics of a good summary.

Step 4:    The groups then read the next selection and change roles, recording their summaries on the group memory chart. This continues until the reading of the text is complete. The teacher may decide to read some of the sections aloud with the entire class and alternate with silent reading of the text, depending upon the ability levels of the students.

## After-Reading Activities

In addition to helping students become more active readers and teaching them to use the strategies of effective readers during reading, ELA teachers can use postreading strategies to help ELLs examine and reflect upon what they have read. In addition, teachers can use postreading activities to help students summarize information, revise their interpretations, draw conclusions, and evaluate the reading. The following postreading activities are designed to help students understand story elements such as plot and character. Once teachers have helped ELLs synthesize the reading material to create a more complete picture, they can then move them to lessons which require deeper levels of literary understanding, such as the activities discussed in Chapter 3.3.

## Story Map (Levels 1, 2, 3, and 4)

Before ELA teachers delve into the literary analysis of a story, they need to determine that students are familiar with the basic elements of a story such as plot, characters, setting, sequence of events, and outcome. Story maps are an excellent tool for helping ELLs organize information and they provide them with the vocabulary with which to discuss a story. In addition, story maps are visual representations that can help ELLs remember what they have read and can allow them the opportunity to use symbols and other graphics to represent abstract ideas. There are several types of graphic organizers that represent story structure available to teachers; depending on the ability level of the learner they may focus on the more simplistic elements of a story's structure or they can include more complex elements such as rising action, climax, falling action, and resolution. English language arts teachers can provide students with a story map before reading and students can fill it out during or after reading. Level 1 students can be given a simplified version of the story in English. Several publishers produce classics aimed at level 1 and 2 students who have a very limited vocabulary. In addition, level 1 and 2 students can fill out the maps using pictures as well as words. Students should be encouraged to work collaboratively with their peers, either filling out their maps together or sharing their results. As ELLs become more comfortable with story structure, they can create their own maps which can be more creative and include more elements, independently or in groups.

## Character Maps and Charts (Levels 1, 2, 3, and 4)

Like story maps, character maps and charts can help ELLs develop a greater understanding of the elements of literature and can promote retention of what they have read. Character maps are visual representations of a character's attributes, both literal, such as physical characteristics, and figurative, such as what the character may represent. Depending upon the level of the language learner, character maps can be modified to include more concrete or more abstract thinking.

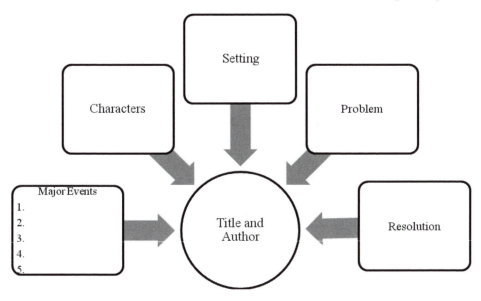

**FIGURE 3.6.** Sample story map.

For a basic character map, students can be asked after reading a story (or during a longer text such as a novel) to place a representation of a character on a sheet of paper. They can draw a picture of the character, cut out a picture from a magazine, or create a symbol representing the character. Students can then surround the character with descriptions of their attributes and/or write a sentence about the character. Students could also create a character map that represents the relationships between characters, perhaps drawing the main character in the center of the map and showing relationships with arrows or lines to other characters. Finally, students can be asked to extend their understanding of characters to include the techniques an author uses to help readers understand a character such as the author's description, the character's words, thoughts, and actions, and what other characters say and think. This information could be placed in a chart and quotations from the text could be used for support.

**ACTIVITY 3.9.** Sample character chart

---

**Character**

---

Description (mine and author's)                Quote: What he/she says


Quote: What others say about him or her        Symbols attached to the character
                                               (visualizing)

---

**Teaching Tip**

Depending upon the ability level of the students, these charts and maps can be used independently or with partners or in small groups. Teachers can introduce the maps and charts by modeling with a more familiar character and then asking students to create maps for additional members of the story. Character maps can be used as post-read aloud activities as well. Teachers should let ELL students have a bilingual dictionary on hand.

**Extension Activities**

- On large pieces of chart paper, students can trace the outline of a peer to use as a model for a character. They can then label different parts of the outline with descriptions of the character; for example, next to the character's heart they could write emotional characteristics.
- In an activity often referred to as the Open Mind, students can be given a graphic organizer that represents the head of a character. In it, students can write or draw the inner thoughts of a character during a particular point in the story.
- Character Bags: Similar to the Open Mind activity, students are given paper bags that represent a character. On the outside, they decorate the bag with the character's external characteristics. On the inside, they can place items, symbols, words, or phrases that represent the character's inner self.

## Dramatic Tableaux (Levels 1, 2, 3, and 4)

Dramatic tableaux is an activity that can combine the understanding of both character and plot and can help ELLs synthesize information from their reading. Dramatic tableaux is a dramatic activity in which students are asked to physically construct a scene from literature through body placement, visual expressions, and possibly the use of props. Students create a freeze frame of the scene and the audience is asked to identify and discuss the scene. Dramatic tableaux draws on many reading comprehension skills: summarizing, identifying what is important, visualizing, and understanding character. In addition, it is an engaging and motivating activity in which all ELLs can participate.

### Steps to Using Dramatic Tableaux:

Step 1:   In groups, students are provided with a scene from a work of literature (this could be from a poem, a short story, or a novel).

Step 2:   Students meet to prepare their tableau. Students can use the five W's and an H to brainstorm their scene:

- Who is in this scene?
- What are they doing? What are they thinking?

- Why is this scene important?
- When (in the story) does this scene take place?
- Where (in the setting) does this scene take place?
- How will you present this scene to your audience?

Step 3:   Students present their tableau to the class. Groups should be given time to set up their scene before the audience is asked to guess the scene. After the scene has been presented, the teacher can facilitate a discussion of the scene and how it relates to the story including reviewing the five W's and an H. In addition, the students representing the characters in the scene could discuss how that character might be feeling and what he/she might be thinking.

Step 4:   The teachers and students can debrief the use of dramatic tableaux: How were the scenes presented similar to or different from what the students had envisioned as they were reading the literature? What reading strategies did they have to use to prepare their scene?

---

### Teaching Tip

Because part of the fun of this activity is guessing which scene is being presented, teachers will want to give the audience time to think about what they are seeing and should encourage students not to "shout out" the answer. Teachers could have students write their guesses on a slip of paper or have students raise their hands, using appropriate wait time before calling on them.

---

### Extension Activities

- Dramatic tableaux can be combined with other postreading activities such as character maps to help students prepare for their scenes.
- As a follow-up activity, students could write a letter to their character discussing the event of the scene in relationship to the story.
- Students could create more than one freeze frame to represent a story or idea.

## Children's Information Picture Books (Levels 1, 2, 3, and 4)

Informational texts can be used in the classroom to help ELLs develop background knowledge they may be lacking compared with other students. Mundy and Hadaway (1999) discuss the use of children's informational picture books to help ELL students build background knowledge about a topic before having students tackle more complex reading material. Unlike some classroom texts, informational picture books are shorter in length, chunk information, and use graphics and illustrations as comprehension aids. Whereas Mundy and Hadaway used picture books to help students understand a science unit on weather, informational picture books are being developed that can help struggling readers (including ELLs) in a variety of content areas.

# 3.3
# Reading Literature

Literature provides students with valuable authentic material that speaks to fundamental human issues that transcend time and culture. Through reading rich literature, students gain familiarity with different linguistic forms, uses, and conventions of the written mode. Furthermore, literature incorporates a great deal of cultural information and can give learners insight into the country of the target language. Extensive reading increases learner's receptive vocabulary and facilitates transfer to active forms of knowledge. Literature also provides a rich context in which to study lexical and syntactic structures and serves as an excellent prompt for oral work. Finally, literature engages students on a personal level. Connecting with literature enables learners to shift the focus of their attention beyond the more mechanical aspects of the language system and inhabit the world of fiction. The study of literature is one of the main activities of the secondary English/language arts classroom; however, most teachers feel unprepared to teach these challenging texts to ELLs. This chapter will provide activities that will allow ELL students to engage in the study of literature.

The National Council of Teachers of English position paper on *The Role of English Teachers in Educating English Language Learners* (2006) recommends that teachers support ELL's literacy development by introducing classroom reading materials that are culturally relevant, by connecting the readings to students' background knowledge and experiences, and by having students read more accessible texts on a topic before moving to complex texts. Thus, we have incorporated adolescent literature into this chapter as well. Because motivation to read adolescent literature is usually strong, teachers are afforded an excellent opportunity to work with ELLs to increase their comprehension strategy use, to make textual connections, and to prepare to study literature that is more challenging. The academic language of literature, such as theme, plot, characterization, imagery, and other literary terms, can be introduced in the course of reading these highly engaging and accessible texts.

## Making Classic Works of Literature More Accessible (Levels 1, 2, 3, and 4)

One of the tasks that teachers find daunting is the fact that they are required to teach a certain curriculum regardless of the level of student abilities in the classroom. For instance, in the county where we teach it is recommended that students read *A Separate Peace*, *A Tale of Two Cities* and *Julius Caesar* in the tenth grade. These are texts with which even our proficient native English speaking students have difficulty. How can we be expected to teach such works to ELLs, particularly those who are in (level 1) the preproduction and (level 2) speech emergent stages? We have read the research that tells us the importance of selecting appropriate texts by matching the reading level of the texts to the reading level of the students, but sometimes this is not an option. In such cases, there are a few ways to assist readers who are not yet proficient enough to read the required texts on their own.

## Reading the Texts as They Are

- Reading to the students: Most students enjoy being read to for set periods of time. Reading aloud models expressive reading and illuminates how unfamiliar words are pronounced. Be aware, however, that listening to a story being read aloud places heavy cognitive demands on ELLs. Stop frequently to review important concepts, clarify vocabulary, and discuss or question the text. English language learners can also benefit by hearing classmates read aloud as much as having the teacher read aloud.
- Listening to books on audiotape or podcast: Many books can be purchased in audio format with the author or a famous actor reading the novel. This option provides the same benefit to the student as having the teacher read to them, and it is a good option for teachers who are not adept at oral reading. This may be a first option for some powerful recordings such as a recording of Martin Luther King, Jr. himself delivering his "I Have a Dream" speech.
- Choral reading: This read-aloud activity involves the repeated recitation of a short text along with motions or gestures to help students dramatize the words. Whereas McCauley and McCauley (1992) do not recommend this strategy for students above sixth grade, Calderon (2007) insists that she has seen it used at the high school level quite successfully. Much depends on the comfort level of your students and the type of text you are reading. Poetry reading is wonderful for choral reading. Students particularly enjoy reading Maya Angelou's (1994) *Phenomenal Woman* in choral fashion.
- Partner reading: In partner reading, students pair up and read to each other. At first, they may choose to alternate at each sentence, stopping at the end of short sections to share and debrief. As their reading confidence grows, they may want to read larger chunks of text to each other. This activity works well if you pair a native speaker with an ELL. The native speaker learns more because, in a sense, he or she is teaching, and we all learn more when we are the expert. The ELL student learns by listening to the native speaker pronounce words and honor punctuation marks.
- Shadow reading: In shadow reading, the ELL student reads aloud quietly with the student (or teacher) who is reading the text to the class (or partner). In this manner, ELLs increase their confidence as they find that it is becoming easier for them to follow along. Encourage them to volunteer to read aloud as the featured reader whenever they feel ready, but do not pressure them. Many ELLs—particularly adolescent ELLs—may be too self-conscious to read aloud.

- Reader's theater: Students take turns assuming roles of characters in the story and dramatizing the action. There are many variations of this activity. Teachers can use the text as it is and select parts with dialogue, or they can have students create dialogue for a scene. The most impromptu variation is when teachers write scenes on strips of paper, and have teams of students act them out with only a few minutes of preparation. For example, when teaching *Great Expectations* the teacher might give students a strip of paper that says *Act out Chapter One where Pip meets the convict for the first time. Your scene should include from where Pip begins to cry at the end of paragraph three to where Pip says, "Goo—good night, sir" to the convict.*

## Modifying the Texts

- Shortening a reading selection: Sometimes it is necessary for teachers to parse texts and have students read only the most important parts. Important portions include the inciting incident, climax, and resolution. Teachers may also want to incorporate sections of text that are rich in literary features or famous lines.
- Summarizing the reading selections: When the text is simply too lengthy or dense, it is feasible to have students read detailed summaries rather than the text itself.
- Rereading the text with cloze activities: Teachers may opt to have students read short segments of text and then have the students read the same segment with blanks inserted where certain words or grammatical concepts can be taught. Have students reread and fill in the blanks. Use this activity to teach the words or concepts.
- Rewriting the text: One activity we have used with great success is to encourage our native English speakers and ELLs at levels 3 and 4 to write modified versions of the text. For instance, one student rewrote *Julius Caesar* (Shakespeare, 1977a) in the format of a children's story while another created a "Classic Comics" version. We have also turned this into a cooperative activity with *Sir Gawain and the Green Knight* (Anonymous, 2007). Each student was assigned a certain number of lines to illustrate and asked to use captions or dialogue boxes. Within 20 minutes students had depicted their section of Sir Gawain's story on 8.5 × 11 inch sheets of paper and posted them chronologically as a border along the four walls of the classroom. Later, these sheets were carefully removed and placed in sheet protectors for posterity and for the reading enjoyment of future ELLs.
- Reading texts translated into the ELLs native language: What students learn while using their native language transfers to their second language (Gersten & Baker, 2000). Many books are available in translation, and with technology such as wireless reading devices (e.g. Kindle) translations are readily accessible. Many texts encourage teachers to ask community volunteers or advanced ELL students to translate texts. A word of caution: This is a very difficult and time-consuming task.

## Other Forms of Texts

- The movie version: There are now many wonderful film adaptations of classic works. ELL students may view the movie rather than read, or some hybrid of reading and watching can be arranged. Watching the film version engages the students with the story while lessening the cognitive load because language is accompanied by visual images. There are numerous BBC films, besides more modern versions, that include actors who are popular with today's students.

**TABLE 3.2.** Recent film adaptations of classic works

| Work title | Year and rating | Director | Famous actors |
| --- | --- | --- | --- |
| Jane Austen's *Pride and Prejudice* | 2005 (PG) | Joe Wright | Keira Knightley<br>Donald Sutherland<br>Judi Dench |
| Jane Austen's *Emma* | 1995 (PG) | Douglas McGrath | Gywneth Paltrow<br>Toni Collette |
| Kazuo Ishiguro's *Remains of the Day* | 1993 (PG) | James Ivory | Anthony Hopkins<br>Emma Thompson |
| C. S. Lewis' *Chronicles of Narnia* | 2005, 2008 (PG) | Andrew Adamson | Anna Popplewell<br>Tilda Swinton |
| William Shakespeare's *Romeo and Juliet* | 1996 (PG13) | Baz Luhrmann | Leonardo DiCaprio<br>Claire Danes<br>John Leguizamo |
| William Shakespeare's *Hamlet* | 1990 (PG) | Franco Zeffirelli | Mel Gibson<br>Glenn Close |
| William Shakespeare's *Othello* | 1995 (R) | Oliver Parker | Laurence Fishburne<br>Kenneth Branagh |
| Mary Shelley's *Frankenstein* | 1994 (R) | Kenneth Branagh | Robert De Niro<br>Helena Bonham Carter |
| Bram Stoker's *Dracula* | 1992 (R) | Francis Ford Coppola | Keanu Reeves<br>Anthony Hopkins |
| William Makepeace Thackeray's *Vanity Fair* | 2004 (PG13) | Mira Nair | Reese Witherspoon |
| J. R. R. Tolkien's *The Lord of the Rings* trilogy | 2001, 2002, and 2003 (PG13) | Peter Jackson | Elijah Wood<br>Orlando Bloom<br>Viggo Mortensen |
| H. G. Wells's *War of the Worlds* | 2005 (PG13) | Steven Spielberg | Tom Cruise<br>Dakota Fanning |
| Virginia Woolf's *The Hours* | 2003 (PG13) | Stephan Daldry | Nicole Kidman<br>Meryl Streep |

## Updating the Classics (Levels 1, 2, 3, and 4)

Enactments are an under-utilized pedagogical technique that is especially motivating for reluctant readers and at-risk youth (Smith & Wilhelm, 2002). This popular postreading activity involves rewriting portions of the text in modern language in screenplay format and creating a movie from the new version. Enactments enliven students' participation because lines must be "translated" and spoken with feeling. Students also enjoy the social aspect of creating scenes in groups where they discuss the text and negotiate meanings. Because each member must have a role in the enactment, each has an interest in the success of the production.

1. Assign students portions of the text (or allow them to choose) to rewrite in modern-day language.
2. Have students create a screenplay for their part of the work.
3. Obtain video cameras from the library or ask the school's video production crew to assist you, and tape the students' scenes.
4. Play the scenes in chronological order on "Premier Day," the day the class views each group's video.

**Teaching Tips**

- Consider having students videotape rather than act out live in class. It is more time efficient and helps avoid wasted class time when students are struck by "the giggles." Some students also enjoy the editing part of the project.
- Allow students leeway with regard to how they recreate their work. One of us had students who created a wonderful African-American English version of *The Great Gatsby* with all of the male students decked out in bowler hats, double-breasted suits, and silk shirts (their prom attire!) and a *Julius Caesar* in which all of the characters were from Brooklyn except for Brutus who was Dominican and spoke parts of his lines in Spanish. Julius Caesar became "Jules," his wife Calpurnia became "Cal," and the conspirators took him to the "Bowl-a-rama" for the death scene. English language learners may incorporate their native language into the dialogue. Once, students created a whole scene in Spanish with English subtitles!

**Extension Activity**

Musical students may enjoy creating a soundtrack to the modernized version. The soundtrack can be composed of original material or popular songs. Ask students to provide the lyrics and explain why the song is appropriate for the chosen scene.

## Using Adolescent Literature as a Bridge to the Classics (Levels 3 and 4)

Young adult novels serve as an excellent bridge to reading more difficult texts. For instance, Sharon Draper's (2001) *Romiette and Julio* effectively parallels and contemporizes Shakespeare's *Romeo and Juliet* (1977b) as does Walter Dean Myers's (2006) *Street Love*. Reading a young adult novel with a similar story and themes to the classic novel builds background knowledge and schema to make the more difficult text accessible to ELL students. It is easier to discuss some of the abstract concepts of themes in relation to the young adult novel than in relation to the classic, on which students are working hard simply to understand the language. For instance, some of the themes of Shakespeare's *Romeo and Juliet* include fate, the individual versus society, the power of love, and civil disorder. Such themes can be introduced in the young adult novels that are paired with the classic and facilitate later discussion of the classics. Here are a few examples of thematic pairings provided to the authors by Joan Kaywell (personal communication, February 10, 2009).

**TABLE 3.3.** Thematic pairings of classic novels and adolescent literature by Joan Kaywell

| Classic | Adolescent literature | Themes/topics in common |
|---------|----------------------|------------------------|
| Lee, H. (1960). *To kill a mockingbird.* New York: Warner Books. | Moses, S. (2003). *The legend of Buddy Bush.* New York: Simon & Schuster. | Based on an actual trial that occurred in 1947 of a black man accused of raping a white woman |
| Gibson, W. (2002). *The miracle worker.* New York: Simon & Schuster. | Trueman, T. (2001). *Stuck in neutral.* New York: HarperCollins. | Special needs relationships |
| Frank, A. (1993). *The diary of a young girl.* New York: Bantam Books. | Filipovic, Z. (2006). *Zlata's diary: A child's life in wartime Sarajevo.* New York: Penguin Group (USA). | Zlata Filipovic is "the Anne Frank of Sarajevo" |
| Hansberry, L. (1994). *A raisin in the sun.* New York: Knopf Publishing Group. | Fogelin, A. (2002). *Crossing Jordan.* Atlanta, GA: Peachtree Publishers. | Conflicts of race and family |
| Bradbury, R. (1987). *Fahrenheit 451.* New York: Random House. | Anderson, M. T. (2003). *Feed.* Somerville, MA: Candlewick Press. | Media and censorship |

---

**Teaching Tip**

Both Kaywell's (1993–2000) series *Adolescent Literature as a Complement to the Classics* and Herz and Gallo's (2005) *From Hinton to Hamlet: Building Bridges between Young Adult Literature and the Classics* offer thematic pairings of young adult novels and classics and provide excellent teaching activities.

---

## Using Adolescent Literature to Make Textual Connections (Levels 3 and 4)

It is easier for ELLs, and all students, to employ the comprehension strategy of making connections with young adult literature. Students can learn the three types of connections (text to self: a connection between the text and the student's own life; text to world: a connection between the text and something that is occurring or has occurred in the world; and text to text: a connection between the text and another story or text) using a T-chart or a double entry journal. Students will first make text-to-self and text-to-world connections with the young adult novel. Later, these connections can be discussed in light of the classic work with which the young adult novel was paired and students can be encouraged to make text-to-text connections between the young adult novel and the classic novel as well.

1.  Explain the making connections strategy to students by describing the three types of connections. Sometimes it is helpful to give students starter sentences:

    - Text to self: This reminds me of when I . . .
    - Text to world: This makes me think about . . .
    - Text to text: This reminds me of something else that I read . . .

2.  Demonstrate the strategy with a graphic organizer. Explain to students that they will choose a quote or summarize a part of the book in the left column and record their connection, or reaction, in the right column. Remind them that these connections should be between the text and their own lives, another text, or the world. Reread a few pages of the text aloud and make a chart of your own connections to demonstrate. Here is an example using Myers's *Street Love* (2006). We have labeled the types of connections. You may want to do the same for your students and ask them to go back through their connections and label them until they become more proficient.

**ACTIVITY 3.10.** Making connections to texts

| Quote or summary from the novel | Connection |
| --- | --- |
| Quote: "My folks are laying lines on me like/ They've written out the part and all/I got to do is get to a place called Start." (Damien on p. 26) | Text to self: This reminds me of when I was younger. My parents always talked about my future like it was set—I had no choice in the matter. This made me mad. I didn't want to get married and have children. I wanted to travel and explore. |
| Summary: In Myers' description of Harlem, he writes about homeless men on the sidewalks. (p. 108) | Text to world: This makes me think about the items in the news about the local church setting up a tent city for the homeless. |
| Summary: Junice talks about how she is destined to repeat the same mistakes as her grandmother and mother. (Junice on p. 26) | Text to text: This reminds me of Juliet in *Romeo and Juliet* when she finds out that her parents are going to force her to marry Paris. |

3.  Read further in the book and ask students to supply the connections and record them as a class.
4.  Allow students to continue the process individually or in small groups. As you continue reading, pause every few paragraphs and ask students to record any connections they have made. Ask students to share their connections before continuing to read.

This activity follows the principles set forth by Freeman and Freeman (1998) for teachers who work with ELLs. They recommend that teachers design curricula around themes, create lessons that have meaning for students, and engage them directly with learner-centered activities that build on students' interests and encourage social interaction that helps develop oral and written language skills. Pairing adolescent literature with the classics and making connections does all of these things.

---

**Teaching Tips**

- Encourage students to summarize as well as use quotes because summarizing is an important academic skill. Require them to include the page number, so they can easily find the reference if they choose to write a paper on the text later. You can select well-written student-written summaries for level 1 and 2 students to read.

- In their article "Helping English Language Learners Look at Stories through Literary Lenses," Carroll and Hasson (2004) use the metaphors of looking in a mirror (text to self), looking under a microscope (text to text), and looking through a telescope (text to world) to describe the three types of connections.

## Using Adolescent Literature to Introduce the Language of Literature (Levels 2, 3, and 4)

The less complex texts of young adult literature are good ways to introduce ELLs to academic language. Robin Scarcella (2003) writes that:

> English learners at the intermediate to high-intermediate and advanced levels in middle school, high school, and college need to learn academic vocabulary . . . Targeted words must be recycled and reviewed so that students can learn their different grammatical forms, registers, associations, and collocations in a variety of contexts. (p. 127)

One way to do this is to introduce students to Freytag's Pyramid (1900) for plot and ask them to practice filling it out based upon a popular television show that they watch.

1. Give students a copy of Freytag's Pyramid that contains all of the elements: exposition, rising action, climax, falling actions, and resolution.
2. Discuss plot structure in light of a young adult novel that you have read. In *Breathing Underwater* by Alex Flinn (2002), these are the parts of plot:

   - Exposition: The reader is introduced to Nick and Caitlin and the setting.
   - Rising action: Nick and Caitlin begin to date. We learn more about their backgrounds. Nick begins to treat Caitlin poorly.
   - Climax: Nick hits Caitlin.
   - Falling actions: Nick is sentenced to anger management class and journal writing. He begins to change how he thinks.
   - Resolution: There is no clear-cut resolution.

3. Once students understand the basic parts of plot, ask them to watch one of their favorite shows and outline the parts of plot on Freytag's Pyramid for discussion in class the next day.

---

**Teaching Tip**

Send a note home letting parents know that watching television is an assignment and invite the family to help the student fill in Freytag's Pyramid. In many cultures, teaching is more teacher-centered and using sitcom TV as an assignment may be new to some parents. Allow level 1 (preproduction) and level 2 (early production) students to complete the Freytag's plot diagram for a show that is produced in their native language.

Title:_____

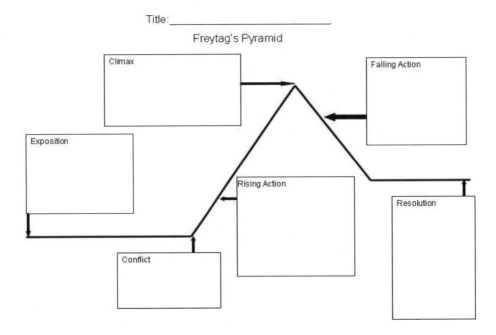

FIGURE 3.7. Freytag's plot diagram.

**Extension Activity**

Young adult novels employ many of the same complex devices as classic literature. During one memorable teaching moment, in the first four pages of *Breathing
Underwater*, students identified 34 literary elements at work: flashback, diction,
imagery, simile, metaphor, symbolism, juxtaposition, sentence structure, repetition,
synecdoche, internal monologue, and allusion, to name just a few! It is much easier
to introduce these terms with young adult literature than with the classics.

## Paideia Seminar (Levels 1, 2, 3, and 4)

An excellent prereading strategy that builds students' background knowledge and motivates
students by sparking their interest in the text is to conduct a Paideia Seminar. These seminars
were first described by Mortimer Adler (1984) and have recently experienced a resurgence in
popularity (Billings & Fitzgerald, 2003) because of a renewed interest in reader response theory
and dialogic classrooms. Terry Roberts and Laura Billings (1999) describe the Paideia Seminar as:

> Formal discussion based on a text in which the leader asks only open-ended ques-
> tions. Within the context of the discussion, students are required to read and study the
> text carefully, listen closely to the comments of others, think critically for themselves,
> and articulate both their own thoughts and their responses to the thoughts of others.
> (p. 41)

An example of how to conduct a Paideia Seminar as a prereading activity for *Romeo and Juliet*
might include focusing on an aspect of the play that interests teens right from the start—gangs.

Certainly, this was the impetus for Bernstein and Sondheim's musical *West Side Story* (Wise, Robbins, & Wise, 1961). The prologue introduces gangs immediately with "from ancient grudge break to new mutiny, where civil blood makes civil hands unclean," and Act I scene 1 starts with a brawl between the two factions. Prior to reading, have students conduct a seminar on gangs in America. To prepare for the seminar, have students study selected materials about present-day gangs. This can include informational brochures, a video documentary, clips from the History Channel show *Gangland*, photographs of gang members, gang tattoos, and gang graffiti, or a presentation by a police officer who specializes in gang activity. Although level 1 and level 2 students may not be able to participate fully in the oral aspect of the seminar, they can analyze photographs and looks at charts of statistics to formulate opinions about gangs in America. They will take away even more if the analysis is done cooperatively. Furthermore, the controversial nature of the question of gangs in America may even encourage students in levels 1 and 2, preproduction and early production, to verbalize their thoughts in the seminar. "Hot" topics encourage participation (Cruz, 2004; Kooy & Chiu, 1998). Level 2 and 3 students will also gain knowledge through the more highly contextualized "texts" of the television show and the police officer presentation.

After students have had ample opportunity to review the material, follow these steps:

1. Arrange students' desks in a circle so students are all facing each other.
2. Tell students the purpose of the seminar is for students to discuss what they think are the most pertinent features of the information they have gathered about gang activity.
3. Set the ground rules first:
   All students will:

   - be given an opportunity to be heard;
   - be treated with respect;
   - avoid making evaluative statements about the comments of others;
   - rely on textual evidence in the event of a disagreement.

4. Ask students to take a few minutes to write brief statements about what they thought were some of the most important features of the material they studied or to record questions about the materials. Have students keep this paper on their desks.
5. Ask for a volunteer to start the conversation. If no one volunteers, use a random selection method to call on someone to share what they wrote on their paper. Alternately, the teacher can also have a question prepared to start the discussion. In the case of a seminar on gangs in America, sample questions might include:

   - Many police departments and gang investigation units choose not to make information about gang tattoos public for fear that gangbangers will use the information. A few police and corrections officers have decided that posting information and pictures, including photos of gang tattoos, on the web will help make tracking gang activity easier. What do you think?
   - Why do you think gang members get these tattoos?
   - What do you think the tattoos mean to gang members?

6. This should spark a conversation. Follow the thread of this thought until it is complete and another one is introduced.
7. Everyone should be allowed to speak, think, and ask questions.
8. To conclude, the teacher can ask students to recap some of the major points of the seminar and discuss the actual procedure itself. Did the students think it went well or that it could be improved? If so, how?

---

**Teaching Tips**

- The teacher may want to sit in the circle to become part of the group rather than the leader.
- Optimally, the role of the teacher is simply to record student comments. However, with the first seminars, teachers will probably need to be more active. The teacher may need to prompt students to analyze the texts by asking open-ended questions.
- The teacher may want to limit the number of resources for the first few seminars so students do not have too much information to synthesize. Sometimes, one good document is enough. If you have level 1 and 2 ELL students, use documents that are highly contextual or pictorial.

---

**Extension Activities**

- The Paideia Seminar can be used with any thought-provoking text, but works best with texts that portray an issue to which there are strong opposing arguments.
- The Paideia Seminar can also be used as a postreading activity. In the case of *Romeo and Juliet*, students can use the text to discuss Juliet's decision to commit suicide or Juliet's parents' decision to force her to marry Paris.

## Close Readings (Levels 1, 2, 3, and 4)

One of the reasons English/language arts teachers give most often for teaching the classics is the quality of the language in which they are written. ELL students of all levels can appreciate rich language as well. It is recommended that you introduce literary terminology with young adult literature because it is less demanding cognitively and reinforce the concepts when studying classic literature.

1. When students are reading, even if it's a modified version of the text with only powerful passages of true text intermingled, encourage them to read with a writer's eye and notice the writer's craft with words. Below are some examples of writers employing literary techniques to enhance their writing:

   - Harper Lee's *To Kill a Mockingbird* (1960: 5): Men's stiff collars wilted by nine in the morning. Ladies bathed before noon, after their three-o'clock naps, and by nightfall were like soft teacakes with frostings of sweat and talcum.
   - Sandra Cisneros's *The House on Mango Street* (2005: 81): Sally is the girl with eyes like Egypt and nylons the color of smoke. The boys at school think she's beautiful because her hair is shiny black like raven feathers and when she laughs, she flicks her hair back like a satin shawl over her shoulder and laughs.
   - Kate Chopin's *The Awakening* (1992: 152): The foamy wavelets curled up to her white feet, and coiled like serpents about her ankles . . . The touch of the sea is sensuous, enfolding the body in its soft, close embrace.

- Chinua Achebe's *Things Fall Apart* (1995: 52): [Ikemefuna] grew rapidly like a yam tendril in rainy season, and was full of the sap of life.
- F. Scott Fitzgerald's *The Great Gatsby* (2004: 189): Gatsby believed in the green light, the orgiastic future that year by year recedes before us. It eluded us but that's no matter—tomorrow we will run faster, stretch out our arms farther . . . And one fine morning—

2. As students read the text, ask them to notice literary features and have them fill out a graphic organizer like this one for the Cisneros passage:

### ACTIVITY 3.11. Close reading of Cisneros' passage

Directions: Record the quote in the left column, the literary device in the center column, and the effect of the literary device in the right column. Ask yourself, what does this device do for the passage or the book as a whole? For level 1, 2, and 3 students a variation of this can be done as a matching exercise.

| Quote | Literary device | Effect |
| --- | --- | --- |
| The boys at school think she's beautiful because her hair is shiny black like raven feathers and when she laughs, she flicks her hair back like a satin shawl over her shoulder and laughs. (p. 81) | similes | The two similes characterize Sally as being beautiful and enjoying the attention she receives because of her beauty. |

3. It is important that this does not become a literary device scavenger hunt, but that students slow down to think about the effect of the devices. Why did the author create the work in such a manner? What was the aim? Activities such as this allow the reader to enter Langer's fourth envisionment stance of stepping out and objectifying the text (Langer, 1995).

---

### Teaching Tips

- Only one-line excerpts have been provided here. When doing this in the classroom, provide ELLs with a more sizeable portion of the text surrounding the quoted material. This way, if the ELL is not able to read the work in its entirety, he or she will have a good feel for the author's style.
- This is a good supported reading activity because it requires readers to slow down and study the text.
- To assist level 1 and 2 students, use realia. For instance, when discussing the Cisneros example, bring in a black satin shawl and a picture of a woman with beautiful long black hair. Ask students to list similarities. Then ask them to think of objects that are similar to their own hair. Level 1 and level 2 students are able to think abstractly and identify objects, so they should be able to participate. They will need to rely on the realia to understand the text, however.

**Extension Activities**

- Students may choose to turn their graphic organizers into critical commentaries later or to use them to compare and contrast two works by different authors or two works by the same author.
- Encourage students to Question the Author (Beck, McKeown, Hamilton, & Kusan, 1998). When they run across literary passages that they find confusing, encourage them not to assume that it is because they are lacking in skill. Sometimes, authors assume too much background knowledge on the part of the audience or do not present their ideas with enough clarity to make them understandable. Sometimes, literary devices do not achieve the desired effect. When this occurs, ask students to rewrite the text to improve it.
- Have students use author examples as models to follow for both syntax and stylistic technique. When they are writing a paper, specify a few types of sentences they should include in the paper. For ease of grading, ask them to highlight each sentence in a different colored highlighter. For instance, you could include the directions: "One sentence should begin with a prepositional phrase and include a simile. Highlight this sentence in green."

## Creating Timelines as a During-Reading Activity (Levels 1, 2, 3, and 4)

Supported reading activities are those that support the thought process during reading. They can be used to help students attend to important concepts and remember information. One useful activity in the reading of lengthy and challenging texts is to stop at the end of chapters to have students create timelines of what occurred. Not only does this encourage students to review what they have read, it also allows students the opportunity to practice using the past tense. Because information can be recorded in short sentences or fragments, less proficient ELLs can participate. Level 1 (preproduction) ELLs can draw graphic representations. Later, as the class moves farther along in the novel, these timelines are a resource to assist students when they attempt to find related passages from earlier in the novel. Furthermore, they allow the teacher to determine if students comprehend the text.

**Teaching Tips**

- Your students' timelines do not need to be as detailed as the one provided, but they should convey the major parts of action.
- Students may work cooperatively on this activity.
- Level 1 students may be provided with a simplified and complete timeline cut into pieces and asked to arrange them in order. Alternately, level 1 students may be asked to create a pictorial timeline rather than one written out in words. Timelines can also be provided to ELLs with less proficiency in a close procedure fashion whereby they fill in the blanks. An example: Jem and Scout visited _____ on his last night in town for the summer.

**FIGURE 3.8.** Sample timeline from Chapter 6 of Harper Lee's *To Kill a Mockingbird*.

**Extension Activities**

- Ask students to illustrate the part of the timeline that they feel was the most significant event of the chapter and have students share.
- Students can practice turning these sentences into questions using the past perfect tense. An example: Whom had Jem and Scout visited on his last night in town for the summer? To what had Scout reluctantly agreed?

# 3.4
# Writing

Whereas the previous two sections of Part 3 contained some writing activities in support of reading and reading comprehension, this section focuses on the art of teaching writing. Many of the activities, however, include peer work and academic talk, and the activities are couched in the process approach to writing because the shift from writing as *product* to writing as *process* has helped ELLs as well as native English speakers (Hedgcock, 2005). The process writing approach breaks writing tasks into five manageable components: prewriting, drafting, revising, editing, and publishing. Three of these stages, prewriting, revising, and editing, are done in collaborative settings where ELLs are able to practice other literacy skills such as speaking, listening, and reading. The following discussion describes the abilities and frustrations of ELLs at each stage of the writing process and makes some research-based suggestions about how to promote ELL students' writing and motivation to write.

The prewriting stage involves brainstorming, listing, mapping, clustering, and drawing. Students learn how to use graphic organizers, which will assist them later in other academic endeavors. All ELLs, regardless of level, can participate in prewriting activities. Level 1, preproduction, students can draw stories and label them with one or two words.

In the drafting stage, the focus for all students is on fluency—getting ideas on paper without concern for "correctness." The goal is to draft without fear. Grammatical accuracy is part of the editing stage in which students and teachers work collaboratively. This enhances ELLs' writing skills, and the supportive interaction helps lower the affective filter and forge personal relationships, creating a community of learners/writers (Cohen, 1986). In classes with ELL students, teachers are advised to teach students to work in peer response groups and as peer partners during the writing process (Peregoy & Boyle, 2001; Pritchard & Honeycutt, 2007). Silva and Brice (2004) cite a variety of factors that influence the effectiveness of peer response groups for ELLs: (1) the language status of the participants, (2) the status of participants in relation to one another,

Nyack College Library

and (3) the modality in which the response is given (i.e. written versus oral, online versus face to face).

The revising process focuses on organization and clarity of meaning, and ELLs are given assistance with elaboration and expression of ideas. The editing process directs attention to grammar, punctuation, and spelling. A growing body of research supports the idea of explicit grammar instruction for ELLs because they do not have an intuitive knowledge of the rules. Ideas for grammar instruction are found in the next section of this book. Ferris and Hedgecock state there is "a positive role for supplemental grammar instruction in L2 writing instruction, which can work in tandem with error correction to facilitate increased accuracy over time" (2005: 272).

Ferris (1999) reports that most ELLs are comfortable with the feedback and the revision cycle of process writing. ELLs accept specific feedback and micro-level revisions better than suggestions for global changes. English language learners do not want the errors labeled or corrected; they simply want feedback that locates the errors and suggestions to revise at the marked location (Ferris & Roberts, 2006). Frodesen (2001) recommends indirect correction through methods such as checks in the margins and underlining. He suggests that teachers focus on errors that stigmatize students, such as errors in noun–verb agreement and the use of double negatives, and limit error correction to a small number of errors. Decisions about feedback should be based on the student's proficiency level, metalinguistic knowledge, and learning style. Weaver (2008) advises teachers to respond to the child first; the content and the conventions follow.

The publishing stage is for sharing and celebration. Sharing and celebration also lowers the affective filter and creates a welcoming environment, a critical factor in student motivation to write and revise. Rodby (1999) found that students were motivated by elements of the environment in which they were studying. Student writing, persistence in revising, and writing skill vary in accordance with the level of comfort they feel in their learning environment. This suggests that curriculum and pedagogy may not be as important as the social organization of the classroom with regard to peer interaction, response techniques, and celebrations.

ELLs in levels 1–2 may feel frustrated because they have difficulty expressing themselves in English. Students will have a very limited expressive vocabulary of 50–2,000 words and will sometimes need to revert to their first language to express themselves. They will typically write in the present tense only and have basic issues with word order (Peregoy & Boyle, 2001). Students may also write one- or two-word sentences, which may be strung together in a way that lacks logical sequence, and many ELLs cannot insert voice into their writing because they cannot distinguish genres and, therefore, will not change form to suit purpose.

Students at the intermediate fluency stage have a stronger vocabulary base and have an easier time expressing themselves. Students at this stage have increased their expressive vocabulary to about 4,000 words and have begun to understand colloquialisms and idioms (Kottler, Kottler, & Street, 2008), yet they will still have difficulties with the various connotations of words and the subtle nuances of meaning. Organization has improved, and they are better able to alter their writing to match the needs of the audience. They will be able to write more and use a variety of sentence structures (Peregoy & Boyle, 2001), but narrative writing will be stronger than expository or persuasive writing.

English language learners at the fluency stage are able to express themselves with relative ease and follow standard organizational patterns of written English. They know several genres of writing and know how to alter register to suit purpose and audience. Their vocabulary is approaching that of a native speaker of their age, and they are able to write lengthy papers using a variety of sentence structures effectively. Although their grammar skills have improved tremendously, they are still apt to need more instruction in grammar (Peregoy & Boyle, 2001). Many teachers work with ELLs who have mastered BICS and have learned to rely heavily on context, facial expressions, and gestures to read and respond to situations. Teachers new to working with ELLs may not realize that there is a vast difference between this type of language exchange and CALP, which is often decontextualized.

Fisher, Rothenberg, and Frey (2007) report that, even after six years in U.S. schools, many foreign-born students still write and read below grade level and perform poorly on standardized tests when they reach secondary school. At the time of writing in 2009, No Child Left Behind required that all students, including ELLs after only two years of sheltered instruction, be held accountable for the same levels of literacy as their native-speaking counterparts. In addition, recent changes in the SAT writing assessment also demand increased levels of proficiency from college-bound students regardless of literacy levels (Panofsky et al., 2005). Despite this increased accountability, research reveals that an alarming number of nonnative English-speaking students fail entry-level writing assessments for college (Rumberger & Gándara, 2000; Scarcella, 2003).

It is imperative that teachers encourage ELLs to write. Level 1 and 2 students can engage in many writing activities:

- cloze activities using familiar paragraphs or narratives;
- creating word lists or captions;
- labeling objects in pictures;
- completing sentences;
- completing graphic organizers;
- transforming information in graphic organizers to sentences;
- completing cartoon strip dialogues;
- word matching;
- word sorts;
- associating sentences with pictures;
- sequencing events based on pictures or short narratives;
- creating a paragraph based on a sequence of pictures;
- writing endings to stories;
- expanding sentences.

The following activities will provide you with ideas for engaging students in writing that will promote literacy and foster a love of language and writing. Level 1 and 2 students can participate in many of the activities if their writing assignments require them to engage in activities that are developmentally appropriate and if they are allowed to work cooperatively. The first activity is a great beginning-of-the-year activity because it lowers affective filters and helps build a warm classroom environment that encourages risk taking. The second activity, Chattaccini: Parts I–III, begins with freewriting and leads into specific revision techniques, and introduces the idea of voice in writing. Next is an activity and graphic organizer focused on expository writing that is required more frequently at the secondary level. There is a brief discussion of ELLs and word processing followed by revision and editing activities.

## Writing with Magnetic Poetry (Levels 1, 2, 3, and 4)

All students have a receptive vocabulary (words they recognize when seen or heard) and a productive vocabulary (words they use to speak or write). Often, students' receptive vocabulary is much larger than their productive vocabulary. Magnetic Poetry encourages students to increase their written vocabulary by presenting them with words they know but may not normally integrate into their writing. It can also introduce them to new words while supporting thoughtful deliberation about word choice and sentence structure. Magnetic Poetry includes words that represent various parts of speech as well as suffixes and prefixes. In our own classes, we have watched students swap suffixes, alter sentence structures, play with parts of speech, and explore nuances of meaning. Placing students in groups to create sentences, poems, and short stories with Magnetic Poetry advances students' communication skills as they negotiate meaning and talk about language with one another. One of the most rewarding benefits, though, is that students are so busy having fun that they often do not realize that they are building their word power and writing skills.

These two activities were adapted from the *Magnetic Poetry in the Classroom: A Guide for Using Magnetic Poetry in Your Curriculum* by Dave Kappell (2009), the inventor.

## Activity One: Team Poetry

1. Divide students into groups of four to five.
2. Give each group a Magnetic Poetry Kit and a surface that will accept magnets.
3. Announce a poem title and give students 10–15 minutes to create a poem.
4. When the allotted time expires give students three to five minutes to figure out how they will read their poem so everyone shares in the oral presentation.
5. Allow class to share their poems.

## Activity Two: Poetry Ladders

Explain to students that, when athletes work out, they often run drills called ladders. In this drill, athletes run in a single line. After a while, the lead runner drops to the end of the line, and the person who was second in line now becomes the leader, setting the pace and allowing others to draft. This is how Poetry Ladders works.

1. Students line up single-file at the magnetic whiteboard in the classroom.
2. On a small table in front of the board are two piles of Magnetic Poetry: the one containing nouns, verbs, and adjectives is face down; the other, containing all other types of words, is face up.
3. The leader approaches the board and has two minutes (use a timer) to blindly choose four pieces from the nouns–verbs–adjectives pile and selectively choose three pieces from the "other stuff" pile to compose a line of verse on the board.
4. This process is repeated with each team member approaching the board at two-minute intervals, selecting their pieces and linking another line of verse grammatically before or after the existing lines.
5. If created lines make no grammatical sense, they are removed from the board.

This process continues until all of the pieces are used up, or it is not possible to create another grammatically correct line.

---

**Teaching Tips**

- Pair level 1 and 2 students with a buddy—if possible, one who speaks their native language.
- Cookie sheets have ferrous surfaces that accept magnets.

- There are many kinds of Magnetic Poetry Kits. They even come in other languages: Spanish, French, Italian, German, Norwegian, Swedish, Dutch, Yiddish, Chinese, and American Sign Language. Level 1 and 2 students may also create lines in their first language. Visit the website www.magneticpoetry.com for more ideas.
- The Magnetic Poetry site has a feature that enables students to create poetry online. Students choose words from a "pile" on the right of the screen and drag them over to a "writing space" on the left. A student can submit his or her piece to the website and email it to up to three people. If a student submits his or her work, he or she is granting Magnetic Poetry permission to include the poem on the website and to use it in packaging and promotional items. Publishing in this manner is a point of pride for many students. Students can also submit anonymously.

**Extension Activities**

- Activity one can be related to the text or topic you are discussing in class. For instance, ask students to create a poem related to an aspect of a text you are reading by making the title a line from the text, a character name, a symbol, or a thematic statement.
- Magnetic Poetry can also be used for grammar lessons much like the LEGO activity in the grammar section.

## Word Choice + Audience = Voice (Levels 2, 3, and 4)

From research on the development of second language writers, it is clear that one of the items ELLs have difficulty with is expanding their expressive vocabulary and altering voice for different audiences. The following activity was presented at the 2008 summer workshop of the Tampa Bay Area Writing Project by Marinés Uscategui (2008). The activity encourages students to employ revision strategies to strengthen their writing and to adjust their use of written language to communicate effectively with a variety of audiences and for a variety of purposes. It provides opportunities for students to practice numerous steps of the writing process as well as reading, active listening, and speaking. The revision techniques are similar to those used by published authors, yet they are not overwhelming, and the "pay off" is high. Finally, the activity allows students choice in their writing topic and relies on students' funds of knowledge by encouraging them to write a personal story.

Uscategui called the activity "Chattaccini." In preparation for this activity, the teacher places spaghetti boxes on students' desks, which are arranged in small groups. Instead of spaghetti in the boxes, they are filled with thin strips of stock paper, each containing a writing topic (describe the movie of your life; describe a moment when you were frightened; etc.). The topics can be teacher created or student generated in a brainstorming activity the day before. Also placed on the desks are parmesan cheese containers. Inside each are slips of paper specifying various types of audiences (your grandmother, a news reporter, the principal, your best friend, an employer, a child, etc.). There should also be a few sticky notes.

## Chattaccini: Part I

1. Tell students to choose a piece of pasta (a writing topic).
2. If a student does not like the first topic, allow him or her to find an agreeable one.
3. Give students 10 minutes to freewrite and encourage them to provide any descriptions they can that will transport the reader into the piece.
4. When 10 minutes are up, have students share their writing with a shoulder partner. As each shoulder partner reads, the listening partner should use a sticky note to jot down words or phrases used by the reader that strike the listener as being especially strong or creative.
5. The teacher can then collect the sticky notes and record stellar words on the board or on a word wall.

## Chattaccini: Part II

1. Ask students to revisit their writing from Chattaccini: Part I and circle all of the adjectives they used.
2. Have students analyze the effect of the adjectives. What do the adjectives add to the work? Are there adjectives that might convey a clearer picture? Give students five minutes to replace weak adjectives.
3. Now have students put boxes around the verbs. Are the verbs really descriptive of the action? Can the student use more descriptive verbs? Does the student have passive verbs rather than active verbs? Give students five minutes to replace weak verbs.
4. Finally, ask students to underline their nouns? Are the nouns concrete? Can they be replaced with more appropriate nouns? Is it a car, or it a Shelby Cobra? Be specific. Give students five minutes to replace weak nouns with specific, concrete nouns.
5. Have students share their old draft and the new draft and compare the two.

## Chattaccini: Part III

1. Ask students to revisit their writing from Chattaccini: Part II. Have them read it again. Once they have read it, ask them who the intended audience was for their piece. How did the audience affect their writing?
2. Discuss audience and voice. How might a piece of writing be different if it were written for your grandmother versus your best friend versus your employer?
3. Ask students to reach in the parmesan cheese container and draw an audience for their paper.
4. Give students 10 minutes to rewrite the piece for the new audience.
5. Ask students to share their new pieces with their shoulder partners. Have them discuss what considerations they made for the new audience versus the previous audience.

## Organizing Academic Writing (Levels 2, 3, and 4)

One of the problems many students have with writing, especially ELLs, is that they do not understand the requirements of certain genres of writing. In cases such as these, having students organize their papers in a graphic organizer can be helpful. Although most teachers decry the standard five-paragraph essay, it is the foundation of most academic expository writing. We complain because not all papers lend themselves to the five-paragraph structure favored by many standardized tests and because the rigid structure squelches student creativity. This activity looks at the structure more as a building block for creative expository writing. The graphic organizer shown in Figure 3.9 enables students to outline expository papers.

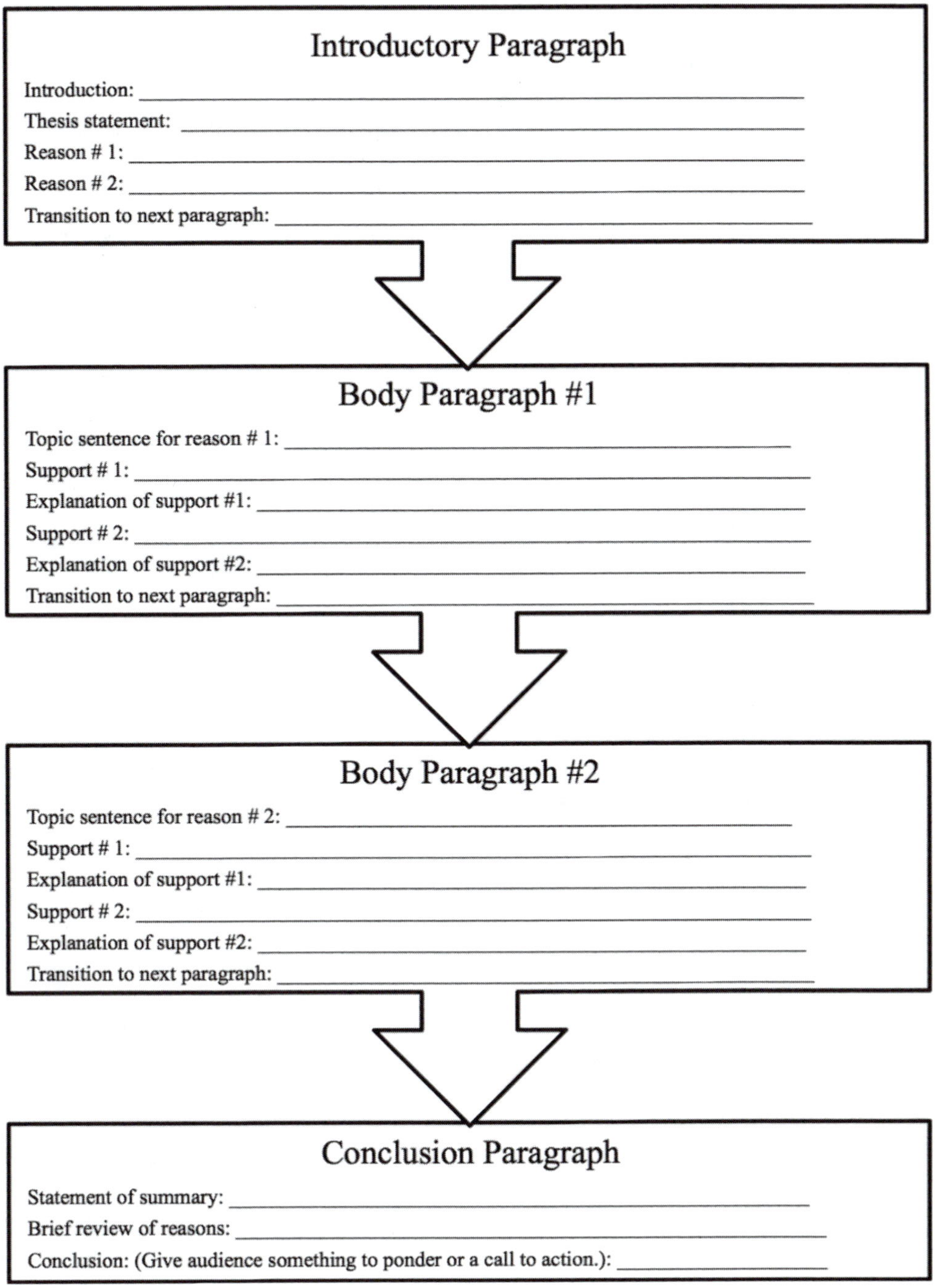

## Introductory Paragraph

Introduction: _____
Thesis statement: _____
Reason # 1: _____
Reason # 2: _____
Transition to next paragraph: _____

## Body Paragraph #1

Topic sentence for reason # 1: _____
Support # 1: _____
Explanation of support #1: _____
Support # 2: _____
Explanation of support #2: _____
Transition to next paragraph: _____

## Body Paragraph #2

Topic sentence for reason # 2: _____
Support # 1: _____
Explanation of support #1: _____
Support # 2: _____
Explanation of support #2: _____
Transition to next paragraph: _____

## Conclusion Paragraph

Statement of summary: _____
Brief review of reasons: _____
Conclusion: (Give audience something to ponder or a call to action.): _____

**FIGURE 3.9.** Graphic Organizer.

**Teaching Tips**

- The organizer can be shortened to cover material needed for one solid paragraph or expanded for a much lengthier paper. Later, graphic organizers can even be altered to accommodate papers with three main topics about which many paragraphs will be written.
- Level 2 ELLs not ready to write papers can convey a great deal of their understanding simply by filling out the graphic organizer. If they are not able yet to transfer the information in the organizer into a paper or paragraph, accept the graphic organizer as their "paper."
- Students can work in pairs to complete graphic organizers.

**Extension Activity**

Graphic organizers can also be used to explain the structure of other types of writing such as newspaper reports that include who, what, why, where, and when all in the first paragraph and then go into details in subsequent paragraphs.

## Composing with Computers (Levels 1, 2, 3, and 4)

When possible, take your students to the computer lab to write their papers. Research on ELLs and writing concludes that word processing has many potential benefits (Panofsky et al., 2005). At the surface level, word processing facilitates the mechanical aspect of getting words on paper and allows for more simple revision through deletions, substitutions, additions, and block moves of text. It also results in a physically attractive final product (Pennington, 2003). At a deeper level, word processing promotes the recursive aspect of writing because students tend to continue to plan as they write, more than they would if they were writing with pen and paper. Aside from the simple types of revisions mentioned earlier, students engage in deep revision when working with word-processing programs. Studies indicate that ELLs spend more time writing and produce lengthier writing when word processing (Ferris & Hedgcock, 2005). Most important, however, is that research by Pennington (2003) indicates that word processing ameliorates some of the fear of writing among ELLs who lack confidence in their writing ability.

**Teaching Tips**

- Not all students in class will have had experience using computers. You may want to conduct a survey to see who has and who has not used a computer. You may ask the media specialist, a business teacher, or technology specialist at your school to provide a workshop on word processing for students who have little to no computer experience before taking the entire class to the computer lab.

- In addition to word processing, ELLs can be engaged in other uses of technology. They can work in small groups to create PowerPoint presentations and participate in class-created wikis and blogs. Level 1 and 2 students can search the internet for pictorial representations to illustrate papers or PowerPoint slide shows. They will also benefit from spell checkers and grammar checkers and explanations.

## Contrastive Rhetoric (Levels 2, 3, and 4)

According to Fisher, Rothenberg, and Frey (2007: 67), contrastive rhetoric is "an approach to teaching writing that teaches students to use language effectively by examining the similarities and differences between Standard English and other languages or vernaculars." Notice that the authors use the expression "and other languages or vernaculars." This means that Standard English is only one of the many forms of English. Pullum (1999) points out that "'dialect' does not mean a marginal, archaic, rustic or degraded mode of speech" (p. 44). It is simply one of many varieties of language, and one is not necessarily better than another. Judgments about "good" and "bad" English are grounded not in linguistics but rather in sociopolitical considerations. Appropriate language is the language that is right at the time, for the purpose, and for the given audience. Some linguists even bristle at the term Standard English because the term implies that other varieties of English are nonstandard; they prefer to use the term "language of wider communication (LWC)" as it was coined by the Conference on College Composition and Communication (1988). In Miles Corwin's *And Still We Rise: The Trials and Triumphs of Twelve Gifted Inner-City Students* (2001), Ms. Moultrie, an English teacher, has this discussion with her predominately African-American students:

> "When I see my mother, I do not say, 'Hello, mother. May I embrace you?'" she says primly. "Naw I say, 'Hey, Mama, wha's happenin'? Gimme some sugar.'
> "It's called situational language. With your friends, you can talk how you want. But in a job interview and in a scholarship interview, you have to speak standard English." (p. 87)

In Weaver's *Grammar to Enrich and Enhance Writing* (2008), she describes a teacher who employs contrastive rhetoric to help students see the difference between the LWC and African-American English and learn to employ one or the other depending upon situational appropriateness. This technique can also be used with students who speak a dialect of English that varies from Standard English on account of language transfer issues, when grammatical rules of the students' native language influence the acquisition of English grammar.

1. Prior to discussing contrastive analysis and code switching with students, the teacher will need to use students' writing as a data source to discern patterns of use in their students' written language.
2. Then, the teacher will create a graphic organizer that contrasts the language of the students with that of Standard English.
3. The teacher will review the graphic organizer with the individual student and have the student write more examples of the student's vernacular in comparison to Standard English.

4. The teacher will discuss the concept of code switching, explaining to students that different forms of language are appropriate for different situations just as certain clothes are appropriate for some situations and not others. For instance, one would not wear an evening gown to do yard work.
5. The teacher will then have students use their individualized code-switching handouts to monitor their own writing. They will fill out the handout each time they self-edit a paper.

**TABLE 3.4.** Using contrastive rhetoric to teach formal patterns of English to native Spanish speakers

Code switching from one vernacular to another.

Directions: Do any of these informal language patterns appear in your paper? If so, place a tick mark in the box, and then go back and code switch to formal patterns. Likewise, do any of these formal language patterns appear in your paper? If so, place a plus sign in the box to indicate that you used the formal pattern.

| Spanish | Informal | Formal | Reason | Paper 1 |
|---|---|---|---|---|
| El jugador que ganó el gol. | The player which scored the goal. | The player who scored the goal. | In Spanish, *que* can mean *that*, *which* and *who*. In English they are three distinct words that confuse Spanish ELLs. | |
| El está en la playa. | He is in the beach. | He is at the beach. | In Spanish, the preposition *en* means *in*, *on* and *at*. *A* means *at* and *to*. Spanish speakers have a difficult time choosing the right preposition. | |
| Juan le envió un ramo de flores. | John to her sent a bouquet of flowers. | John sent her a bouquet of flowers. | In Spanish, the indirect object is placed between the subject and the verb. In English, the indirect object is placed between the verb and the direct object. | |
| No le gusta nada que escribe. | He no like nothing that he writes. | He does not like anything that he writes. | Spanish routinely uses double negatives and places the negative before the verb. English does not use double negatives any more. We used to in Shakespeare's time! | |
| Yo vi a la Señora Jones en la cafetería. | I saw the Mrs. Jones in the cafeteria. | I saw Mrs. Jones in the cafeteria. | In Spanish, speakers distinguish a person in absence by using an article. In English, speakers use the same words whether the person is present or absent. | |

**Teaching Tip**

To help ELL students become aware of the differences between formal and informal English, ask students to create a T-chart graphic organizer where they list situations where formal English should be used on one side and places where informal English would be more appropriate on the other side. Discuss their lists and draw parallels to language.

**Extension Activities**

- Encourage students to use this compare–contrast method to study vernaculars other than their own. They will find that there are numerous differences in the way people speak—regional, ethnic, gender, racial, and more.
- Ask students to rewrite lines of text switching character dialogue from one vernacular to another. Then ask students how the different vernaculars influence their opinion of the character. In one of our classrooms, students rewrote scenes from *Julius Caesar* in various vernaculars, from "gangsta" to Brooklyn, and had a blast. They had to study the other vernacular and create a graphic organizer like the one here and apply the rules of the language consistently. Students' comprehension was measured based upon their "translations" of the text.

## Read-Around-Groups or RAGs (Levels 2, 3, and 4)

Read-Around-Groups (RAGs) are one way that students can receive peer feedback on their papers and offer feedback to others. They are nonthreatening, thanks to the anonymous nature, and they can be used to accomplish a variety of tasks. For students to participate, each student must have a draft of a paper they have written. Students should be told in advance that others will be reading their papers. Instead of using their names, they should put a four-digit number in place of a name. For ELLs there are many benefits to RAGs: (1) they get to see the type of writing that their peers are doing; (2) they are not held accountable for reading entire papers; (3) they get to practice their speaking and listening skills as they negotiate the selection of the best paper from each group; and (4) they may even have their paper selected, which will boost their confidence.

To conduct RAGs:

1. Place students in groups of four.
2. Have each group select a leader to collect papers and pass them to the next group and a recorder who will keep track of the best paper in each set of papers that is read.
3. To begin the activity, the group leader collects all of the papers of its own members and passes them to the group to the right.
4. Give the groups a specific task to perform. This task may vary. See the extension activities. One task might be to read each paper in a set of papers silently and select the best paper from that set. Tell students they will have approximately 90 seconds to read as much of each paper as they can and that you will let them know when it is time to rotate papers within the group and when the group should be done reading that set of papers. Call times out. Students will

be reluctant to stop reading as there will be parts left unread owing to the short time period. Assure them that this is all right.

5.  The group leaders accept the papers from the group on the left and pass them out to the members of their own group. Each group member reads each paper in the set of papers it has received (spending 45 seconds on each). The group is then given one minute to select the best paper in the set. The recorder writes down the four-digit number of the best paper before the group leader collects all of the papers and passes that set of papers to the next group.

6.  This process continues until each group has read every set of papers but their own. When they receive their own set of papers back, all groups should be done reading all of the papers in the class.

7.  Give the groups time to read the papers of their own members, but don't ask them to rate them. This might cause too much tension among members.

8.  By the time this activity is finished, each person in the RAGs will have read the paper of every other class member.

9.  The teacher then calls on the recorder from each group to report the numbers of the papers that were voted best. Write them on the board. If a piece of writing is chosen more than once, put a check mark next to the four-digit number each time it is called out.

10. Ask the writers of the two or three most selected papers to share their writing with the class. Before they read, ask the class to listen carefully and to be prepared to discuss the merits of each piece.

11. After each piece is read aloud, ask the class why they think that paper was chosen as one of the favorites. With the class, make a list of the characteristics of that paper that helped it receive the most votes.

12. Have the class select the three most important characteristics listed and use those characteristics to create a rubric for revising the pieces of writing from this RAGs session.

13. Once the revision process is completed, students may want to participate in another RAGs session!

---

**Teaching Tip**

Set time limits that are a little shorter than necessary to keep students on task. Emphasize that it is okay if they do not read each piece in its entirety as long as they get a feel for the paper. Stick to the time limits and call them out. RAGs may not go smoothly the first time you try it but will be easy to accomplish once students are used to the procedure.

---

**Extension Activities**

-   RAGs can be used for specific revisions as well. Rather than asking students to select the best paper from each group (as we did in step 5), ask students to read for the paper that uses the best vivid imagery, the best use of personification, or the best word choice. Or ask students to read for the most interesting story or the most heartwarming story, disregarding the mechanics of writing. Narrow the focus so that students practice different skills and so that different students, including your ELLs, have their papers recognized.

- RAGs can also be used to edit final drafts: Pass papers to the right within the groups. Groups do not exchange papers. Turns should last one minute. At each turn, readers will make a small pencil check in the margin on any line containing a surface error. At the end of each turn, readers initial in the margin where they stopped reading and pass the paper to the next reader, who continues at that spot. When the writer gets his or her own paper back, he or she can edit to eliminate or correct any identified problems. This activity aligns with Ferris and Roberts's (2006) research, which notes that ELLs prefer feedback that locates the errors and asks students to revise at the marked location.

- You can also use Spandel and Stiggins's (1990) Six Traits Rubric and ask RAGs to read for one of the items on the rubric: ideas and content, organization, voice, word choice, sentence fluency, or conventions.

# 3.5
# Grammar

Knowledge of a student's background allows you to tailor instruction to meet his or her needs, and it is, therefore, helpful to know some basic concepts about the structure of a student's native language. Student grammar errors are often a result of language transfer. For instance, in Spanish a student would say, "No me gusta nada que escribo" or literally, "I do not like nothing that I write." Native language patterns of syntax, such as placing the negative particle before the verb and using double negatives, standard in Spanish, will often transfer into students' attempts to speak English. Sound patterns may also transfer. For instance, many English words that begin with an "s" sound that is followed by a consonant such as "school" and "ski" begin with an "e" in Spanish, so it is not uncommon to hear native Spanish speakers say "eschool" and "eski." Language arts teachers are not required to know the underlying concepts of language structures of multiple languages, but many of these structures can be discovered through a close analysis of students' written and spoken language. Systematic errors can be detected just as they would for a native speaker.

Most ELLs develop what is known as an *interlanguage* (Selinker, 1972), an emerging language that combines features of the first and second languages and may reflect errors that are actually attempts to acquire the new language. The errors result from language transfer, over-generalization of rules, simplification of rules, and creative innovations with language as the ELL tries to make him- or herself understood (Weaver, 2008). The production of these errors indicates that the student is working to acquire the language and should be viewed as a positive indication. It is important to not over-emphasize errors or uphold grammatical correctness because this will raise the affective filter and discourage students from taking risks with their speaking and writing.

English language learners acquire language patterns in a systematic yet idiosyncratic fashion. Table 1.1 outlines the order of the patterns of language that ELLs will learn (Pienemann, 1989; 2007; Krashen, 1981a). If you teach a grammatical concept before an ELL is developmentally ready to learn it, chances are slim that the concept will be acquired and applied (Terrell, 1991).

It is better to decipher patterns in your students' writing and speaking that differ from Standard English, select those that are most frequent or stigmatizing, and group students for instruction as needed.

English shares cognates, sentence structures, word orders, and sounds with Latin, Greek, German, and Romance languages. *Mal* is a Latin root meaning *bad*; it means the same thing in Spanish. Many English words with negative connotations have the prefix of *mal*: *malevolent, malignant, malfunction, malign*. Students whose native language is a Romance language may have an advantage over non-Romance language speakers because there are many similarities among our languages.

It is critical to know the level of students' ability in their native language because it is easier for ELLs to learn reading and writing in English if they have already begun to master these areas in their native language. Many ELL students come from countries embroiled in political conflict that has interrupted the formal schooling of its children; others come from rural regions where formal schooling was unavailable. A further consideration is whether or not the student socializes with English speakers. If the student is constantly surrounded by speakers of his or her native language, it will take much longer for that student to develop BICS and even longer to develop CALP. Furthermore, knowing an ELL's English proficiency level—level 1, preproduction; level 2, early production; level 3, speech emergent; or level 4, intermediate fluency—is crucial when creating differentiated learning activities.

Buddy systems, pairing nonnative speakers with native English speakers, and social events organized to welcome ELLs and their families can open venues for communicating in English and create a warm learning environment and lower the affective filters that would otherwise impede language acquisition.

There is a difference between *learning* a language and *acquiring* a language (Krashen, 1981a). Think of your own attempts to study a second language. You may have taken five years of Spanish in grades 8–12 and two semesters in college, yet find it impossible now to conjugate verbs with ease; *learned* Spanish is not the same as *acquired* Spanish. We agree with Scarcella (2003), who states that "knowledge of grammar without the ability to apply it is useless." Chapter 1.2 of this book outlines five principles for creating an effective learning environment for second language learners. These principles play a crucial role in grammar instruction.

After reading about interlanguage and developmental patterns of acquisition, you may wonder if it is possible to accelerate ELLs' learning of English grammar through formal instruction. Research indicates that instruction based upon structural grammatical features can increase the speed of acquisition, but that instruction cannot push ELLs to learn more than they are developmentally ready to acquire. Pedagogical intervention cannot alter the order of the grammatical patterns of language that ELLs will learn (Gass & Selinker, 2001). Constructivist approaches whereby learners construct strategies and build skills for themselves are more effective than teaching a concept in isolation, providing practice and testing (Gass & Selinker, 2001; Krashen, 2003; Andrews et al., 2006). Some theorists believed that students would naturally acquire grammar rules (Krashen, 1981b), but even these theorists now concede that there is a place for explicit grammar instruction in limited amounts and at the right time developmentally (Krashen, 2003).

This shift in thinking is one of the results of studies conducted with students that Rumbaut and Ima (1988) have characterized as "Generation 1.5," children who left their native country during a crucial period of their language acquisition and academic development. Even after six years in U.S. schools, many Generation 1.5 students, despite earning passing grades, still write and read below grade level and perform poorly on standardized tests (Fisher, Rothenberg, & Frey, 2007). Scarcella and Rumberger (2000) note that not all students will naturally acquire the rules of a language; some need focused grammar instruction if they are to perform well in academic settings (Samway, 2006).

In the following grammar activities, we have attempted to incorporate research-based best practices in grammar instruction for ELLs. English language learners and native speakers will benefit from engaging in grammar instruction. The following activities include listening to and analyzing popular music, studying grammatical structures by playing with LEGOs, viewing famous works of art, learning from literary giants, conducting surveys, and writing editorials for the school or local newspaper. The activities can be done cooperatively in heterogeneous groups.

## Grammar from Nursery Rhymes to Hip Hop (Levels 1, 2, 3, and 4)

At the secondary level, most students are very interested in music and popular culture. Teachers can use this to their advantage by allowing students to analyze the lyrics of popular songs. During this activity, teachers can have students practice the art of code switching by having students translate the lyrics into Standard English. They can also introduce some grammatical concepts when rewriting the lyrics into complete sentences and by looking at the structure of the sentences within the lyrics. We model this activity using the tried and true nursery rhyme "Mary Had a Little Lamb." You can use this to model for the class, and then have the class vote on a popular song to analyze.

First, share the lyrics with the class:

Mary Had a Little Lamb

1.    Mary had a little lamb its fleece was white as snow;
2.    And everywhere that Mary went, the lamb was sure to go.
3.    It followed her to school one day, which was against the rule;
4.    It made the children laugh and play, to see a lamb at school.
5.    And so the teacher turned it out, but still it lingered near,
6.    And waited patiently about till Mary did appear.
7.    "Why does the lamb love Mary so?" the eager children cry;
8.    "Why, Mary loves the lamb, you know," the teacher did reply.

Then, have the class discuss the lyrics and whether or not they are written in Standard English. In the case of this song, the lyrics are Standard English; however, it is extremely formal English. You may choose to have the students translate some of the lines into conversational English instead. This could lead to a good discussion of language register. When students choose a popular song, chances are that changing registers will be from less formal to more formal. Students may rewrite lines 5 and 6 in this manner: "The teacher put the lamb outside, but the lamb waited patiently for Mary."

Each song will lend itself to discussing different grammatical features. With this song, there are numerous items to discuss in terms of grammatical concepts. Below is a list of grammatical concepts that could be taught with each line:

- *line 1*: run-on sentences; the possessive form *its* versus the contraction *it's*; verb tense; the irregular verb *to be*; the placement of adjectives; the use of the semi-colon;
- *line 2*: verbs in the infinitive form; complex sentences; introductory clauses/dependent clauses; independent clauses and the proper use of conjunctions;

- *line 3*: pronoun references; use of the comma and *which* versus *that*;
- *line 4*: complex sentences; introductory clauses/dependent clauses; independent clauses and verbs in the infinitive form;
- *lines 5 and 6*: compound sentences; idiomatic expressions such as "turned it out"; adverbs;
- *line 7*: punctuation of dialogue; adjectives and the placement of adjectives;
- *line 8*: punctuation of dialogue and the use of tag questions.

Of course, you would not want to cover all of these topics, but it is easy to see how lyrics can easily lend themselves to engaging grammar instruction. This song seems to beg to be used in discussing complex sentences since it contains two:

- Sentence A: Everywhere that Mary went, the lamb was sure to go.
- Sentence B: It made the children laugh and play, to see the lamb at school.

A complex sentence consists of one independent clause and one or more dependent clauses. In sentence A, the dependent clause is "everywhere that Mary went," and the independent clause is "the lamb was sure to go." When the dependent clause comes before the independent clause (as in sentence A), the dependent clause should be followed by a comma. Sentence B is actually written incorrectly in that it does not require a comma. An easy way to have students test to see whether a sentence is a complex sentence is to ask them if they can flip-flop the sentence and the sentence still makes sense. For instance, sentence A could be written in its original order, or it could be written as "The lamb was sure to go everywhere that Mary went." In the reordered version, notice there is no comma needed.

---

### Teaching Tips

- Caution the class about appropriateness of lyrics or preselect a few songs from which the students can choose.
- Rely on urbandictionary.com to define some of the slang language in the songs.
- Use one of your favorite songs for this activity. It will allow the students a glimpse of you as a person and help to further lower the affective filter.
- For level 1 and 2 students, this activity is better served with a short and repetitious song such as "Three Blind Mice." Students will understand the lyrics if you act them out using realia and gestures.

---

### Extension Activities

- Have students write their own sentences following the sentences of the lyrics as a model for structure.
- Song lyrics are excellent sources for teaching poetic devices. In this song, you can point out the lamb's "fleece was white as snow" is a simile. You can also use songs to discuss some abstract literary elements such as theme and mood. The theme of this song is about requited love, and the mood is upbeat.

- Use song lyrics to teach about different genres. Students may choose to rewrite "Mary Had a Little Lamb" as a newspaper report, a short story, or an editorial. Then they can use a graphic organizer to compare and contrast the components of the original and new versions.

## Studying Parts of Speech with Artwork (Levels 1, 2, 3, and 4)

As a prereading activity, find a piece of artwork that relates to a similar topic present in the text you are about to read. For instance, William Aiden Walker has a series of paintings called *Cabin Scenes*. In "Cabin Scene IV," the painter depicts an African-American man and woman outside their cabin. The time period is the post-Reconstruction south and portrays living conditions very much like those Janie Crawford, of Zora Neale Hurston's *Their Eyes Were Watching God* (2006), experienced.

Show the artwork to the students. Brainstorm words to create word walls of various parts of speech to describe the painting. In the case of "Cabin Scene IV," the following words could be elicited from students:

- *nouns*: palm tree, man, woman, laundry, fence, dog, chickens, pig, pot, fire, palmetto, shack, wood, hat, kerchief, dress, pants, jacket, skirt, clouds, sky, chimney;
- *verbs*: sit, feed, eat, cook, wash;
- *adjectives*: green, red, blue, black, brown, pointy, dilapidated, hungry, African-American.

Once the word lists are created, have students work in pairs to create sentences to describe the painting. From the sample word list, students could create multiple sentences depending on the students' proficiency levels:

- The man sits.
- The woman feeds the chickens.
- The pig eats.

Advanced students may write more complex sentences:

- The man sits and watches the woman feed the chickens.

Students could then be encouraged to lengthen their sentences:

- The man in the jacket and hat watches the woman in the dress feed the hungry red and brown chickens.

Students are pre-learning vocabulary and building background knowledge. When they read Chapter 2 of *Their Eyes Were Watching God*, they have a picture in their minds of the place Janie lives with her Nanny. They are also learning parts of speech and word order in English sentences.

**Teaching Tip**

The fine art transparencies publishing companies include with teacher texts can provide contextual support for ELL students.

**Extension Activities**

- Teach students synonyms while doing this activity. For instance, *dilapidated* is an adjective for the cabin. Discuss synonyms and their different shades of meaning: *decrepit, rundown, ramshackle, falling apart* and *falling to pieces*. This is also a good opportunity to introduce idioms such as *the worse for wear* and *on its last legs*.
- This activity can be done as a stand-alone activity or in conjunction with any reading selection. One painting to use when teaching Dickens's *A Tale of Two Cities* (2007) is Jean-Pierre-Louis-Laurent Houel's *Prise de la Bastille*. You can also show portraits of historical figures mentioned in reading selections such as Adolph Ulrich Wertmuller's portrait *Marie-Antoinette (1755–93) of Habsbourg-Lorraine, Archduchess of Austria, Queen of France and Navarre, 1788*.

## Sentence Combining (Levels 2, 3, and 4)

Sentence combining involves the combination of two or more sentences into a single, more sophisticated sentence. Although research on the teaching of grammar and the best way to teach grammar has often been contradictory, research has consistently supported the use of teaching sentence combining as a method of improving student writing (Strong, 1996; Andrews et al., 2004). Sentences can be combined by (1) employing punctuation such as semi-colons, colons, and dashes, (2) creating compound sentences with conjunctions such as "and," "so," and "but," (3) reducing one of the sentences to a phrase such as an appositive or to a subordinate or dependent clause.

Suppose your students wrote a summary of the scene in *To Kill a Mockingbird* where Mayella took the stand and wrote this paragraph:

Mayella was nervous. She was on the stand. The lawyer was Atticus Finch. He asked Mayella lots of questions. He asked Mayella to tell the jury what happened. Mayella asked Tom to chop up the chiffarobe. She paid him a nickel. Mayella looked at the judge. Mayella cried.

Model sentence combining for the students:
- Reduce one sentence to a phrase:

Mayella was nervous. + She was on the stand. = Mayella was nervous on the stand.

- Reduce one sentence to an appositive:

The lawyer was Atticus Finch. + He asked Mayella lots of questions. = The lawyer, Atticus Finch, asked Mayella lots of questions.

- Combine sentences using conjunctions:

Mayella asked Tom to chop up the chiffarobe. + She paid him a nickel. = Mayella asked Tom to chop up the chiffarobe, and she paid him a nickel.

- Combine sentences by turning one into a subordinate clause:

Mayella looked at the judge. + Mayella cried. = As Mayella looked at the judge, she cried.

- Combine sentences using punctuation:

Mayella was nervous. + She was on the stand. = Mayella took the stand; she was nervous.

Give students the opportunity to try sentence combing on their own:

- Combine these sentences using a conjunction:

He asked Mayella to tell the jury what happened. + Mayella asked Tom to chop up the chiffarobe.

- Combine these sentences by turning one into a phrase:

Mayella looked at the judge. + Mayella cried.

- Ask students to rewrite their summary using at least three of the sentence combining techniques:

    Sample response:

Mayella was nervous when she was on the stand. The lawyer, Atticus Finch, asked her lots of questions. He asked Mayella to tell the jury what happened, and she said she asked Tom to chop up the chiffarobe for a nickel. As Mayella looked at the judge, she cried.

---

**Teacher Tip**

Level 2 students will be able to participate in this activity if the sentences are simple. Sentences can also be prewritten with each sentence on a different color of paper. Cut sentences into individual words for students to combine with the words of a sentence on another color. For example:

Mayella's father is angry. + Mayella's father is Burris. = Burris is angry.

---

**Extension Activities**

- As students peer read each other's work, have them highlight sentences that they think their peer could easily combine.
- Discuss rhetoric with students and the fact that sometimes short and concise sentences are more powerful and desirable. Simply because we can combine sentences does not always mean we should combine sentences.

---

## Grammar in LEGO Land (Levels 1, 2, 3, and 4)

This activity was adapted from an idea presented by Amy Benjamin in Brock Haussamen's *Grammar Alive! A Guide for Teachers* (Haussamen et al., 2003) and relies on the power of visuals and manipulatives in constructing knowledge.

### Activity One

- Obtain LEGOs and sort them by color.
- Affix words to the LEGOs so that all blue LEGOs have prepositions on them, white have pronouns, green have verbs, yellow have nouns, etc.
- Put students in mixed proficiency groups of three or four.
- Ask students to create as many sentences as they can with the LEGOs.
- For level 1 and 2 students, provide a limited number of simple and frequently used words.
- Once students have created as many sentences as possible, ask students to look at the order of the colors of their LEGOs.
- Write down any patterns that students notice.
- Use this to introduce the idea that English is a subject–verb–object (SVO) language and to point out other patterns in English word order.

### Activity Two

- Ask students to create as many "stories" as they can with two-word sentences. Share examples with them: Julius Caesar's "I came. I saw. I conquered," or—in your best sportscaster's voice—"He runs. He shoots. He scores!"
- Students will notice that their sentences are all made up of one white LEGO and one green LEGO.
- Explain the concept of subject and predicate.

### Activity Three

Build upon the two-word sentence of "he scores" by placing it with a subordinate clause and forming three different types of sentences:

- He scores, raising his fist in victory. (subject–verb upfront)
- After practicing corner shots for weeks, he scores. (delayed subject)
- He, the captain of the team, scores. (separated subject and verb)

---

**Teaching Tips**

- You may choose to label some LEGOs with words while labeling others with parts of speech to allow students more options when creating sentences. Like the blank Scrabble tile, students can substitute these blanks for any word of that part of speech.
- To add to your LEGO collection, go to www.lego.com.

---

**Extension Activities**

- Use the color-coded parts of speech to teach a number of grammatical patterns.
- Encourage students to create ways of using the LEGOs to teach grammatical concepts.

---

## Imitating Our Favorites (Levels 3 and 4)

A popular expression that has come about in the teaching of grammar and writing is "reading with a writer's eye." To do this, once students have read a text to decipher the meaning, reread to analyze the craft of writing, studying how the author uses language (Bean, Chappell, & Gillam, 2005). Studying an author's craft can lead to rich writing that incorporates rhetorical features such as imagery and figurative language. It can also be used to teach grammatical concepts by pulling out sentences from the texts you are reading to model different sentence structures.

Here are a few examples from short stories:

**ACTIVITY 3.12. Analyzing texts with a "writer's eye"**

| Short story and author | Grammatical feature and explanation | Example from short story |
|---|---|---|
| Desai, A. (1999). Games at twilight. In *Prentice-Hall Literature: Platinum*. Englewood Cliffs, NJ: Prentice Hall, pp. 3–13. (Original work published in 1978) | *Parallelism*: the repeated use of a grammatical pattern within a sentence or a series of sentences | Parallelism of verb and prepositional phrases: *A band of parrots suddenly fell out of the eucalyptus tree, tumbled frantically in the still, sizzling air, then sorted themselves out into battle formation and streaked away across the sky.* (p. 4) |
| Jacobs, W. W. (1999). The monkey's paw. In *Prentice-Hall Literature: Platinum*. Englewood Cliffs, NJ: Prentice Hall, pp. 31–37. (Original work published in 1902) | *Adverbs of manner*: answer the question "How?" and modify verbs | *"Never mind, dear," his wife said, soothingly.* (p. 31) |
| Stephenson, C. (1999). Leiningen versus the ants. In *Prentice-Hall Literature: Platinum*. Englewood Cliffs, NJ: Prentice Hall, pp. 43–58. (Original work published in 1938) | *Past perfect tense*: a verb that indicates an action was completed before another time or action and is formed by adding the helping verb "had" to the verb's past participle | *Long after the launch had disappeared, Leiningen thought he could still hear that dimming, imploring voice.* (p. 44) |

Find examples of a grammatical concept in the work you are reading and use them as models to explain the concept to the class. Then, as a class, create new sentences about the text you are reading that imitate the modeled structure. In pairs or small groups, have the students create original sentences following the same structure.

---

**Teacher Tip**

As you are preparing to teach a text and rereading it in preparation, read with a writer's eye and notice repetitive sentence structures used by the writer. Focus only on two to three types of structures and color-code them with highlighters, so you can find them easily when you want to use the examples as models. After ascertaining common errors in your ELL and native English-speaking students' writing, look for examples that would benefit them.

---

**Extension Activity**

When you ask your students to create written responses to the work you are reading, ask them to model their response on the style of the author who wrote the work. If you have studied more than one grammatical structure, you may be specific: Ask students to include two sentences containing parallelism and one sentence that contains an adverb of manner.

---

## Preparing Students to Write Research Reports (Levels 1, 2, 3, and 4)

Grammar instruction should have the goal of not only facilitating students' verbal communication skills but also preparing them for academic writing. One type of academic writing is the research paper, which often calls for students to write in passive voice without using the first-person pronoun. A fun activity to help prepare students for this type of writing is to have pairs of students survey classmates, friends, and family members about a topic that the students choose on their own. Sample survey questions might be as follows:

- What is your favorite song?
- Who is your favorite actor?
- In what country were you born?
- Do you think the food in the school cafeteria is good?

Each member of the pair must survey five or more people. Once surveys are completed, partners combine their information to write a short report based upon their findings. A sample report might look like this:

Ten George Washington Junior High School students were asked to name their favorite male actor. Heath Ledger was the favorite of three of the students, while Owen

Wilson and Will Smith were each named twice. Djimon Hounsou, Josh Hartnett, and Leonardo DiCaprio each received one vote.

---

**Teaching Tips**

- Have students practice their interviewing and note-taking skills in class with each other before sending them out in the school or community to ask their survey question. This will boost their confidence in speaking and get them adjusted to recording information while listening.
- Brainstorm a list of many questions with the class and allow pairs to create their own question or choose one from the list.
- Bring in a model from a professional research journal or the newspaper so that students know that this is the type of academic writing they will have to do.
- Level 1 and 2 students can also assist in the survey. They can learn to ask the question, and have the respondents write down their answers on a clipboard. They can record the answer themselves if the answer is a yes or no response. Shy students, however, may not want to participate.

---

**Extension Activities**

- Students can create opinion surveys based upon issues related to the texts they are reading. Opinion surveys related to *Romeo and Juliet* might include questions such as the following:

  - Is it ever okay to date someone without the blessings of your family?
  - If someone harms your friend, should you seek revenge?
  - Do you believe in fate?
  - Do you believe in love at first sight?

- Students can create opinion polls about issues outlined by their school or local paper that affect their community. The whole class can create survey questions related to the same issue and compile their findings into one report that can be sent as a letter to the editor.

# 3.6
# **Vocabulary Development**

Vocabulary is a major component of reading comprehension for all students. The more ELL students develop their vocabularies the better able they are to make sense of what they read. Poor vocabulary is a detriment to students' academic success and poor academic vocabulary can be found in many ELLs (VandeWeghe, 2007). When reviewing the literature about effective vocabulary instructions, several components and recommendations emerge:

- Teachers should create language-rich and word-rich environments.
- Vocabulary can be developed through wide reading of a variety of texts.
- In addition to promoting wide reading, teachers should also intentionally teach selected vocabulary.
- Vocabulary can be developed through direct methods such as pre-instruction of words required for a specific text.
- Students need multiple exposures and multiple opportunities to learn vocabulary words in authentic contexts.
- Students need to be actively engaged in word-learning tasks.
- Students need to develop word-learning independence and this can be taught through explicit strategy instruction.

Many of the characteristics listed as effective vocabulary instruction can be used in the ELA classroom and represent best practice in ELA instruction. English classrooms lend themselves to word-rich environments through providing students with a wide range of texts and a wide range of opportunities to encounter these texts, by teaching students a variety of strategies to understand new vocabulary encountered in a range of texts, and by helping students to become actively engaged in literacy experiences. The NCTE Standards for the ELA (NCTE & IRA, 1996) have several standards that relate directly to the practices listed in the aforementioned recommendations:

> Standard 1: Students read a wide range of print and non-print texts to build an understanding of texts, of themselves, and of the cultures of the United States and the world; to acquire new information; to respond to the needs and demands of society and the workplace; and for personal fulfillment. Among these texts are fiction and nonfiction, classic and contemporary works.

> Standard 2: Students read a wide range of literature from many periods in many genres to build an understanding of the many dimensions (e.g. philosophical, ethical, aesthetic) of human experience.

> Standard 3: Students apply a wide range of strategies to comprehend, interpret, evaluate, and appreciate texts. They draw on their prior experience, their interactions with other readers and writers, their knowledge of word meaning and of other texts, their word identification strategies, and their understanding of text features (e.g., sound–letter correspondence, sentence structure, context, graphics).

In order for students in ELA classrooms to meet these standards, they must learn strategies for developing their vocabulary knowledge. This is especially relevant to ELLs, who frequently come to school with limited English vocabulary knowledge. Knowing a wide range of words and how to use them effectively is important for ELLs in that it provides the foundation they need to read and understand a wide variety of texts, it expands their ability to communicate and participate in class activities and in the world outside the classroom, and, most important, it empowers them socially.

Wallace (2007) revealed several important challenges ELA teachers need to take into consideration when planning instruction:

- The Learning Predicament: English language learners need extensive reading for developing vocabulary but they also lack the appropriate vocabulary to participate in extensive reading. Therefore, ELLs will need explicit vocabulary instruction in order to participate in the reading tasks they encounter in school.
- Needed Vocabulary Development: Teachers can expect a significant gap between ELLs and their English-only peers, which requires "continued attention toward vocabulary development" (p. 190).
- Vocabulary Breadth and Depth: English language learners not only know fewer words than their English-only counterparts, but they also "know less about the meaning of these words" (p. 190).
- Vocabulary Strategies:

  - Use of cognates: If the student's first language shares cognates with English, teachers can take advantage of this relationship and teach the use of cognates in vocabulary development.
  - Basic words: Teachers need to be aware of students' tier 1 word knowledge (basic words that are learned in the students' home or community). If students do not have the appropriate tier 1 knowledge, they will have difficulty comprehending texts.

- Review and Reinforcement: English language learners need opportunities for vocabulary instruction in their second language through teacher-directed instruction and student-led reinforcement activities.
- Vocabulary and Comprehension: Vocabulary knowledge is partially responsible for student reading comprehension.

Wallace's (2007) results offer suggestions related directly to ELLs (such as the teaching of cognates) but also demonstrate that many of the strategies for effective vocabulary instruction for students whose first language is English are also effective for ELLs. In *When Kids Can't Read: What Teachers Can Do*, Kylene Beers (2003: 179–200) provides several suggestions for teaching vocabulary to students who struggle with reading, and many of these can be applied to ELLs:

1. Assign word study, not word memorization.
2. Teach students how to use the context as a clue.
3. Teach word parts.
4. Turn vocabulary study into a word hunt.
5. Use graphic organizers.
6. Use logographic cues (graphics as a tool for remembering words).
7. Read Aloud and Use SSR.
8. Ask the Right Questions.

In our experience, the "traditional" model for teaching vocabulary in an ELA classroom was to give students a list of 20–25 words that were not necessarily related to the week's lessons (or using a separate vocabulary workbook completely unrelated to the curriculum), having students copy the definition of the words from the dictionary, possibly giving a brief lecture on the meaning of the words in which most of the conversation comes from the teacher, and ending with a quiz on the words at the end of the week. Fortunately, much has changed and teachers now have a variety of methods for teaching vocabulary to choose from. This chapter will examine several strategies for effective vocabulary instruction in ELA classrooms and show how they can be applied to help ELLs develop their vocabulary knowledge and skills.

## Types of Vocabulary

Deciding what vocabulary words to teach in an ELA classroom can be daunting. English language learners come to mainstream classrooms with a range of vocabulary knowledge, and it is the English teacher's task to determine what type of vocabulary instruction will best lead to improving ELLs' literacy skills in reading, writing, listening, and speaking. Burke (2008) identifies two domains of vocabulary: expressive, which we need to have to effectively speak and write, and receptive, which we need to have when we read or listen. Students may be able to determine the meaning of a word when they are reading, for example by using context clues, but that does not mean they are able to use it themselves in their speech or writing. English language arts teachers need to make decisions about not only what vocabulary to teach but also how they want their students to be able to use it. For some lessons, ELLs may need to use the vocabulary to comprehend a text, but for other lessons students may be asked to incorporate that vocabulary into their writing and speech. Before teaching word meanings to ELLs, teachers will need to clarify what they want students to be able to know and do with that vocabulary.

An additional way to think about the types of vocabulary students will encounter and need to learn was developed by Beck, McKeown, Hamilton, and Kusan (2002). They categorized words into three levels called tiers:

- Tier 1 words are learned through spoken language.
- Tier 2 words are encountered in written texts.
- Tier 3 words are content specific.

Depending upon the needs of the ELL, teachers may have to teach all three levels of vocabulary. In order to promote ELLs development of tier 1 words, ELA teachers should provide frequent and regular opportunities for students to talk and interact with their peers. In addition, English teachers can use activities such as reading aloud, playing tapes of stories, and showing films to help ELLs improve their receptive vocabulary. For daily lesson planning, ELA teachers will want to focus on tier 2 words—words students will encounter in the texts they will read and words they will need to develop their writing abilities. However, teachers may also need to teach tier 3 words when it comes to content-specific vocabulary such as literary terms, genre-specific terms (for example, words related to science fiction stories or Shakespearean language), and terms related to background knowledge (for example, historical terms related to the setting of a story or literary allusions). In addition to considering tiers of vocabulary knowledge, ELA teachers can consider three categories provided by Graves and Prenn (1986), which require progressively more sophisticated skills by the student:

- Known concepts: These are concepts that the student is familiar with but hasn't acquired the word for or concepts students may have in their oral vocabulary but haven't identified in written form.
- Synonyms/antonyms or multiple meaning words: Synonyms and antonyms can be used to help students understand unknown words. Teachers can go beyond simply asking students to define words and ask them to provide a synonym and antonym. In addition, teachers can encourage students to find synonyms and antonyms in their first language for English words. Words that contain multiple meanings can be especially difficult for ELLs who may have knowledge of one definition of a word but are unable to comprehend the word in another context.
- Unknown concepts: Typically tier 3 words; these words require direct instruction of the concept by building background knowledge and providing examples.

## Word Knowledge Check (Levels 1, 2, 3, and 4)

One way to find out what types of words the ELLs in your classroom are familiar with is to use a word knowledge check. Parabakht and Wesche (1997) created a five-point scale for students to demonstrate their knowledge of a word. Consider modifying the word knowledge check for your ELLs if a five-point scale seems too sophisticated.

**ACTIVITY 3.13.** Word knowledge check for Richard Rodriguez's *Hunger of Memory* (1982)

| | I never saw it before | I heard it but don't know what it means | I am familiar with the word but don't know it well (I think I know what it means) | I know it well | I can use it in a sentence |
|---|---|---|---|---|---|
| anglicized | | | | | |
| diminutive | | | | | |
| wrath | | | | | |
| benign | | | | | |
| vulnerable | | | | | |
| ghetto | | | | | |
| translation | | | | | |
| confidential | | | | | |
| intimacy | | | | | |

---

### Teaching Tip

Teachers can use multicultural literature that incorporates English and vocabulary from other languages to validate student' native languages as well as to let them be the "experts" about language. Rodriguez's text discusses his own experiences with his conflicts between holding onto his Hispanic heritage and wanting to assimilate into American culture. Rodriguez's text is written in English but intermingled with Spanish vocabulary.

---

English language arts teachers can use a variety of strategies to teach these different types of vocabulary words as well as strategies to help students become more word conscious. Before discussing specific strategies and activities, here are a few teaching tips/guidelines for teaching vocabulary to consider.

---

### Tips for Teaching Vocabulary

- Preteach important vocabulary words that are necessary for student understanding of the lesson.
- Choose vocabulary words from the texts students will encounter in the curriculum, not from isolated word lists.
- Choose a few words to teach well, rather than a long list of words that students may learn only superficially.
- Provide opportunities for students to make connections: connections to themselves, to words in their own language, to visual images, and to their background knowledge.

- Display important vocabulary terms visually around the room.
- Model the use of key vocabulary in class in formal and formal discussions.
- Teach a "word of the day."
- Play word games. Find resources that play with language such as poems, songs, and tongue twisters.
- Encourage and reward students who are using key vocabulary in daily activities.
- Teach a variety of strategies for learning the meaning of words. Allow students the freedom to choose the strategies that work best for them.
- Teach vocabulary in multiple lessons and make connections across lessons.
- Immerse students in a language-rich environment. Read aloud to students. Model the characteristics of an effective and engaged reader.
- Foster reading outside class. Encourage independent reading. Keep a class-room library with texts that are engaging and appropriate for ELLs.
- Allow students the opportunity to discuss their understanding (or lack of understanding) of vocabulary, before providing them with definitions of new words.

## Fostering Word Consciousness (Levels 1, 2, 3, and 4)

Teachers need to motivate students to learn new words in authentic contexts. Students should be made aware of the new words they encounter and be encouraged to incorporate new words into their vocabulary. Graves and Watts-Taffe (2002) identified several ways to integrate word consciousness into daily instruction, which can be integral parts of an ELA classroom, two of which were mentioned in the teaching tips: modeling attention to word usage and promoting word play. Another recommendation by Graves and Watts-Taffe is to involve students in word investigations. Students can be encouraged to act as researchers who examine the different ways vocabulary is used in their daily lives.

## Helping Webster Become Bilingual (Levels 1, 2, 3, and 4)

This activity is meant to broaden students' vocabulary and improve their listening and viewing skills by having them record words they hear during the day with which they are unfamiliar. These words then become the basis for their dictionaries. The activity also debunks deficit thinking about ELL students because in this activity being bilingual is an asset. It also incorporates small group work that builds students' speaking skills.

Prior to doing this activity, students will need to have familiarity with the way dictionary entries are formatted.

1. Ask your students, both ELLs and native English speakers, to listen closely to language for one week and to write down every word that they hear that they are unfamiliar with. If they do not know how to spell the word, encourage them to ask the speaker of the word. If the word was on television, ask them to record the context in which the word was mentioned and ask an adult for help later. If it was in print, ask them to bring the text to class. Tell students they should record 30 words during the week. If you have very gifted native speakers, they may need to look for unknown words actively.
2. Have student alphabetize their lists to turn in to you at the end of the week. Check the words for correctness and appropriateness.

3. Return the word lists to their owners, and give each student a booklet that contains 32 double-sided blank pages. You can create these booklets from regular copy paper, and they should be small enough that you can staple the "binding" in the middle.

4. Tell students to write one word from their list on the top of the left-side page, leaving room for more writing.

5. Tell students that each set of pages is going to become a dictionary entry. On the left side of the page, the student will include the following in addition to the word: pronunciation, syllabication, part of speech, definition. Extra credit can be given for etymology.

6. On the right hand side, students will create a graphic image of the word or a symbol to help them remember the word. They will also include a translation of the word into another language. You will need to group students so that students who speak more than one language are available to assist monolingual students.

7. In the opening pages of the dictionary, students should include a one-page introduction stating how the dictionary can be used and a one-page pronunciation/abbreviation guide. If any dictionaries were used to help create definitions, an end page should include citations for those sources.

8. Ask students to design attractive covers for their dictionaries that include a title, the student's name, and class period.

---

**Teaching Tip**

It may be preferable for students in early stages of language proficiency (levels 1 and 2) to write their dictionaries in their native language and have the right hand side contain the English translation.

---

**Extension Activities**

- Students can also create dictionaries for subject-specific words such as literary terms or words related to photosynthesis or even "testing words" such as *compare/contrast*.

- Students may also want to create jargon dictionaries. Allow students to pick topics in which they are interested: guitar playing, video games, snowboarding, jewelry making. Ask them to create a dictionary of words that are commonly associated with that topic. For instance, guitar players sometime refer to their guitar as an "axe."

- Another idea is to have students create dictionaries of "teen speak"—modern language with which adults might be unfamiliar. Caution students about classroom appropriateness.

---

## Word Walls (Levels 1, 2, 3, and 4)

Although typically used as a strategy for elementary school students to help them develop their understanding of site words, word walls can easily be adapted for the secondary classroom and can foster word consciousness. Teachers can place on the wall important vocabulary words that will be necessary for understanding a particular text, words related to a unit of study, or words associated with literary genres. Students can create illustrations of the terms and place them on the word wall, create sentences using the words, and record examples of the terms they encounter in their reading or in daily life. For example, when beginning a unit on poetry, a teacher can put the terms for literary devices on the word wall (onomatopoeia, simile, metaphor, alliteration, etc.) and then students can write examples from the poems they read onto sentence strips and put them next to the terms on the word wall. Students can also put examples of these devices in daily life such as lyrics from songs that use the same literary devices. Students should be encouraged to cut out examples of vocabulary terms from magazines and newspaper articles and place them on the word wall. English language learners will benefit from the visual reinforcement of vocabulary words and the connections to other texts and authentic language experiences this strategy promotes.

## Cognates (Levels 1, 2, 3, and 4)

English language learners can use knowledge of their native language as a scaffold to learning in English. One aspect of students' native language that ELA teachers can use for students whose home language is one of the Romance languages (e.g. Spanish, French, or Italian) is the teaching of cognates. Cognates are vocabulary items in two different languages that share a common origin and have similar pronunciations, spellings, and meanings in the two languages. There are many words in English that contain cognates in other languages. Students can use their vocabulary background knowledge in their native language to better understand vocabulary in English. Teachers can draw attention to cognates through modeling and discussion, and they can use other strategies such as word walls and visual representations such as graphic organizers to help

**ACTIVITY 3.14. Sample Spanish and English cognates**

| English | Spanish |
| --- | --- |
| accident | accidente |
| bicycle | bicicleta |
| concert | concierto |
| decide | decidir |
| exclaim | exclamar |
| family | familia |
| group | grupo |
| honor | honor |
| important | importante |
| list | lista |
| much | mucho |
| natural | natural |
| ordinary | ordinario |
| patience | paciencia |
| really | realmente |
| special | especial |
| totally | totalmente |
| uniform | uniforme |
| vegetable | vegetales |

students remember the meanings of cognates when they are reading. Understanding and recognizing cognates can build ELLs' confidence in their vocabulary knowledge as well as teach them valuable comprehension skills.

## Draw the Word: Visual Representations (Levels 1, 2, 3, and 4)

English language learners (especially levels 1 and 2) should be encouraged to create visual representations of words to help develop their understanding of word meanings. Using pictures and symbols can help ELL students remember words longer and better than memorizing a definition. Students can incorporate word images onto vocabulary flashcards or integrate them into graphic organizers and word maps.

## Semantic Maps (Levels 1, 2, 3, and 4)

Students can create visual maps, often referred to as semantic maps, to represent relationships between words, words that share common roots, and words that share meanings. English language learners can use semantic maps to help them learn words associated with a particular concept or to learn roots so that they can later decode words using those roots. An example of a word map using morphology, gaining information about the meaning of new words using knowledge of their prefixes, roots, and suffixes, is a vocabulary tree (Beers, 2003). Students draw the tree to represent their growing knowledge of a root word and its related vocabulary terms.

### Steps to Creating a Vocabulary Tree:

Step 1:   Teachers choose a root word that they want students to study and students place it at the bottom of the tree (the root).

Step 2:   Under the word students write the definition (alternatively, level 1 students can draw a picture or illustrate it in some way).

Step 3:   On the branches of the tree students write words that contain that root and their definitions. In addition, students write the word in a sentence.

Step 4:   Off of the branches, students create leaves that record where they have encountered the word, for example in a piece of literature, in a conversation, in a song, etc.

Beers (2003) also suggests creating class vocabulary trees where students add words to the tree to share with their peers.

## Vocabulary Squares (Levels 1, 2, 3, and 4)

Another visual strategy to help ELLs develop their vocabulary knowledge is the vocabulary square. Students divide their paper into four quadrants and place information about the word in the boxes. Teachers can modify the vocabulary square to contain information they deem important, depending upon the needs of the language learner. For example, students could put the word and its English definition in one box and then in another box they could put the word in their native language. In addition, students could draw a picture depicting the meaning of the word in another square. The example below also has students create an analogy using the word, which can help them remember things that are similar to the vocabulary word as well as reinforce their understanding of literary devices. Students could put their vocabulary squares on index cards with the word on one side and the squares on the other and then practice with them as flashcards.

**ACTIVITY 3.15.** Sample vocabulary square

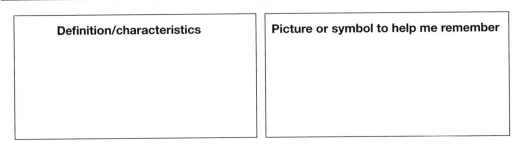

| Definition/characteristics | Picture or symbol to help me remember |

**Word or concept**

| Analogy (A _____ is like a _____ because _____) | Examples/nonexamples |

## Words in Context (Levels 1, 2, 3, and 4)

Whereas ELL students can use many strategies to learn words that are given to them in word lists, they also need to practice making inferences about the meaning of words through the context in which they are written. Beers (2003) points out that creating a definition of a word from its context is more difficult that it may appear and requires skills that less proficient readers may not have achieved. However, she does state that some authors will provide clues that can help readers determine the meaning of a word in context: definition/explanation clues, whereby the author provides the definition in the sentence, restatement of synonym clues, whereby the author provides an additional term for the word or restates the word in simpler terms later in the text, contrast or antonym clues, whereby the author provides an opposite meaning for a word, and gist clues, whereby readers have to understand the overall meaning of a passage and then guess the definition of the word using inferencing (pp. 186–187). Teachers can explicitly teach the types of context clues authors may provide to students and model how to look for these clues.

One strategy ELLs can use for determining the definition of a word through context is the student VOC strategy (Billmeyer & Barton, 1998). The steps to the VOC strategy are as follows:

Step 1:    Students write the sentence of the unfamiliar word.
Step 2:    They make a prediction about the meaning of the word based on the sentence.

Step 3:    They consult a source to find a definition of the word (students may use heritage language dictionaries here as needed).

Step 4:    Students write a sentence using the word.

Step 5:    Students determine a way to remember the word's meaning; like the Vocabulary Squares strategy, students could draw a picture or create an analogy to help them remember.

**ACTIVITY 3.16.** Example student VOC from *To Kill a Mockingbird* by Harper Lee

**Word: chattels**

"So Simon, having forgotten his teacher's dictum on the possession of human chattels, bought three slaves and with their aid established a homestead on the banks of the Alabama river some forty miles above St. Stephens."

Prediction: the sentence mentions slaves and refers to possession of humans, so maybe it has something to do with slavery.

Source: Webster's online: chattel. Slave.

Regardless of the time period owning chattel was wrong.

Chattel reminds me of chains. Slaves were brought here in chains.

## Vocabulary Bookmarks (Levels 3 and 4)

Another way to help ELL students identify words they don't understand and use the context to determine word meanings is through vocabulary bookmarks. There are many variations of the vocabulary bookmark; some teachers will give students a bookmark and have them identify the word and the page number where the word occurs in their reading. Later, the teacher and students can revisit the words they chose, find the words in the text, and use a strategy such as the student VOC to determine the meaning. The following example of a vocabulary bookmark asks students to go one step further and make a guess about the meaning of the word as they are reading as well as to record any clues that helped them arrive at their guess. Teachers can print out copies of the bookmark and have students keep them with them as they read. Vocabulary bookmarks are useful to ELLs because they give them ownership over which words they may encounter and find difficult, whereas ELA teachers may not always be aware of what words in a text may provide difficulty for students.

**ACTIVITY 3.17.** Sample vocabulary bookmark

| Word | Page # | Guess and clues |
|------|--------|-----------------|
| chattels | 4 | something to do w/slavery<br>*slaves, possession, humans* |
| | | |
| | | |
| | | |
| | | |

## Vocabulary Charades (Levels 1, 2, 3, and 4)

A fun activity that engages students and can promote creative thinking is vocabulary charades. Like regular charades, students draw a vocabulary word randomly and act it out for the class while the class guesses the word. Students can work in pairs or in groups to act out a skit that conveys the meaning of the word or concept. In addition, students could use the activity of Dramatic Tableaux, discussed in Chapter 3.2, whereby they create a frozen scene that represents the meaning of the vocabulary word. Similar to vocabulary charades, students can play vocabulary pictionary in which they draw the word on the board or chart paper while their team guesses the word being represented. These activities are great for ELLs because they are kinesthetic and nonverbal.

## Vocabulary Bingo (Levels 1, 2, 3, and 4)

This activity works especially well when a teacher wants to review a larger group of vocabulary words that students have studied over time. Students are given a blank bingo sheet and they write their vocabulary words onto the sheet in whatever order they would like. The more words there are available for students to choose from, the longer the game is likely to last. Because students are choosing their own words, they can choose words with which they feel most knowledgeable, which can boost their confidence while playing. This encourages students of all levels to build their vocabulary. The teacher (or a student volunteer) reads off a definition of the word and students place their marker on the appropriate vocabulary word. Teachers can use students' vocabulary flashcards to choose the words to call out. The first student to get bingo (all the words in a row, column, or diagonal) wins and the teacher should be sure to check that the student has chosen the correct word to match the definition. This game is easy to create and students really enjoy it; teachers can offer inexpensive prizes for the winner such as pencils or other school supplies or could give a reward such as a free homework pass.

**ACTIVITY 3.18.** Sample vocabulary bingo board with words from *To Kill a Mockingbird*

| Morbid | Taciturn | Literate | Furor | Tyranny |
|---|---|---|---|---|
| Mortifying | Desolate | Fluently | Peril | Wrathful |
| Oppressive | Devoid | Free Space | Justice | Tedious |
| Diction | Civil | Chiffarobe | Benignly | Impudent |
| Heathen | Obituary | Martyred | Purloined | Eluded |

**Teaching Tip**

Students could create their bingo board the day before (or for homework) and illustrate the words with symbols or drawings to help reinforce their understanding of the word meanings and help them make associations between words and other concepts.

## Wide Reading and Reading Aloud (Levels 1, 2, 3, and 4)

Although it is important for students to develop depth of understanding of vocabulary through specific and intentional teaching of selected word meanings, ELLs can also develop their vocabulary through wide reading of a variety of texts. English language arts teachers should encourage students to read often both inside and outside school. One way English teachers can expose language learners to a language-rich environment is through reading aloud. Reading aloud allows teachers the opportunity to model effective reading of texts including pronunciation and comprehension. In addition, read-alouds can help ELLs gain important background knowledge for a unit of study. Reading aloud also improves listening comprehension, listening vocabulary, and creates interest in reading. Calkins (2001) suggests several times and places when reading aloud can be used to improve students' reading comprehension: reading aloud to begin the day, reading aloud within mini-lessons, reading aloud in support of whole-class book studies, and reading aloud to help students talk and think about texts.

Fisher, Rothenberg, and Frey (2007) offer several suggestions for teachers to create effective read-alouds:

1. Select books which are appropriate for readers' interests and ability levels.
2. Preview and practice reading the text aloud.
3. Establish a purpose for reading aloud.
4. Model fluent oral reading while conducting a read-aloud.
5. Read with animation and expression.
6. Use guided reading techniques such as stopping and asking questions.
7. Make connections between the read aloud and other texts the students are reading.

English language arts teachers should take advantage of read-aloud time in the classroom by encouraging discussion and interaction with the text, by following up with a reading activity such as having students draw the action of the story or share a personal response or connection, and by discussing new vocabulary terms that appeared in the text.

Another way to encourage wide reading in the ELA classroom is through Sustained Silent Reading (SSR). Dedicating class time to SSR models for students the importance of reading and can promote positive attitudes about reading. English language arts teachers can build a classroom library that contains high-interest, accessible texts for ELLs including multicultural literature, adolescent literature, and graphic novels. Teachers should encourage independent reading outside school as well and reward students for their outside reading. Using a reading survey such as the one described in Chapter 3.2 can help teachers get to know their students' reading interests and help them make recommendations to students about which texts to choose. If teachers decide to invest their time in SSR, they should consider reading along with students; although there are certainly lots of tasks to take care of in an English classroom, reading during silent reading time really sends the message that reading is important and worthwhile.

## Dictionaries (Levels 1, 2, 3, and 4)

In order to encourage ELLs to improve their vocabulary knowledge, students must learn strategies to become independent word learners. Using a dictionary is an important skill for all students in ELA classrooms. Teacher should model how to use a dictionary and have bilingual dictionaries in their classroom. Although not everyone agrees about the effectiveness of stopping to look a word up in the dictionary, students need to know there are resources available to them when they find an unfamiliar word that affects their understanding of a passage (Fisher, Rothenberg, & Frey, 2007).

# 3.7
# Speaking

Oral language fluency is the ability to communicate in the target language in a broad range of situations in a way that is easily understood. This includes both informal conversational language and being able to talk about academic subject areas. The American Council on the Teaching of Foreign Languages (ACTFL) is a good resource for helping to understand and measure second language proficiency. ACTFL has a rubric that measures oral language proficiency on a scale from 0 to 5, where 0 signifies no functional competence and 5 represents oral competence equivalent to that of an educated native (ACTFL, 1999).

Oral language, along with listening, accounts for the bulk of our interaction every day, far more than reading or writing. Loban is quoted as saying, "We listen a book a day, talk a book a week, read a book a month, and write a book a year" (W. Loban quoted by Peregoy & Boyle, 2001: 105).

In our experiences with observing teachers, traditional classrooms are heavy on teacher talk time, with the teacher talking up to 95 percent of the time. Teachers need to understand the importance of increasing the opportunities for student talk (or peer talk) time in class. Allowing time for students to synthesize what is being taught in their own words helps them to teach one another. Peer talk is easier for the ELLs to understand and will provide a model to assist in developing their speaking skills.

Here are some suggested strategies that teachers can try in order to help increase the amount of student talk time in class:

- Plan what you will say in advance to reduce the amount of teacher talk.
- Plan questions that will engage your students in meaningful discussions.
- Plan a range of questions, from yes/no and choice questions that can be answered by preproduction and early production students, to more complex "Why" questions that can challenge the speech-emergent and intermediate fluency students.

- To maximize student talk time, have students discuss the questions in small groups of three or four before posing questions to the whole class.
- Designate a speaker for small groups and rotate that responsibility.
- Give small groups the opportunity to report their answers to the class orally.

The quantity of talk time is important, but equally crucial is the quality of talk time. Does the student talk time mostly involve dialogue practices, drills, grammar activities, choral repetition, and answering teachers' artificial questions? Or does the talk resemble more authentic communication?

Most classroom language is artificial communication, and a great percentage of this communication is done in the form of "display" questions, in which the teacher already knows what the expected answer is, and is simply testing the student. For example:

- Teacher: Who wrote *Hamlet*?
- Student: Shakespeare.
- Teacher: Very good!

A more authentic exchange might look like the following:

- Teacher: Who is your favorite English writer?
- Student: Shakespeare.
- Teacher: Which of Shakespeare's works do you like best?
- Student: *Hamlet*, because I like stories about ghosts.
- Teacher: I know what you mean; I like ghost stories too.

It can be argued that the second exchange is still artificial because the student did not offer this information as part of a regular conversation, but the student provided an answer the teacher did not already know. It is important for teachers to respond in a manner that shows they are listening and care about what the student has to say (Horwitz, 2008).

The following activities are selected whole-language techniques that are particularly effective at promoting oral language. We will illustrate these techniques in the context of teaching ELA and give samples of language objectives for each where appropriate. We hope that this will not only give you some practical ideas that you can incorporate in your lessons, but also inspire you to apply these principles to your own ideas and lessons.

## Creating Language-Teaching Opportunities (Levels 1, 2, 3, and 4)

Creating situations in the classroom when real-world language can be practiced is paramount. This can be done by finding the language-teaching opportunities in each classroom session. One way to accomplish this is to think about what social situations could be created in the classroom. Make a conscious effort to find situations that will lend themselves to real-life conversations. Ask questions that will help identify what language skills students will need in order to participate actively in the activity that is being planned:

In this lesson are students going to need to:

- ask each other questions?
- answer questions?

- give information?
- share ideas?
- discuss a topic?
- give their opinions?
- agree/disagree politely with their peers?
- organize a skit?
- work cooperatively on a group project?

There will be specific types of language that are needed for each situation above. Examples of themes from *The Merchant of Venice* that can be used to practice realistic oral exchanges include:

- asking to borrow objects from peers;
- going to a bank and asking to borrow money and discussing interest rates and repayment schedules;
- giving borrowers conditions for lending objects;
- collecting money or objects that were borrowed;
- making excuses for not being able to meet lending conditions;
- asking a peer for an extension for returning something that was borrowed.

---

**Teaching Tips**

- For each lesson, teachers can provide level 1 and 2 students with chunks of language or formulaic expressions they can use to participate in the conversation. Chunks of language are unanalyzed pieces of useful everyday conversation that can be used prior to learning particular language structures and register that comprise the speech chunks.
- Teachers can also rehearse the situations where students will need these chunks, and model the correct application of the various expressions.

---

## Steps to Creating Language-Teaching Opportunities

The High School Literature class is being introduced to *The Merchant of Venice* by William Shakespeare (1977c).

Step 1:    The teacher introduces the play with the following quote, "I will buy with you, sell with you, talk with you, walk with you, and so following, but I will not eat with you, drink with you, nor pray with you" (William Shakespeare, *The Merchant of Venice*, 1596–7). The teacher asks the class to predict what the play is about. For level 1 and 2 students, the teacher will turn the class's predictions into yes/no questions. "Do you think this play is about buying something?"

Step 2:    The teacher will tell the class that the story is about lending and borrowing money. The teacher elicits ways that people ask to borrow something and puts these suggested formats on the board. The teacher then asks students to identify whether it is a polite way or not. Language objective: *Students will learn how to borrow things politely.*

Step 3:    Using the phrases on the board, the teacher asks the students to improvise asking to borrow things from each other, and listens for their responses. The teacher takes note of the types of responses that students give to one another. Language objective: *Students will learn how to respond to requests to lend something to someone.*

## Jazz Chants (Levels 1, 2, 3, and 4)

Jazz Chants were first introduced by Graham (1978) and are the rhythmic expression of Standard American English as it occurs in situational contexts. Using Jazz Chants is an effective way to get students to practice the rhythm of oral English. English is a stress-timed language (in contrast to the languages such as Portuguese and Spanish that are syllable timed). Using Jazz Chants is a way to help ELLs acquire and practice the timing of the language. Chants can also help ELLs be introduced to chunks of language, practice vocabulary, better understand idiomatic expressions, and contextualize specific grammatical structures and situational contexts. Chants are generally set up as conversational exchanges in order to practice patterns and vocabulary in a context that they may be exposed to outside the classroom. The chant depends on repetition and learned responses.

Chants can be used effectively to help students learn and remember problematic grammar forms. There are several websites that give teachers ideas of how to create their own chants. We have all learned the chant, " 'i' before 'e' except after 'c'." Our learning of how to recite the alphabet can also be seen as a chant. Jazz Chants are successful with middle and high school students, too. Teenagers enjoy and respond to sports cheers and raps, and both fall nicely into the category of Jazz Chants.

### Steps for Presenting Chants:

Step 1: The teacher helps the student understand clearly the situational context of the chant. The teacher explains any new vocabulary that will be used in the chant, introduces idiomatic expressions, and explains the cultural nuances that underlie this topic. Language objective: *Students (all levels) will learn chunks of language that are useful for everyday or classroom situations.*

Step 2: The teacher models the first line of the chant at a normal rate of delivery and using the natural inflections and asks the students to repeat it. This procedure should be used throughout the chant. The teacher may wish to repeat each line several times, especially lines that may give some pronunciation difficulties. Language objective: *Students will practice the chunks of language that they learned in step 1.*

Step 3: The teacher then establishes a clear beat by clapping, using rhythm sticks, or snapping his or her fingers, and encourages the students to catch the rhythm as well. The teacher continues the beat, repeating step 2. Language objective: *Students (all levels) will learn the stress-timing of the chunks of language that they learned in steps 1 and 2.*

Step 4: In order to give the students a sense of the conversational exchange that is taking place, the class is divided into two groups. Step 3 is repeated, having the first group repeat after the teacher one set of lines, and the second group repeating after the teacher the response. The teacher's voice continues to provide the model. Language objective: *Students will practice the new chunks of language in regular conversational exchanges using the stress-timing that they learned in step 3.*

Step 5: Finally, the chant is conducted as a dialogue between the teacher and the class. The teacher establishes a clear beat, gives the first line of the chant, and the students, in unison, respond with the second line of the chant. This should be repeated until the students are comfortable enough to respond without being dependent on the text.

> Language objective: *Students will be able to recite the new chunks of language in regular conversational exchanges using the stress-timing that they learned without having to look at the print version.*

If this seems repetitive to you, just imagine, as a native speaker of English, if you were learning some phrases in Chinese. As it is a tonal language, it would take much practice and repetition to feel comfortable reproducing the phrases while simultaneously getting the rhythm and tones right. The key to a successful chant is repetition.

---

**Teaching Tips**

- The book and accompanying tape titled *Grammarchants* (Graham, 1993) goes through all the grammatical structures from the verb *to be*, to the future tenses, to present perfect, comparatives, and superlatives. It is especially effective in helping students practice using contractions.
- LaVon Bridges and Alice Write share original jazz chants for middle and high school students on their website *LitSite Alaska* (http://litsite.alaska.edu/workbooks/jazzchants.html). A fun example is *We are the Rogers Park Wolves* used to teach students about animals of Alaska. It reinforces the use of the present simple tense as a form to express regular habits. It uses *always*, which is habitual, along with *like to*, which shows preferences. The chant incorporates key vocabulary and rhymes it with common words familiar to teens such as *pack/Jack, food/dude, howl/pal*, and so on.

---

## Using Music in ELA (Levels 1, 2, 3, and 4)

Singing and reciting poetry are activities that can help ELLs develop speaking skills because they help reduce anxiety and inhibition. Music with English lyrics is popular throughout the world, and the themes provide a wide range of topics to discuss and vocabulary to learn. Adolescents respond to songs and poetry related to topics of interest, and those that incorporate humor. Research supports the usefulness of music for ELLs. A study on the characteristics of pop songs found that they shared characteristics that made them a rich source of learning for ELLs: they are repetitive, relatively simple, conversation like, and vague enough to be interpreted in personal ways by the listeners (Richard-Amato, 1996).

### Steps for Presenting a Song in Class:

Step 1:    Play the song through once, letting the students listen to the words. Language objective: *Students will become familiar with the song on a superficial level.*

Step 2:    Ask general questions such as: What is the song about? What words or phrases did you hear repeated? Language objective: *Students will be able to compile and organize vocabulary from the song into a graphic organizer. Level 1 students will be able to learn a few new words, relating them to contextual clues provided by the teacher and other students.*

Step 3:    Give the students a copy of the lyrics. If you would like, leave some key words blank for them to fill in. Language objective: *Students will be able to follow along reading the words as they hear the words.*

Step 4:     Play the song again allowing the students to see the words and hear the music. Discuss: What words did you not understand when you heard the song without the printed lyrics? Language objective: *Students will be able to add a few more words to their vocabulary from hearing the discussion.*

Step 5:     Play the song a third time and encourage the students to sing along. Language objective: *Students will be able to practice saying the words in song form.*

Step 6:     Discuss and explain the lyrics and, as a follow-up, get the students to relate the themes to their own lives or to the lives of others they know. Language objective: *Students will be able to talk about themselves (level 1 students can be helped to learn a few short phrases about themselves).*

## Teaching Conditionals and Promises with *Napoleon Dynamite* (Levels 1, 2, 3, and 4)

Theme songs from movies on American pop culture or songs from classic movies are rich resources that make students eager to use their oral language skills. *Napoleon Dynamite* (2004) is a favorite film of many high school students. It is the story of an awkward high school student from a dysfunctional family. He helps his best friend Pedro, an immigrant student from Mexico, run for class president and win a surprising victory against one of the most popular cheerleaders in school. During a school assembly, candidates for class president give their campaign speeches and are required to put on a skit. After delivering his speech, a dejected Pedro feels that all is lost since he did not know about the skit requirement. Suddenly, Napoleon spontaneously performs an energetic dance routine to the song "The Promise" by the popular band When in Rome. Napoleon gets a standing ovation from the audience and saves Pedro's campaign. Here is an excerpt from a lesson incorporating "The Promise" (When in Rome) from the film *Napoleon Dynamite*.

Step 1:     Give a short synopsis of the film plot (see synopsis provided). Language objective: *Students will be able to share parts of the film that they liked, and add to the story orally.* Teacher can rephrase statements students make into yes/no and choice questions for the level 1 and 2 students to be able to share their opinions as well. Example: "Did you think the part about Napoleon's dance routine was funny?"

Step 2:     Play the film clip of the dance routine and the song "The Promise." Ask students to pay attention to the words and write down 10 of the words that they hear. Language objective: *Students will be able to tell the teacher some of the words and the teacher will write the words on the board; level 1 and 2 students will have an opportunity to learn new words here and start noticing them in the song.*

Step 3:     Write the following structures on the board and have the students match vocabulary words with these two chunks. Language objective: *Students will learn these two chunks that relate to making promises and conditions.* Learning chunks of language is a very good strategy for level 1 and 2 students.

- I'll always . . .
- When you are . . .

Step 4:     Play the song again for the students to sing along. Provide the lyrics for the students to sing along (lyrics can be found on the internet). Language objective: *Students will practice the grammatical forms of conditionals and promises orally by singing the song. All levels of ELL students can sing along.*

## Role Play with TV Commercials (Levels 1, 2, 3, and 4)

Drama comes from the Greek word for *to do* or *to act*. Drama acts out stories. The speech and action of drama recreate the flow of human life. Drama crosses cultural boundaries by uniting students in a single project or activity that is fun and nonthreatening and can include the following activities: pantomime, movement and dance, using puppets, role play, and reader's theater, just to name a few. Drama helps to develop both verbal and nonverbal (paralinguistic) skills.

Role play can be used in various ways in the ELA classroom. It can reduce inhibitions, getting students who are normally shy to step out of themselves as they take on a role, pretending to be someone else. This activity provides students with valuable experiences of rehearsing real-life situations within the safety of their classroom. Role-playing can be either an impromptu activity or more elaborate, if they actually study the lines and then put on a presentation for the class. The latter type can be used effectively with level 1 and 2 students and can help them gain self-confidence in speaking English in different situations. Using a TV commercial to create dialogues is a good way to connect daily life with popular literature.

### Steps for Role Play:

Step 1:    The teacher shows a part of a TV commercial—and pauses where two people start a dialogue.

Step 2:    Students in pairs or triads create dialogues. *Level 1 and 2 students are paired with fluent students who can help them learn some phrases.*

Step 3:    Students present the dialogues they have created to the rest of the class. *All students can participate in this fun activity.*

Step 4:    The teacher then plays the dialogue of the commercial for the class to compare with what they created.

## Connecting Storytelling and Literature (Levels 1, 2, 3, and 4)

All cultures in the world have some form of storytelling and the tradition of passing down stories from one generation to the next. These stories can be family-specific or of a broader nature. The fact that all families have certain favorite stories can be used very effectively to get students talking in class. Storytelling also has an added benefit as it allows teachers to get to know their students on a more personal level and provides an opportunity to bring students' home culture into the classroom. The use of oral tradition, starting with an English language learner's home culture, and then transitioning into literature and the classics, is an effective tool in helping students build the schema needed to better understand new subject matter introduced.

A good way to begin is to encourage students to collect stories from their families and have them share their stories with the class. When the literature in class is dealing with issues from everyday life, such as in *The Grapes of Wrath* (Steinbeck, 2002), students' personal stories of family migration and immigration can be collected and told.

### Example of Storytelling using *The Grapes of Wrath*

Step 1:    Start the lesson by showing the class a picture, as using visuals to start a lesson is a great way to level the playing field no matter what the language proficiency of the student. They will be able to relate to a photograph at some level.

Step 2:    Help the class build a common vocabulary for talking about the picture. Build a semantic map with all the words that are provided by the students because visually seeing the words and how the words relate to one another is a good way to provide contextualiza-tion for new vocabulary that is presented to ELLs.

Step 3:    Have students bring in photos of family trips that they have taken and tell a story about their trip. Level 1 and 2 students can be given a sheet that has the formulaic phrases that they will need minus their personal details to fill in: "This is a picture of my family in _____." "We enjoyed _____ on this trip."

Step 3 alternative: If the student doesn't have a photo, this can also be substituted with a drawing or an object that reminds them of their trip.

Step 4:    Discuss the travel of students in relation to the travel of the Joads in *The Grapes of Wrath*.

## What's in the Bag? (Levels 1, 2, 3, and 4)

Games provide a fun way to practice recurring patterns of language and can generally be played by ELLs once they have been taught some basic "chunks" of language.

What's in the Bag? is a game that helps students practice asking questions. Bring an unusual object to class that is related to something from the ELA lesson. Allow students to ask questions about the object. The teacher can comment on the questions and provide clues. A variation can be to conduct this as a "20 questions" in which the answers to the questions have to be either "yes" or "no."

### Sample Activity Using a Song from *The Sound of Music*

Step 1:    Bring an object that you really like to class in a brown paper bag.

Step 2:    Allow students to ask yes/no questions about the object. For your ELLs, you will want to provide sample structures for this kind of question: Is it _____? (provide some adjectives). Can you _____ it? (provide some verbs).

Step 3:    Comment on the questions to help ELLs understand the questions that were asked and the answers that you give.

Step 4:    Play the song "My Favorite Things" and give them the words to sing along (lyrics can be found on the internet).

Step 5:    Ask students to bring an object to class that is one of their favorite things. Even ELLs at the beginning levels can participate in this and answer yes/no questions about their favorite object.

## Watch, Role-Play, Improvise (Levels 1, 2, 3, and 4)

The use of joke telling and humor in general is a much more sophisticated form of language, but there are many opportunities to employ humor in an ELA class that will help generate oral language. For example, students can be asked to find plays on words to share with the class. Many humor-infused activities can be used as debate starters or as discussion foci. Others can encourage learners to produce English in creative and meaningful ways. Fortunately, the internet is a good resource for humor. Just enter "humor" and the topic of choice into a search engine. Then, make sure the humor you choose is content and age appropriate.

### Steps for Watch, Role-Play, Improvise:

Step 1:    Have students watch examples of situational humor.

Step 2:    Ask students to comment or explain the sketches to familiarize ELLs with the mechanics of humorous situations.

Step 3:    Have students role-play the sketches they have watched, create similar ones, and improvise their own (level 1 students can help act it out).

## Fumble Rules (Levels 1, 2, 3, and 4)

Rules are generally structurally simple, making them easy for ELLs to understand. Rephrasing a rule in a way that violates that rule is always fun and increases the memorability of the rule. You can give rules to the ELLs and ask them to create their own versions that actually violate the rules. Here are a few examples:

- Don't use no double negatives.
- Verbs has to agree with their subjects.
- A writer must not shift your point of view.
- Reserve the apostrophe for it's proper use and omit it when its not needed.

---

**Extension Activities**

- More rules can be found at www.creativeteachingsite.com/humorgrammar.htm. Have the students try to spot the error in each of the phrases.
- Students can work out the corrections in groups of ELLs paired with fluent English speakers.

---

## Funny Rhymes (Levels 1, 2, 3, and 4)

All students enjoy a good laugh, and most enjoy playing with language. One activity that capitalizes on these two ideas is the creation of funny rhymes. In this activity, the teacher provides rhymes to the class with blank spaces to be filled in with a rhyming word. Here is an example of a funny rhyme:

- If your husband bakes a cake, watch out for the mess he'll _____. (make)

Learners can complete the rhyme, and then discuss gender stereotypes or division of labor at home. This is a good vocabulary-building activity for all language levels. For level 1 and 2 students, provide the words for them to match.

## Multiple Choice Questions (Levels 1, 2, 3, and 4)

Another way to infuse language learning with humor is to have students create nonsensical selections for multiple choice questions. A good source of humorous versions of multiple choice options is the TV show "Who Wants to Be a Millionaire?" or its website. To help participants relax, the first question always has a humorous D option:

The postal abbreviation RFD stands for what?

A: Rural Free Delivery
B: Recover From Destination
C: Received From Donor
D: Road made From Dirt

Provide ELLs with examples like the one above and have learners create their own D option and present the question and the multiple choice answers to their classmates. This activity can also be used to review material being studied in class.

## Puns: Explain, Complete, Construct (Levels 3 and 4)

Explaining puns is meaningful because some puns are not easy to get. This makes them especially suitable for classes with ELLs because they may not be the only ones that need a language explanation. Explaining puns makes speaking meaningful and raises learners' awareness of how humor is attained. The explanations of puns will often lead learners to interesting debates.

Here are some explanation-friendly puns:

- What did the grape say when it got stepped on? It just let out a little whine.
- Did you hear about the guy whose whole left side was cut off? He's all right now.
- Sign on the lawn at a drug rehab center: "Keep off the Grass."
- Time flies like an arrow. Fruit flies like a banana.

Once learners have been exposed to the way puns are constructed, they may enjoy completing a given pun themselves. Start with familiar or content topics, such as the ones below. Their inventiveness will surprise you.

- We'll never run out of math teachers because they always _____. (multiply)
- To write with a broken pencil is _____. (pointless)
- When the power went off during an exam at a school, the students were _____. (de-lighted)

Once learners have a firm grasp on puns, they can construct their own. Also, in a more demanding task, you may provide learners with the first line of the pun, but leave the punchline to their creativity.

- What did the tall tower say to the low tower?

You can also use the same structure to focus on content matter concepts:

- What did the comma tell the semi-colon?

ELLs will start generating their own jokes in a creative oral composition genre.

## Word Play (Levels 3 and 4)

Many ELLs enjoy word play and can begin with guided tasks, such as making a proverb humorous by elaborating its casual style. Take any proverb that suits the content of the literature you are studying and ask learners to rephrase it in a way that is as elaborate as possible. For example, if your class is reading *The Odyssey*, the proverb "A rolling stone gathers no moss" would be an excellent conversation starter. Does the class agree with the proverb? Does the proverb prove to be true in light of Odysseus' travels? Once students have discussed the proverb, they may produce something along the lines of "A revolving petrified mineral conglomerate accumulates no simple nonflowering plant bryophyte." Of course, students will need to have thesauri handy! Later, students' elaborated versions may be used to make their classmates guess the initial proverb.

# 3.8
# Listening and Viewing

Listening comprehension is the ability to separate meaningful units from the stream of speech that one hears (Diaz-Rico & Weed, 2006). Listening, along with reading, is classified as a receptive skill, but it is far from being a passive activity. Intuitively, we know that listening comprehension is developed by listening to the target language and that there are specific skills involved with becoming a good listener. For ELLs, learning listening strategies can help improve listening comprehension. The ELA teacher is presented with many opportunities to help ELLs develop their listening comprehension skills in the target language. Meaningful input that is comprehensible to ELLs can in turn become output in the target language.

Here are some simple strategies that can be taught to ELLs to help them develop good listening skills (Richard-Amato, 2003).

- Focus attention as completely as possible on what is being said.
- Relax and let the ideas flow into your mind.
- Don't be upset if you don't understand everything.
- Try to connect what you hear to what you already know.
- Listen for key words and ideas.
- Ask the speaker to repeat or to speak more slowly, if necessary.
- Try not to be afraid to ask questions about meaning when it seems all right to do so.
- Make guesses about what is being said.
- In conversation, check out your understanding by using confirmation checks. (Example: Is this what you are saying?)
- Whenever possible, pay attention to the forms fluent speakers are using. (How are they different from the forms you use?)

- Write down what you have learned—new words, meanings, concepts, structures, idioms, etc.—in a notebook.
- Find a buddy with whom you can compare lecture and discussion notes later to see if you missed any important points that were made.
- Find opportunities to listen outside class by watching television shows and movies, going to lectures, etc.

The great news about listening comprehension for ELLs is that it is the generally the first competency acquired by learners who are constantly exposed to the spoken target language. With 17 years of experience teaching English in another country, one of us has observed that students who are not exposed to the target language in spoken form do not acquire listening comprehension. These students tend to depend on the written form in order to comprehend. In real life, people generally communicate orally rather than in written form when the person is present. The following principles seem to apply to improve listening comprehension:

Principle 1:  The quantity of listening activities matters. The more listening the learners do, the better they become at comprehension. It is important to expose listeners to a variety of speakers, both native and nonnative, and to a variety of genres of speech, including formal and informal, academic and interpersonal. Listeners should also be exposed to a variety of regional dialects, accents of speakers from various countries that speak English, and accents of second language learners from other countries. Finally, language learners should have access to a variety of modes of audio: from telephone conversations to radio programs, to live informal conversations, to structured lectures, films, documentaries, and music. The use of technology can help learners have easy and free access to a great variety of authentic listening through podcasts, online radio, films, and television. Having read hundreds of interviews with ELLs, we find that, when they are asked what has helped them the most in learning English, many have responded that watching television programs and listening to music in English has been what has really helped them the most. Bear in mind that this is a self-reported perception about their personal experience.

Principle 2:  The quality of listening activities matters. Listening activities should be meaningful, interesting, and engaging in order to motivate learners. The learners need to clearly see a purpose for the activities. The listening activities should be real, or at least realistic (see explanation of this distinction in the chapter on speaking). One way to make listening more interesting is to make sure that they are learner-centered topics that students want to discuss. When language acquisition is socially motivated, and a creative process, it requires a high degree of personal engagement (Richard-Amato, 2003). The difference between the kinds of language that makes quality listening activities is illustrated by Goodman (1986), who contrasted what makes language easier or more difficult (Table 3.5).

If you stop and think about the diverse activities that go on in an ELA classroom, a great majority of them involve listening comprehension. Take a literature class as an example. The following are some of the typical activities:

- The teacher gives an oral presentation introducing the class to a writer or poet (while students listen and take notes).
- The teacher reads a short story or poem to the class (the students listen).

**TABLE 3.5.** Indicators of easy versus difficult language

| It's easy when: | It's difficult when: |
| --- | --- |
| It's real and natural. | It's artificial. |
| It's whole. | It's broken into bits. |
| It's sensible. | It's nonsense. |
| It's interesting. | It's dull and uninteresting. |
| It's relevant. | It's irrelevant to the learner. |
| It belongs to the learner. | It belongs to someone else. |
| It's part of a real event. | It's out of context. |
| It has social utility. | It has no social value. |
| It has a purpose for the learner. | It has no discernable purpose. |
| The learner chooses to use it. | It's imposed by someone else. |
| It's accessible to the learner. | It's inaccessible. |
| The learner has power to use it. | The learner is powerless. |

Adapted from Goodman (1986).

- The teacher shows a film about the life of the writer (the students watch and listen).
- The class discusses a film or reading (the students listen to peers talking about the film or reading).

Given the importance of listening comprehension in the ELA classroom, it is paramount to support ELLs in the often overlooked ELA strands of listening and viewing. One way to do this is through sheltered instruction, which can be defined as an approach that provides language support to students while they are learning academic subjects (Diaz-Rico & Weed, 2006). Although sometimes sheltered instruction can mean classes consisting solely of nonnative speakers of English who operate at similar English proficiency levels (Echevarria, Vogt, & Short, 2004), in this text, the focus is on sheltering instruction for the vast majority of nonnative English speakers who are actually being taught in classrooms that are made up of both native English speakers and nonnative English speakers of various language proficiency levels. In the state of Florida, for example, this constitutes over 10 percent of the K–12 school population and includes students from 202 different home languages (Florida Department of Education, 2008).

Sheltering listening activities for ELL students can mean various things. Instruction for language learners simply means that the teacher will provide contextual clues in the form of gestures, pictures, realia (objects), simplified language, adjusting the speech rate, and so on, to make the input more comprehensible to the language learner. Sheltered instruction goes beyond just providing "good teaching" that incorporates best practices. It distinguishes itself in that it incorporates knowledge of second language acquisition into teaching and provides language objectives that include learning the academic language skills, developing strategies for learning how to learn (metacognitive strategies), and, at the same time, acquiring the necessary vocabulary, grammar, syntax, phonology, and morphology. The following three activities are examples that illustrate the use of sheltering listening in a literature class.

## Oral Presentation of a Poem (Levels 1, 2, 3, and 4)

The following activity uses "The Road Not Taken" by Robert Frost for the example:

Step 1:    The teacher provides pictures of different kinds of roads and asks students to describe them (write words that describe the roads on the whiteboard for the preproduction and early production students to identify with the pictures). Provide pictures of crossroads, paths, in wooded areas, and so on, to introduce the vocabulary of the poem. Language objective: *Students (all levels) will learn at least seven new words related to the poem.*

Step 2:  The teacher reads the poem "The Road Not Taken" the first time, asking the students to listen for any emotions (for the level 1 and 2 students, provide a print copy and an emoticons chart in your classroom that they can point to showing what mood they feel is portrayed). Language objective: *Students will be able to identify the mood of the poem by the expressions the teacher uses to read the poem.*

Step 3:  The teacher asks the students to listen as the poem is read aloud a second time, paying attention to identify what vocabulary words were used that were already on the board. Language objective: *Students will be able to hear and identify some of the words they learned in step 1.*

Step 4:  The teacher asks students to help add to the list of vocabulary words that were already on the board by highlighting the ones that were already written on the board, and adding new ones to the list. Language objective: *Students will be able to identify the new words orally and use one of the words in a sentence (for level 1 students the teacher will provide a fill-in-the blank statement that will work with various new words: "The path was _____").*

Step 5:  The teacher passes out copies of the poem with some of the key words blanked out (suggested words can include ones that give key concepts in the poem, such as: *diverged, sorry, long, other, perhaps, step, doubted, sigh,* and *less*). The teacher reads the poem again, and the students can try to fill in the missing words. Language objective: *Students will be able to fill in the blank words in the poem. For the ELL students, make sure that the words that have been blanked out are provided in scrabbled order, either on their handout or on the board.*

Step 6:  The teacher talks about the meaning of the poem with the class, explaining the difference between literal and ironic interpretation and providing examples of literal versus ironical interpretation by showing the irony in everyday situations: if you Google the words "the irony of fate" and click on "images" you will find examples you can use to start the discussion. Language objective: *All students will understand what irony is, and how it is used in this poem (for level 1 and 2 students, provide pictures or cartoons that illustrate irony).*

---

**Teaching Tip**

There are many photos available online. One example of this is a photo of a "Dead End" sign with a cemetery in the background.

---

## Showing Films (Levels 1, 2, 3, and 4)

The following is an example using *A Lover's Quarrel with the World* (1963), a film about the life of Robert Frost. It was completed just prior to Frost's death at the age of 88 and includes his speaking engagements at Amherst and Sarah Lawrence Colleges. The film combines Frost's work with scenes of his life in rural Vermont and includes the poet's reminiscences on his career. It is 55 minutes in length.

Step 1:    Before showing the film, the teacher asks some pre-viewing questions. The teacher will use the K–W–L format as a graphic organizer to find out what students already know about poets (K) and what they want to know about Robert Frost in particular (W). Language objective: *Students will be able to draw on their previous knowledge to answer oral questions such as:*

- What would you like to know about Robert Frost? For your preproduction and early production students, take responses from other students to this question and transform them into yes/no questions to ask them. For example, if a student responds "I would like to know if he had a family," this response could then be transformed into a yes/no question to ask: "Would you like to know if he had a family?").
- What sort of things do you think the film will show? These prediction-type questions model higher-order thinking and study strategies that will help students become familiar with the American system of education, which is based on this kind of thinking. The great majority of questions asked to ELLs tend to be display-type questions that really do not ask for their opinions. They are just expected to give back information they have heard. For level 1 and 2 students, the teacher can ask choice questions for which the answer is in the question, such as: "Do you think the film will be interesting or boring?"

Step 2:    The teacher gives the students a handout that will guide them as they are watching the film, so they can collect the important information.
        Sample questions can include:

- When was Robert Frost born?
- Where was Robert Frost born?
- How long did he live?
- What does he say about his own work?
- What do others say about his work?
- What do you think he is most famous for?

---

**Teaching Tip**

For level 1 and 2 students, the worksheet should be modified to include multiple choice answers rather than fill in the blank questions. Language objective: *Students will be able to fill in the information about Robert Frost as they are watching the film about his life, as adapted for each language proficiency.*

---

## Class Discussion Using Small Groups (Levels 1, 2, 3, and 4)

In a class with ELLs present, it is important that all students are given an opportunity to speak. One way to lower the affective filter is to allow students to discuss the questions to be asked in small groups prior to the whole-class discussion. The affective filter is lowered even more when groups of students are allowed to choose a speaker for the group. Language learners will gain more from the interaction when they do not have to worry about speaking in front of the class. Additionally, group work often creates a warm learning environment, an environment in which ELLs will be more willing to eventually become the group reporter to the class.

The following example illustrates how to conduct a group discussion on the Frost poem and film used in the last two activities:

Step 1:    The class is divided into groups of three students with each student given a role: a speaker, a writer, and a reader. The groups discuss the questions. The reader reads the questions aloud for the group. Each group discusses the questions while the writer records the group's responses. Language objective: *Students will be able to understand their colleagues speaking in a small group setting, and respond as appropriate to their language level.*

Step 2:    The teacher conducts a whole-class discussion giving each group the opportunity to share their responses. The speaker for each group reports the responses of their group back to the class. Language objective: *Students will be able to understand their colleagues and teacher in the whole-class setting, and respond as appropriate to their language level.*

## Podcasting for ELLs (Levels 1, 2, 3, and 4)

The word *podcasting* comes from combining the words *iPod* and *broadcasting*. The simple and very accessible technology has made it possible for ELLs to have easy access to authentic listening sources in the target language on any topic that may be of interest to them. Teachers may take advantage of these resources as a data bank for listening comprehension exercises.

An example of resources for ELA is the "Literature to Go" series of podcasts from the University of South Florida (http://itunes.usf.edu/), a free collection of stories and poems, organized by grade from kindergarten to twelfth grade, in MP3 format that can be downloaded to an iPod. There are printable text versions of each passage with accompanying activities. Another interesting source is "English Feed," a podcast produced by Kenneth Beare (http://esl.about.com) that focuses on grammar and vocabulary issues and provides great listening practice. It allows listeners to subscribe to the feeds so that they will receive new episodes automatically.

Not only can teachers access materials from the countless sources that are available online, they can also create their own podcasts with very little equipment. There is a lot of technical support available online to help teachers create podcasts. One popular site is called Tech-Ease, which can be found in the University of South Florida's iTunes U page (http://itunes.usf.edu/). It is a collection of tutorials on the latest technologies for educators. Follow the links to the COEDU section when navigating to the iTunes Store page, select the "Podcasting" tab, and you will find free video clips that will take you through all the various steps in the process of making podcasts from either computer platform.

## Total Physical Response (TPR) (Levels 1, 2, 3, and 4)

Total physical response (TPR) is a strategy that is very effective in engaging even preproduction students. Students who are going though the "silent period" of language acquisition can participate in meaningful listening activities while the teacher monitors their comprehension without the need for oral feedback. Total physical response is a language teaching strategy that introduces new language through a series of commands to enact an event (Graham, 1993). Learners actively listen to oral language as they simultaneously see it modeled. Listening is practiced in a very nonthreatening atmosphere.

## Principles of the TPR Method

- Physical cues are provided in listening activities that assist the student in comprehension.
- Concepts are best learned through doing something. There is an important connection that is made in the brain from activity to language.
- It is acceptable for students to be in the "silent period" of language acquisition (level 1), and they should be able to participate even when they do not feel comfortable speaking.
- Copying from others is okay. It is not cheating to get cues from others; in fact, it is very much a part of life.

Total physical response is used every day by teachers who may not even realize that what they are doing is called TPR: the teacher gives commands and models each step carefully. The ELL student can observe others following the directions, and this in turn can give the ELL student confidence and teach them these important commands without singling him or her out. ELL students at the intermediate fluency level (level 4) may appear to be fluent in English and teachers can forget that they will struggle in understanding the academic language in the classroom. If the teacher follows some simple principles of TPR, students will have a much easier time understanding what is going on and at the same time be assisted in acquiring the academic language necessary to thrive and not just survive.

## Examples of TPR

- Teacher: OK, everybody, take out your grammar books. (ELLs can observe the class taking out their textbooks and follow the lead).
- Teacher: Now turn to page 51. (ELLs can start opening their book on cue and can look over at the student next to them, observing that their book is open to page 51.)
- Teacher: I want you to do questions 1–5. Here is how you do this, let's do number 1 together ... The teacher models what academic answers will look like by doing one for the speech-emergent and intermediate fluency students to be able to start developing academic-quality work.

## Readers' Theater (Levels 1, 2, 3, and 4)

Another technique for ELA teachers to present literature orally and help language learners develop their listening comprehension skills is using Readers' Theater, a minimal type of theater in which the "actors" perform spontaneously without rehearsing. It relies on facial expression and body movements, and not on costumes or props.

In Readers' Theater, students act out roles in the literature. The narrator (the teacher or a good reader in the class) reads a script, pausing for each line. The students who listen and watch others act out roles will easily be able to make a connection between the words they are hearing and the actions they are seeing. Level 1 and 2 students can gain confidence and language ability and are able to demonstrate their listening comprehension by participating, even without speaking. The same principles that apply to TPR also apply to Readers' Theater for ELLs.

There are many online resources that offer scripts to be used for educational purposes free of charge. Texts can be copied, adapted to the grade level and proficiency level of the target students, and used in class. The book titled *Readers' Theater in the Middle School and Junior High Classroom* by Lois Walker (1996) is a teacher's guidebook of ideas, giving step-by-step instructions on how to use Readers' Theater in the classroom.

# 3.9
# Developing a Unit of Study for a Complete Work

So far, the chapters of this text have discussed the five strands of ELA as if they were discrete skills to be taught one at a time. We know, however, that a comprehensive curriculum integrates reading, writing, speaking, and listening throughout the entire unit of study. This chapter discusses how to design a unit of study for a complete work using the activities and strategies discussed in Chapters 3.2–3.8.

## Thematic Units

According to Smagorinsky (2008) a conceptual unit of instruction dedicates a period of time "to sustained attention to related ideas" (p. 111). This chapter will discuss a specific type of unit, the thematic unit, in which lessons are designed around an overall theme. Designing instructional units around a specific theme has several advantages for ELA teachers and their ELL students:

- Unit themes allow for students to make personal connections to particular topics. Students, including ELLs, can use their background knowledge about a topic to help facilitate new learning.
- Unit themes allow students to see a "big picture" and connect lesson ideas together. They can make individual lessons appear more meaningful and relevant to students.
- Unit themes allow teachers to incorporate a variety of texts into the curriculum. Rather than organizing a unit around a particular genre of literature, such as the short story, teachers can bring in a variety of texts to connect to a theme such as poetry, short stories, novels, nonfiction, and visual media and technology.
- Unit themes allow for interdisciplinary teaching. English language arts teachers can work with teachers in other content areas to create a unit which connects across disciplines and

curriculum. English language learners can benefit from interdisciplinary teaching because they are provided with more opportunities to build background knowledge and to make meaningful connections.

- Unit themes allow students to become responsible for their own learning as they construct their answers to the key unit questions and ideas, rather than simply memorizing facts in isolation.
- Unit themes can tie in key vocabulary that can be repeated across lessons.

The theme for the unit presented in this chapter will be *Growing Up*. This is a theme that all students in secondary school should be able to identify with regardless of language ability or background. Because we believe that ELLs can benefit from a unit being anchored by studying a whole-class novel, the primary text for this unit is *To Kill a Mockingbird* by Harper Lee. Lee's novel was chosen for a number of reasons: (1) it is perhaps the most commonly taught classic American novel in the United States and chances are that most ELA teachers will be called upon to teach it at some point in their career; (2) it is an engaging text told in the first person through a charming narrator with a strong voice; and (3) in addition to an entertaining storyline, the novel is well written and uses a variety of literary techniques that lend themselves to teaching students the beginnings of literary analysis. Typically, Lee's novel is taught in the upper middle or lower high school grades. Depending upon the maturity level of the students, teachers may consider changing the theme from *Growing Up* to *Coming of Age*.

According to Smagorinsky (2008), a conceptual unit is not simply a collection of related texts; rather it "involves students in conversations that deepen as they progress through the texts, activities, and discussions" (p. 112). The unit should engage students in the exploration of key questions and key concepts with which students are continually developing and revising their understandings.

## Components of a Unit Plan

The typical components of a unit plan are a rationale, goals and objectives, an assessment plan, and lessons and activities. These components will be discussed in this chapter in three ways: (1) through a general discussion of the practices of creating a unit of instruction in an ELA classroom; (2) through the specific aspects of unit planning that need to be considered when teaching ELLs; and (3) by providing examples from the thematic unit *Growing Up*. When planning a unit for a class that contains ELLs, teachers can use the key questions presented by Freeman and Freeman (2000) in their article "Meeting the Needs of English Language Learners":

1. Is curriculum organized around big questions?
2. Are students involved in authentic reading and writing experiences?
3. Is there an attempt to draw on students' background and knowledge? Are students given choices?
4. Is the content meaningful? Does it serve a purpose for the learner?
5. Do students have the opportunity to work collaboratively?
6. Do students read and write as well as speak and listen during their learning experiences?
7. Are students' primary languages and cultures valued, supported, and developed?
8. Are students involved in activities which build their self-esteem and provide them with opportunities to succeed? (pp. 3–7)

These are questions ELA teachers should be asking themselves while they are conceiving their unit of study and throughout the teaching of the unit.

## The Unit Rationale

There are several reasons to create a rationale for teaching a conceptual unit. Simply stated, teachers need to know why they are teaching what they are teaching. From a planning standpoint, your rationale can help guide your decision making: it helps you determine which texts to choose and which objectives to teach and helps you create a framework for which to plan the lessons and activities. In addition, teachers need to be able to articulate to students why they are studying a particular subject and how it relates to students' lives and their education. Teachers also have to explain to a variety of people the curricular choices they make and the pedagogical methods they use. There are a multitude of decisions teachers make when determining what to teach and how to teach it:

- What are the state standards I am expected to teach?
- What are the district, school, and grade level expectations for my subject?
- What are the needs and ability levels of my students?
- What specific aspects of my community need to be considered?

English language arts teachers also sometimes have to face questions about censorship. If a particular text might be considered objectionable to a student or group of students, parents, or members of the community, having a clear and justifiable rationale is essential. One resource English teachers can use to help support their justification for using a particular text or film is the compact disc *Rationales for Challenged Books: Prepared by NCTE in Partnership with IRA* (NCTE & IRA, 1998).

Although creating a written rationale for a unit may seem daunting, teachers should at least have a mental rationale prepared. When preparing a rationale teachers can use the simple, yet time-honored, method of the five W's and an H.

- Who is my audience for this unit? What are the needs of my students? What are their ability levels? What backgrounds and experiences do they bring to the classroom? What prior knowledge do they have?
- What will I teach? Which texts will I use? What materials are available to me? When teaching ELLs we need to consider both language and content objectives as well as the levels of language proficiency of the students.
- When will I teach this unit? There are certain times in a school year when a particular unit may be most effective. Standardized testing can affect curriculum planning. In addition, teachers can take into account the curriculum of other content areas.
- Where am I teaching? Teachers can consider the needs of students in relationship to their community. How can I connect with all learners' home cultures?
- How will I teach this unit? What methods will I use? How can I best support all my learners and best integrate reading, writing, listening, speaking, and viewing into my lessons and use appropriate and authentic assessment measures?

Smagorinsky (2008) offers several types of justifications for teaching a unit which are also extremely helpful. The following are a few examples he provides. For a more complete list, see *Teaching English by Design: How to Create and Carry Out Instructional Units.*

- Responding to the psychological needs of students. Literature often explores aspects of the human condition: topics such as growing up, creating an identity, friendship, and family relationships are all possible unit themes which can make connections to students' lives.
- Considering the cultural significance. Unit topics can center on important cultural events in history such as the Civil Rights movement, topics such as Immigration, and can be centered on students' own cultural experiences through themes such as diversity and cultural boundaries. In addition, a unit could explore a cultural aspect of literature such as local or regional authors.
- Considering literary significance. Teachers may choose to focus on a literary period or genre and its significance to students' cultural literacy, for example studying Shakespeare. (pp. 141–143)

The unit theme of *Growing Up* most closely aligns with the psychological needs of students; students, in one way or another, can identify with the joys, trials, and tribulations of maturing. However, because the novel *To Kill a Mockingbird* deals with issues such as racism and discrimination, teachers can explore elements of cultural significance as well.

## Unit Goals

Teachers need to consider their overall goals for instruction that they want to carry out throughout the unit and the student learning outcomes that will result from the instruction. At the same time, teachers need to ask themselves how they will assess these goals. Unfortunately, instruction in ELA classrooms has not always matched assessment: teachers frequently began planning with the text they wanted to teach or the activities they wanted to use. Without considering the goals and learning outcomes as well as the way students will prove they have accomplished these goals, it is difficult to determine if learning has actually taken place. For ELLs teachers need to consider both content and language goals. The following are some questions to help you get started thinking about unit goals:

- What do I want my students to know and be able to do at the end of the unit?

    - What do I want students to know about literature?
    - What reading skills do I want students to develop during this unit?
    - What writing skills do I want students to develop during this unit?
    - What listening and speaking skills do I want students to develop during this unit?

- What language skills do I want my students to develop throughout the unit?
- How will I know how well students have accomplished these goals?

### Sample Content Goals for *Growing Up* Unit

1. Students will understand that through literature we can understand ourselves and others.
2. Students will engage in strategies to comprehend literary text: to identify, analyze, and apply knowledge of the structures and elements of literature.
3. Students will identify, analyze, and apply knowledge of the purpose, structure, and elements of expository texts.
4. Students will engage in activities to make meaning of texts through personal response.

5. Students will demonstrate knowledge of composing processes.
6. Students will use writing to generate meaning and clarify understanding.
7. Students will practice and develop their writing skills using the six traits: ideas and content, organization, voice, word choice, sentence fluency, and conventions.
8. Students will make connections between ELA texts and developments in society and culture.
9. Students will use ELA to become familiar with their own and others' cultures.
10. Students will show an ability to construct meaning from media and nonprint texts.
11. Students will show an ability to engage in meaningful discussions for the purpose of interpreting and evaluating ideas.
12. Students will learn reading strategies to access and understand texts.

Teachers of ELL students also need to consider language objectives in addition to content objectives; although these need to be considered in daily lesson planning, having overall language goals for the unit is also important. The objectives for English language proficiency vary on the level of the English language learner. Teachers will need to consult their state standards for specific language objectives that correspond to the proficiency levels of their students.

## Essential Questions

In addition to creating unit goals Freeman and Freeman (2000) suggest that teachers with ELL students organize their curriculum around "big" questions (p. 3). The purposes of using guiding questions, often referred to as essential questions, in unit planning are the same as those listed for organizing units around themes: to help students see the purpose of what they are learning and make connections between lessons and ideas; to help students learn key vocabulary in context; to help students make connections between the curriculum and their own lives; and to involve all language proficiency levels of ELLs (students can explore essential questions dealing with universal topics regardless of their proficiency levels). Essential questions are not necessarily related to specific content—they can be more general, as students need to be able to connect to them, to their lives, and to other content. Essential questions should be thought-provoking and open-ended, should require students to call on background knowledge and content knowledge, and should be revisited throughout the unit.

### Sample Essential Questions for *Growing Up* Unit

- What obstacles do we encounter as we grow up?
- What role do our family, friends, and other adults have in our development as we grow?
- How does our family heritage and our community influence who we are and whom we become?
- What factors influence our "education" as we grow up? (School, home, life lessons, etc.)

## Assessment

Before planning specific lessons, teachers need to consider the goals and how they will assess them. Students should be assessed in a variety of ways and ELA teachers must consider all aspects of ELA: reading, writing, listening, speaking, and viewing. English language learners can benefit from alternative and performance assessments such as presentations, dramatic activities, projects, and portfolios. Many of the activities discussed in this text are designed to be collaborative so students should be assessed appropriately; of course, ultimately the goal is for students to gain and develop independence but, if students are not ready to perform without assistance, they should not be assessed independently. In addition, teachers should consider providing a balance between informal, low-stakes assessments that help students develop fluency such as quick writes, journals, reading logs, and small group activities and more formal activities in which students have time to prepare and revise a final product such as an essay, project, or presentation. When assessing ELLs, teachers must also take into account students' language proficiency level (preproduction, early production, speech emergence, and intermediate fluency), and create appropriate modifications to assessment activities. The following are suggestions for assessments for a *Growing Up* unit. Students at levels 1 and 2 can participate in the activities but may not be able to complete all assessments; assessments will need to be modified for their specific English proficiency level. The important thing to remember is that students are given choices about assessment so that they can demonstrate success and their content knowledge in a variety of ways.

## Formal Assessment Ideas for *Growing Up* Unit

- A written paper addressing one of the essential questions and how it relates to the novel: Students can use the five paragraph essay format described in Chapter 3.6. Students at lower proficiency levels could address the question and the text through an alternative assessment, such as filling out a graphic organizer or choosing and ordering sentences that are provided by the teacher.
- Cultural influences project: Students create a presentation illustrating how their cultural heritage, family background, and/or community have influenced who they are. Students can choose to give an oral report, create a PowerPoint presentation, create a collage or other graphic representation, write a poem, etc., depending upon their ability level. Students should make connections to one other text studied in class such as the literature circles text or *To Kill a Mockingbird*.

## Informal Assessment Ideas for *Growing Up* Unit

- Participation in literature circles: Depending upon the level of the student, teachers can collect role sheets, reading logs, double entry journals, etc. Students can also be encouraged to self-assess their contributions to discussion.
- Literature circles presentation: Each group presents their literature circles book to the class. For presentation ideas see Chapter 3.2.
- Reader responses to class novel: *To Kill a Mockingbird*. Students can keep a reading log to record their reactions to the class novel. Other reader response activities such as Talking to the Text and double entry journals can be used. See Chapter 3.2.
- Participation in various low-stakes reading and writing activities including collaborative activities (filling out graphic organizers, creating maps and charts, participation in dramatic activities, readers' theater, etc). Students can be given credit for participation and completion.

## Lessons and Activities

These are in no way exhaustive or prescriptive, but we have included examples of how the various strategies and activities presented in Chapters 3.2–3.8 can be applied to the study of a whole-class novel as part of a unit with the theme *Growing Up*. In addition, we have provided a sample lesson plan template that considers best practices in teaching ELA with best practices in teaching ELLs modified from B. Cruz, S. Thornton, and Dr. Joyce Nutta, University of South Florida.

**LESSON PLAN 3.1.**

|  | Preproduction | Early Production | Speech Emergence | Intermediate Fluency |
|---|---|---|---|---|
| Content Objective: Should be valid for all language levels | | | | |
| Language Objective: The goal should be one level above students' present level | | | | |
| Preparation: What materials can you identify to provide comprehensible input for each level? | | | | |
| Procedures: How are you going to provide comprehensible input in your delivery? What strategies will you use? | | | | |
| Assessment: How are you going to access at each of the language levels? | | | | |
| Home–School Connection: What activity can you use to connect with all learners' home cultures? | | | | |

In an effort to show how the activities in this text can be integrated into a unit of instruction, we have listed activities from Chapters 3.2–3.8. By structuring them as before-, during-, and after-reading activities centered around the novel, we hope that we can better demonstrate the interrelatedness of reading, writing, speaking, and listening and their roles in the ELA classroom. In addition, we hope that you can see how these activities and strategies we discuss can be modified to accommodate the many and varied texts you will use in your curriculum. It is also important to note that many of these activities require listening and speaking even when they are listed as reading and writing activities. The chapter number where you can find these activities and strategies is listed next to its title.

## Activities and Strategies to Use before Students Read *To Kill a Mockingbird (TKAM)*

- Jazz Chants 3.7: Using songs from the 1930s as an introduction to the novel, you can have students practice their oral language skills through Jazz Chants.
- Concept Map for *Growing Up* 3.2: By creating a concept map for the unit theme of *Growing Up*, students can activate their prior knowledge before beginning their exploration of the unit theme and reading the novel.
- Anticipation Guide for *TKAM* 3.2: In order to better understand some of the main issues and themes in *To Kill a Mockingbird* students can fill in and discuss an anticipation guide such as the one provided in Chapter 3.2.
- Literature Circles 3.2: Before reading *TKAM*, students can participate in literature circles using young adult novels that share the theme of *Growing Up*. Here are some possible literature circles novels that are also multicultural and/or deal with the same time period:

  - *Bud, Not Buddy* by Christopher Paul Curtis (1999).
  - *Bless Me, Ultima* by Rudolfo Anaya (1972).
  - *The Absolutely True Diary of a Part-time Indian* by Sherman Alexie (2007).
  - *Roll of Thunder, Hear My Cry* by Mildred D. Taylor (1976).
  - *Out of the Dust* by Karen Hesse (1997).
  - *Esperanza Rising* by Pam Munoz Ryan (2002).

- PACA for the Great Depression 3.2: Before beginning to read *TKAM*, you can give students nonfiction text selections about the Great Depression. The PACA is a prereading activity designed to build background knowledge and help students read informational texts.
- Parts of Speech with Artwork 3.5: This grammar activity can also be a prereading activity. Students could be shown artwork related to the themes or setting of *TKAM*.
- Reciting Poetry with "The Haunted Oak" 3.7: In order to develop their oral language skills, students can practice reciting the poem (similar to the reciting music activity) by Paul Laurence Dunbar. The poem is related in theme to *TKAM* and it contains repetition and rhyme, which makes it fun to recite.
- Author's Promise Activity 3.2: This is a prereading strategy teachers can use to help students access the text, ask questions and make predictions, and involves teacher read-aloud (3.3). An example from *TKAM* is provided in 3.2.

## Activities and Strategies to Use during the Reading of *TKAM*

- Sheltered instruction with a poem 3.8: Using the listening activity provided with the Frost poem "The Road Not Taken," students can discuss how the poem relates to *TKAM*. For example, how did Atticus take the "road not taken" when he agreed to take on Tom Robinson's case?
- Reading aloud, shadow reading, audio tapes, and film 3.3: Chapter 3.3 discusses several ways to help students access a work of literature when they do not have the reading proficiency required to read the text. (An audio version of *TKAM* is available, read by Sissy Spacek.)
- Talking to the Text, Double Entry Journals 3.2: Chapter 3.2 discusses several during-reading strategies to help students slow down while they read and connect to the text.
- Close Readings 3.3: Teachers can model how to conduct a close reading of a text using passages from *TKAM*.

- Character Charts 3.2: Students can fill out character charts and create character maps for the characters in *TKAM*.
- Contrastive Rhetoric 3.4: Students can examine the speech patterns of the characters in *TKAM* and rewrite them in Standard English (especially the children's speech).
- Directed Reading Sequence 3.2: Teachers can give students nonfiction selections describing the Scottsboro Trials (real trials in the 1930s that closely align with Tom Robinson's trial) and have students use the DRS to comprehend the selections.
- Timelines 3.3: In order to better understand the plot, students can create timelines for the events in each chapter of *TKAM*.
- Role Play 3.7: Students can develop their speaking skills by role-playing the various events in the novel.

## Activities and Strategies to Use after the Reading of *TKAM*

- Magnetic Poetry 3.4: Students can create magnetic poems that illustrate the themes from *TKAM*.
- Literature Circle presentations 3.2: Students can give presentations sharing their literature circle texts with the class.
- Dramatic Tableaux 3.2: In order to remember the plot and better understand the characters, students can create tableaux representing important scenes from the novel.
- Soundtrack—song lyrics grammar activity 3.5: Students can create a soundtrack for events in the novel and then examine the grammar of the lyrics of one of the songs.
- Music 3.7: As a speaking activity, students can share the songs they chose and the lyrics with the class. Students can sing along with the music.
- Five-paragraph essay 3.4: Students can write an essay answering one of the Essential Questions and relating it to the novel.
- Chattaccini 3.4: Students can be given topics from *TKAM* and use this writing activity to develop fluency and generate ideas for their essays.
- Read-Around Groups (RAGS) 3.4: Students can read and respond to each other's essays through this peer revision activity.
- Paideia Seminar 3.3: Students can use the novel as their text for this discussion activity. Students could discuss and debate the questions: Should they keep the information about Boo quiet? Why was Tom Robinson found guilty?
- Storytelling 3.7: In order to develop their oral language proficiency, students could share a story from their background that has shaped who they are as a person. This can be part of the cultural influences project.

## Concluding Remarks

As you think about unit design in your own ELA classroom and you think about the specific ELLs you will be and currently are working with, we hope you remember that, for the most part, what is good teaching for English-proficient students is often what is good teaching for ELLs; good teaching, however, also takes into account the second language developmental needs of the ELLs in our classrooms, not only teaching them the content matter but also helping them increase their English language proficiency as well. We hope that you can use these strategies in your classroom to promote reading, writing, speaking, and listening regardless of the type of students you have. And we also hope that after reading this book you can take all of the wonderful and engaging things you do in your classroom and have a few more ideas about how to make them work for ELLs.

# Resources

# Internet Resources for Teachers

The following are general ELL teaching resources that can be found on the internet. Annotations have been provided to assist you in your selections. The sites have been selected for accuracy, credibility, and durability. We have tried to give priority to sites whose sponsors have longstanding reputations for service to the public good (e.g. professional organizations, museums, government organizations, and colleges and universities). Nonetheless, keep in mind that, because the internet is fluid, you will need to review content carefully. Should a URL not work, enter the resource's name into a search engine to find an updated web address.

## Professional Organizations and Journals

American Council on the Teaching of Foreign Languages: www.actfl.org/
Computer-Assisted Language Instruction Consortium: https://calico.org
*Heritage Language Journal*: www.heritagelanguages.org/
*Internet TESL Journal*: http://iteslj.org/
Modern Language Association: www.mla.org/
National Association for Bilingual Education (NABE): www.nabe.org
Teachers of English to Speakers of Other Languages (TESOL): www.tesol.org

## Research Centers and Institutes

Center for Applied Linguistics: www.cal.org
  CAL's self-described mission is "improving communication through better understanding of language and culture." Links to research reports, resources, and training services are all provided.

Center for Research on Education, Diversity and Excellence (CREDE)
   Government-funded center designed to conduct research and disseminate knowledge to improve the education of marginalized students. Individual research projects are housed at various universities, for example Center for Applied Linguistics (www.cal.org/crede); Center for Multilingual Multicultural Research (www-rcf.usc.edu/~cmmr/crede.html); UC Berkeley (http://crede.berkeley.edu).

Dr. Cummins' ESL and Second Language Learning Web: www.iteachilearn.com/cummins/
   This website, based on the work of Jim Cummins, makes available research and publications on second language learning and literacy development.

Educational Policy Information Clearinghouse: www.eplc.org/clearinghouse_ell.html
   Links to information resources, research, and reports are provided on this site. Users can also sign up for a free news service.

An ELT Notebook: http://eltnotebook.blogspot.com
   This blog for English language teachers of all levels of experience serves as a forum to exchange ideas, opinions, and teaching strategies.

Language Policy Research Unit: www.language-policy.org/blog/
   This website "supports interaction among researchers, policy-makers, other decision-makers in the area of language policy and planning for education and society." Links to census data, professional journals, and book reviews are included.

Let Everyone Participate: www.lep.gov/
   LEP.gov promotes fair language access to federal programs and serves as a clearinghouse, providing and linking to information, tools, and technical assistance regarding limited English proficiency and language services.

National Clearinghouse for English Language Acquisition and Language Instruction Education Programs: www.ncela.gwu.edu/
   Funded by the U.S. Department of Education, this clearinghouse collects, analyzes, and disseminates information about language instruction educational programs for ELLs.

National Institute on the Education of At-Risk Students: www.ed.gov/offices/OERI/At-Risk/index.html
   The At-Risk Institute supports a range of research and development activities designed to improve the education of students at risk of educational failure because of limited English proficiency, poverty, race, geographic location, or economic disadvantage.

Office of English Language Acquisition (OELA): www.ed.gov/about/offices/list/oela/index.html
   The two-fold mission of OELA is to ensure academic success for ELLs and immigrant students by attaining English proficiency and to assist in building the nation's capacity in critical foreign languages.

Tapestry at the University of South Florida: http://tapestry.usf.edu/
   Series of free video lectures by experts in the field of teaching English to speakers of other languages. Topics include Legal Issues and ESOL, Special Education and ESOL, Content Instruction, and Dialect Diversity.

## Classroom Teaching Resources

BILING: Forum for Discussion of Research on Bilingualism and Bilingual Education: http://lists.asu.edu/archives/biling.html
   Searchable archive of discussions on related issues and topics.

Culture Grams: www.culturegrams.com/
   Although this site requires a registration fee, many school libraries and districts opt to sub-

scribe so that the entire faculty has access to these highly informative profiles purporting to provide "an insider's perspective on daily life and culture, including the history, customs, and lifestyles of the world's people."

Dave's ESL Café: www.eslcafe.com

This "Internet Meeting Place" can be accessed by teachers and students alike. The easily navigated site offers resources such as idioms, pronunciation help, a photo gallery, and an "idea cookbook" for teachers.

Differentiated Instruction: www.frsd.k12.nj.us/rfmslibrarylab/di/differentiated_instruction.htm

Links, strategies, and tools for effectively reaching all students in a heterogeneous educational environment.

ELL/ESOL Resource Downloads: www.missouri-pirc.org/esol_downloads.html

This bilingual (English/Spanish) site from Missouri offers a range of downloadable resources for parents and educators.

ELL Links for the Linguistically Diverse Educator: www.western.edu/faculty/kwieseman/ELL/LDE_Strategies.htm

This gateway site provides dozens of annotated links to assist those who work with ELL students. In addition to information about helpful organizations and federal mandates, links to print resources, strategies for ELL survival, and ideas for instruction are provided.

English Forum: www.englishforum.com/00/teachers/

Links for ESL teachers, dictionaries and reference books, and online exercises and quizzes that can be used with students.

English Language Learning: www.isbe.state.il.us/bilingual/htmls/ellparents.htm

Created by the Illinois State Board of Education, this site provides resources (print and video) in several languages.

ESL Connect: www.eslconnect.com/links.html

This gateway site offers links to scores of other useful ESL sites. The sites are helpfully organized by topics such as ESL Lessons, Homework Help, Crosswords and Puzzles, and English Teaching Ideas.

ESL-Kids: www.esl-kids.com

Free printable flashcards, worksheets, and games that can be used with ELL students.

ESL Kidstuff: www.eslkidstuff.com

Although geared for elementary students, this site nonetheless provides some useful materials such as flashcard images, games, and printables.

ESL Lesson Plans and Resources: www.csun.edu/~hcedu013/eslplans.html

Links to dozens of lesson plans, resources, and other learning activities.

ESL Lounge: www.esl-lounge.com

Teachers can download free lesson plans, learning activities, and worksheets for ESL classroom teaching. Other resources include board games, flashcards, and song lyrics ready for use.

ESL Printables: www.eslprintables.com

This website offers teachers an opportunity to exchange resources such as worksheets, lesson plans, and learning activities. For each contribution you send, you can download 10 printables free of charge.

ESL Teacher Resources (Purdue University): http://owl.english.purdue.edu/owl/resource/586/01

Links to professional resources, both theoretical and practical. The list includes links to organizations and journals of interest to language teachers and language policy developers, as well as online teaching and reference materials.

Gateway to 21st Century Skills: www.thegateway.org

Free and easy access to thousands of lesson plans and other teaching resources.

Help!Kits | ESCORT: www.escort.org/?q=node/149
  Downloadable resource guides to help busy teachers with practical, research-based advice on teaching ELL students.
its-teachers: www.its-teachers.com/
  Quarterly online magazine for English language teachers. In addition to articles and research, you will also find practical classroom applications.
Kathy Schrock's Guide for Educators: http://school.discovery.com/schrockguide/world/worldrw.html
  Links to a wealth of resources for foreign language instruction and ESL education.
Lanternfish: http://bogglesworldesl.com
  Printable teaching resources such as worksheets and flashcards are provided, along with real-world language applications.
Learn English Through Song: www.letslets.com/teach_english.htm
  Designed as a supportive resource for ELLs, this website teaches English grammar, vocabulary, and pronunciation using specially written English language songs.
Letters from Home: An Exhibit-Building Project for the Advanced ESL Classroom: www.postalmuseum.si.edu/educators/4b_curriculum.html
  Intended for grades 8 and above, these enrichment materials help build language and communication skills. The dynamic power of personal letters is highlighted in this collection while students develop English proficiency.
Linguistic Funland: Resources for Teachers and Students of English: www.tesol.net/tesl.html
  Materials, activities, and links are provided in addition to "fun sites" that can be utilized by teachers in the classroom.
Longman English Language Teaching: www.longman.com
  The Great Teachers web page on this site provides teachers' resources, sample exams, and helpful teaching tips.
Mark's ESL World: www.marksesl.com/?source=sft
  A "gateway" site featuring links for teachers, students, and the international ESL community.
Resources for English as a Second Language: www.usingenglish.com/
  The ESL Teacher Resources section provides handouts and printable materials, professional articles, lesson plans, and links to other sites. Tests and quizzes are also available on the site as is a discussion forum for other ESOL educators.
Selected Links for ESL Teachers: http://iteslj.org/ESL3a.html
  In addition to lesson plan and assessment ideas, this site includes language-appropriate readings for students, articles and research papers, and games and activities for language learning.
Tapping into Multiple Intelligences: www.thirteen.org/edonline/concept2class/mi/index.html
  This online workshop allows visitors to explore how multiple intelligences can be used to accommodate ELLs.
Teaching and Learning English Using Online Tools: http://www2.alliance.brown.edu/dnd/dnd_links.shtml
  Created by the NYC Board of Education and Office of ELLs as well as the Education Alliance at Brown University, this site offers a gateway compendium to sites that allows teachers to think about how to incorporate and embed language learning for ELLs into their content classes.
Teaching Diverse Learners (TDL): www.lab.brown.edu/tdl/index.shtml
  TDL is dedicated to enhancing the capacity of teachers to work effectively and equitably with all students. It includes information about teaching and learning strategies; assessment; policy; strategies for working with families; and organizations.
teAchnology: http://teachers.teach-nology.com/web_tools/

Games, glossaries, and printable page-making tools are some of the resources available to teachers on this site.

TESOL CALL-IS (Computer-Assisted Language Learning Interest Section): www.uoregon. edu/~call/cgi-bin/links/links.cgi

Collection of "starter sites" that include K–12 resources, content-rich sites, class activities and techniques, and student-centered sites.

## Culturally Responsive Teaching

Educating All Our Students: www.ncela.gwu.edu/pubs/ncrcdsll/edall.htm

This final report for the National Center for Research on Cultural Diversity and Second Language Learning outlines effective instructional strategies for linguistically diverse students.

Teaching Diverse Learners (The Education Alliance, Brown University): www.lab.brown.edu/tdl/ tl-strategies/crt-research.shtml

The Education Alliance, Brown University, provides a list of research-based strategies and links to promote culturally responsive instruction and learning.

Principles for Culturally Responsive Teaching: www.alliance.brown.edu/tdl/tl-strategies/crt-principles.shtml

A definition and discussion of what is entailed in a culturally responsive pedagogy.

## Clip Art and Images

In addition to the large search engines (Altavista, Google, Yahoo!, etc.), the following are useful sites to access royalty-free clip art and line drawings for educational use.

Classroom Clip Art: http://classroomclipart.com/

A source for free clip art, pictures, and illustrations for use in the classroom.

Clip Art Collection for Foreign/Second Language Instruction: http://tell.fll.purdue.edu/ JapanProj//FLClipart

A royalty-free collection of clip art and line drawings for educational use. Categories include verbs, adjectives, food, sports, and events.

Clipart ETC: http://etc.usf.edu/clipart/index.htm

An online service of Florida's Educational Technology Clearinghouse—with 43,000 pieces of free clip art and growing every month.

Kathy Schrock's Guide for Educators: Clip Art Gallery: http://school.discovery.com/clipart/index. html

Free clip art plus animated clips from Discovery Education.

Kid's Image Search Tools: www.kidsclick.org/psearch.html

Special image databases for art, astronomy/space, animals, and history/society.

My Florida Digital Warehouse: http://myfdw.com

A copyright-friendly database of media assets for students and teachers.

NCRTEC: Using Pictures in Lessons: www.ncrtec.org/tl/camp/lessons.htm

A collection of lesson plans that demonstrate ways pictures and graphic resources can be used effectively in the classroom.

# Literature for Teachers

This section will provide an annotated list of some reader-friendly research articles and texts that offer practical findings and advice on related topics. Although the main findings are synthesized and included in our book, especially in Part 2, this section is intended as further reading for teachers who would like to read more on specific subjects/topics. Also provided is a list of instructional materials that teachers can use in classrooms to help accommodate ELLs.

## Best Practice in ELL Instruction

Chamot, A. U. and O'Malley, J. M. (1987). The Cognitive Academic Language Learning Approach: A bridge to the mainstream. *TESOL Quarterly*, 21 (2): 227–249.
> The Cognitive Academic Language Learning Approach (CALLA) is an instructional model that was developed to meet academic needs of students learning English as a second language in American schools.

Faltis, C. J. and Wolfe, P. M. (Eds.). (1999). *So much to say: Adolescents, bilingualism, and ESL in the secondary school.* New York: Teachers College, Columbia University.
> Resource for secondary teachers on how to improve education for language minority students. Practical suggestions for content area teachers are based on research findings.

Fern, V., Anstrom, K., and Silcox, B. (n.d.). Active learning and the limited English proficient student. *Directions in Language and Education*, 1 (2). Retrieved August 9, 2007, from www.ncela.gwu.edu/pubs/directions/02.htm.
> The conclusions of a focus group that studied active learning and its implications for ELLs.

Genesee, F., Lindholm-Leary, K., Saunders, W., and Christian, D. (Eds.). (2006). *Educating English Language Learners: A synthesis of research evidence.* New York: Cambridge University Press.
> A review of scientific research on the learning outcomes of ELLs in U.S. schools.

Linquanti, R. (1999). Fostering academic success for English Language Learners: What do we know? www.wested.org/cs/we/view/rs/514.

A synthesis of authoritative sources that begin to answer questions such as: What instructional practices and programs work best for ELLs?

Lucas, T. (1993). What have we learned from research on successful secondary programs for LEP students?: A synthesis of findings from three studies. *Focus on middle and high school issues: Proceedings of the Third National Research Symposium on Limited English Proficient Student Issues*. Washington, DC: U.S. Department of Education.

Patchen, T. (2005). Prioritizing participation: five things that every teacher needs to know to prepare recent immigrant adolescents for classroom participation. *Multicultural Education*, 12 (4): 43–47.

A practical guide to helping teachers get to know their students and understand the process of adapting to a new culture.

Tambini, R. F. (1999). Aligning learning activities and assessment strategies in the ESL classroom. *Internet TESL Journal*, 5 (9). http://iteslj.org/Articles/Tambini-Aligning.html.

The author discusses the alignment of instructional objectives and learning strategies in the context of a lesson plan.

TESOL (1997). *ESL standards for preK–12 Students*. Alexandria, VA: TESOL.

In conjunction with *Integrating the ESL standards in classroom practice: Grades 6–8* and *Integrating the ESL standards into classroom practice: Grades 9–12,* the standards can help content area and language arts teachers plan for instruction.

Thomas, W. P. and Collier, V. P. (2002). *A national study of school effectiveness for language minority students' long-term academic achievement.* Berkeley, CA: Center for Research on Education, Diversity and Excellence.

Findings on a longitudinal study that examined the long-term academic achievement of students who participated in different language support programs.

Truscott, D. M. and Watts-Taffe, S. (1998). Literacy instruction for second-language learners: A study of best practices. *National Reading Conference Yearbook*, 47: 242–252.

Investigation and discussion of strategies used by general classroom teachers considered effective with ESL students.

Walqui, A. (2000). Strategies for success: Engaging immigrant students in secondary schools. Retrieved January 17, 2009, from www.cal.org/resources/digest/0003strategies.html.

Ten principles are given for developing effective teaching and learning contexts for immigrant adolescents.

## Cultural Information

Axtell, R. E. (1997). *Gestures: The do's and taboos of body language around the world*. New York: John Wiley and Sons.

Informational guide about gestures and signals, organized by country.

Center for Applied Linguistics (2006). *Refugee families and refugee youth*. Washington, DC: CAL.

Two videos—*A New Day* and *Be Who You Are*—help refugee families and refugee youth adjust to their new lives in the United States. Family adjustment, school life, and learning English are some of the topics covered.

*CultureGrams*. (2006). New York: Ferguson Publishing Company.

Concise cultural reports covering 25 categories, including history, religion, family, and economy.

Dresser, N. (1996). *Multicultural manners: New rules of etiquette for a changing society*. New York: John Wiley and Sons.

An overview of the correct behavior to use in a wide range of cross-cultural situations.

Flaitz, J. (2006). *Understanding your refugee and immigrant students: An educational, cultural, and linguistic guide*. Ann Arbor, MI: University of Michigan Press.

This book is focused on the 18 countries that contribute a majority of refugees and immigrants to the United States and includes interviews with students, information about specific schooling traditions, and country profiles.

Henze, R. and Hauser, M. (2000). *Personalizing culture through anthropological and educational perspectives*. Washington, DC: Center for Research on Education, Diversity and Excellence.

The premise of this book is that teachers can use students' prior knowledge and skills as rich resources for teaching and learning, helping to create culturally responsive schools.

Ioga, C. (1995). *The inner world of the immigrant child*. Mahwah, NJ: Lawrence Erlbaum and Associates.

Incorporating the voices and artwork of immigrant children, this book is a teacher's description of the cultural, academic, and psychological adjustments that these students must make.

Levitan, S. (Ed.). (1998). *I'm not in my homeland anymore: Voices of students in a new land*. Toronto: Pippin Publishing.

Collection of short stories written by immigrant students, reflecting on their experiences.

Mace-Matluck, B. J., Alexander-Kasparik, R., and Queen, R. M. (1998). *Through the golden door: Educational approaches for immigrant adolescents with limited schooling*. McHenry, IL: Delta Systems Publishing Group.

This book examines the needs of recent immigrant students who enter middle school and high school with little or no prior formal schooling and with low literacy skills. The critical features of successful secondary school programs for these students are described and guidelines for school administrators and teachers are provided.

Padron, Y. N., Waxman, H. C., and Rivera, H. H. (2002). *Educating Hispanic students: Obstacles and avenues to improved academic achievement*. Berkeley, CA: Center for Research on Education, Diversity and Excellence.

This report examines factors that must be considered when planning for effective instruction of Hispanic students.

Short, D. and Boyson, B. (2004). *Creating access: Language and academic programs for secondary school newcomers*. Washington, DC: Center for Applied Linguistics.

This book will help district personnel create a newcomer program or enhance an existing program.

## Teachers' Manuals and Guides

Akhavan, N. (2006) *Help! My kids don't all speak English*. Portsmouth, NH: Heinemann.

This book explains how to set up a "language workshop" that helps to expand students' language skills and thinking strategies. Although it has an elementary focus, the sample lesson plans, classroom-tested units of study, and ready-to-use graphic organizers included are nonetheless helpful and can be modified for older students.

Brownlie, F., Feniak, C., and McCarthy, V. (2004). *Instruction and assessment of ESL learners: Promoting success in your classroom*. Winnipeg: Portage and Main Press.

This handbook for teachers provides suggestions for orienting the ELL to a new school, how to assess the ELL, how to modify lesson plans, and how to involve parents.

Cary, S. (2000). *Working with second language learners: Answers to teachers' top ten questions*. Portsmouth, NH: Heinemann.

This easy-to-use book explores topics such as students' cultural backgrounds, encouraging reluctant speakers, and teaching grade-level content to ELLs.

Echevarria, J., Vogt, M., and Short, D. (2007). *Making content comprehensible for English learners: The SIOP Model* (third edition). Boston: Pearson, Allyn & Bacon.

Using a sheltered instruction approach, the authors offer guidelines for implementing their program. An accompanying CD features classroom clips, reproducible resources, and interviews with the authors.

Helmer, S. (2003). *Look at me when I talk to you: ESL learners in non-ESL classrooms*. Toronto: Pippin.

Exploration of the underlying fundamentals of communication and how culture influences messages sent.

Law, B. and Eckes, M. (2000). *The more-than-just-surviving handbook: ESL for every classroom teacher*. Winnipeg: Peguis Publishers.

Written for both elementary and secondary school teachers, this book provides strategies for working with ELLs in the regular classroom.

O'Malley, J. M. (2002). *Authentic assessment for English Language Learners: Practical approaches for teachers*. Reading, MA: Addison-Wesley.

Offers alternative assessment strategies for ELLs that can be used with all students.

Reiss, J. (2005). *Teaching content to English Language Learners*. White Plains, NY: Pearson.

This practical book helps content area teachers apply second language learning theories in their classrooms. Emphasis is on making content more accessible, strengthening vocabulary, and increasing student participation.

Samway, K. D. and McKeon, D. (1999). *Myths and realities: Best practices for language minority students*. Portsmouth, NH: Heinemann.

This book dispels common myths related to ELL students by providing basic background information on issues such as second language acquisition, legal requirements for educating linguistically diverse students, assessment and placement.

Short, D. J. (1991). *How to integrate language and content instruction: A training manual*. Washington, DC: Center for Applied Linguistics.

This manual, intended for teachers, administrators, and teacher educators, presents strategies for integrating language and content. Topics include materials adaptations, lesson plan development, and assessment issues.

Walter, T. (2004). *Teaching English Language Learners: The how to handbook*. White Plains, NY: Longman.

This user-friendly book includes discussions on culture, language acquisition, literacy development, and academic/content area development. A list of resources is also included.

## ESOL Textbooks

Brisk, E. (2006). *Bilingual education: From compensatory to quality schooling*. Mahwah, NJ: Lawrence Erlbaum Associates.

This textbook synthesizes the available research on bilingual education, in an effort to demonstrate that bilingual education is "possible and desirable."

Carter, R. and Nunan, D. (2001). *The Cambridge guide to teaching English to speakers of other languages*. London: Cambridge University Press.

Leading figures in the field contributed to this book on applied linguistics and language studies with particular emphasis on TESOL.

Diaz-Rico, L. T. and Weed, K. Z. (2006). *The crosscultural, language, and academic development handbook: A complete K–12 reference guide* (third edition). Boston: Pearson, Allyn & Bacon.
A textbook that can be used in any introductory ESOL methods course for pre-service or in-service teachers.

Garcia, E. (2002). *Student cultural diversity: Understanding and meeting the challenge* (third edition). Boston: Houghton Mifflin Company.
Garcia puts a focus on culturally responsive pedagogy, including plenty of classroom applications and strategies.

Gonzalez, V., Yawkey, T., and Minaya-Rowe, L. (2006). *English-as-a-second-language (ESL) teaching and learning.* Boston: Pearson, Allyn & Bacon.
Provides theoretical and practical discussions of best approaches and strategies for increasing the academic achievement of at-risk English language learners.

Ovando, C. J., Combs, M. C., and Collier, V. (2006). *Bilingual and ESL classrooms: Teaching in multicultural contexts.* New York: McGraw-Hill.
This classic text integrates theory and practice to provide comprehensive coverage of bilingual and ESL education.

Parker, F. and Riley, K. (2005). *Linguistics for non-linguists: A primer with exercises* (fourth edition). Boston: Allyn & Bacon.
Provides pre-service and in-service teachers with the basic elements of applied linguistics in a way that beginners will be able to understand and apply to the classroom.

Rhodes, R. L., Ochoa, S. H., and Oritz, S. O. (2005). *Assessing culturally and linguistically diverse students: A practical guide.* New York: The Guilford Press.
Provides very practical tools and techniques for assessing ELLs and culturally diverse students in K–12 classroom settings.

Richard-Amato, P. A. (2003). *Making it happen: From interactive to participatory language teaching, theory and practice* (third edition). New York: Longman.
A practical guide to methods of teaching ESL that provides ways to create meaningful interaction in the classroom.

Zainuddin, H., Yahya, N., Morales-Jones, C. A., and Ariza, E. N. (2002). *Fundamentals of teaching English to speakers of other languages in K–12 mainstream classrooms.* Dubuque, IA: Kendall Hunt.
This book includes discussions on culture shock, how languages influence culture, differences in verbal and non-verbal communication, and teaching styles.

## Legal Issues

Bureau of Student Achievement through Language Acquisition (SALA). (2008). *Consent decree: League of United Latin American Citizens (LULAC) et al. v. State Board of Education Consent Decree, United States District Court for the Southern District of Florida, August 14, 1990.* Tallahassee, FL: Florida Department of Education. www.fldoe.org/aala/lulac.asp.
The Florida ESOL consent decree provides a structure that ensures the delivery of comprehensible instruction to which ELL students are entitled.

González, J. M. (2002). *Bilingual education and the federal role, if any . . .* Tempe, AZ: Language Policy Research Unit, Education Policy Studies Laboratory, Arizona State University. www.language-policy.org/content/features/article1.htm.
This article addresses bilingual education in the context of the No Child Left Behind Act.

National Clearinghouse for English Language Acquisition. (2006). *Resources about assessment and accountability for English Language Learners.* Washington, DC: NCELA. www.ncela.gwu. edu/resabout/assessment/index.html.

This article provides an introduction to the issues, a bibliography and webliography, and a web and library pathfinder.

U.S. Department of Education, Office for Civil Rights. (2000). *The provision of an equal education opportunity to limited-English proficient students.* Washington, DC: Author. www.ed.gov/ about/offices/list/ocr/eeolep/index.htm.

An important document explaining Title VI requirements, and compliance issues.

## Language Arts-Focused Research

More citations of English/language arts ESOL-focused research can be found in the references section for Part 2.

Christy, J. (2000–2005). *Helping English language learners in the English and language arts classroom: Teaching today.* New York: McGraw-Hill. Retrieved February 13, 2009, from www. glencoe.com/sec/teachingtoday/subject/help_ELL_lit_la.phtml.

This site gives general strategies for the English classroom, plus skill builders for grammar, literature, and writing.

eTeach. (2008). *Language arts instruction and English language learners.* Retrieved January 17, 2009, from: www.phschool.com/eteach/language_arts/2001_12/essay.html.

Topics of this article include differential preparation for second language schooling and second language literacy development.

Kasper, L. F. and Singer, R. (2001). *Unspoken content: Silent film in the ESL classroom.* Retrieved January 17, 2009, from http://lkasper.tripod.com/unspoken.pdf.

An article that affirms the value of using popular film, and, in this case, silent film, as a resource for enhancing English language learning.

The Education Alliance at Brown University. (2005). *Approaches to writing instruction for adolescent English language learners.* Retrieved January 17, 2009, from www.alliance.brown.edu/ pubs/writ_instrct/apprchwrtng.pdf.

A discussion of recent research and practice literature in relation to the nationwide standards on writing.

## Home–School Collaboration

Chang, J. M. (2004). Junior historians: Doing oral history with ESL and bilingual students. *TESOL Journal,* 2 (4): 7–9. Retrieved February 16, 2009, from www.ncela.gwu.edu/pubs/tesol/tesol-journal/juniorhi.htm.

This article provides a rationale for oral history approaches, and shows teachers how to get started.

Gonzalez, N., Moll, L., Floyd-Tennery, M., Rivera, A., Rendon, P., and Amanti, C. (1993). Funds of knowledge for teaching in Latino households. *Urban Education,* 29 (4): 443–470.

Provides theoretical and practical discussions of best approaches and strategies for increasing the academic achievement of at-risk ELLs. Authors include pertinent case studies, thought-provoking questions, and activities. Especially interesting is the history of immigrant ESL students in the United States.

Moll, L., Armanti, C., Neff, D., and Gonzalez, N. (1992). Funds of knowledge for teaching: Using a qualitative approach to connect homes and classrooms. *Theory and Practice*, 31 (2): 132–141.
A report that shows that, as a result of research, teachers have come to view their students as competent participants in households rich in cognitive resources.

## Teacher Training and Professional Development

Association for Supervision and Curriculum Development. *Differentiated instruction resources.* Retrieved February 16, 2009, from www.ascd.org/research_a_topic/Education_Topics/Differentiating_Instruction/DI_Resources.aspx.
A collection of resources on differentiated instruction including articles, books, videos, workshops, and professional development online courses.

Brown, J. E. (2002). Audio books in the classroom: Bridging between language arts and social studies. *The Alan Review*, 29 (3): 58–59.
Good ideas for how to use audio books with language arts and social studies.

Crandall, J. (1992). Content-centered instruction in the United States. *Annual Review of Applied Linguistics*, 13: 111–126.
An article about the approach whereby the second language is used as the medium for teaching and acquiring subject-specific knowledge.

González, J. and Darling-Hammond, L. (2000). *Programs that prepare teachers to work effectively with students learning English.* Retrieved February 16, 2009, from www.cal.org/resources/digest/0009programs.html.
This article describes pre-service and in-service programs that prepare teachers to work effectively with English language learners.

Haynes, J. (2004). *Tips on communicating: Show your school's mainstream teachers and students how to communicate with your newcomers from the very first day.* Retrieved February 16, 2009, from www.everythingesl.net/inservices/tipsoncommunicating.php.
A practical article showing teachers how to facilitate communication with non-English-speaking students from the very first day of class.

Northwest Regional Educational Laboratory. (2001). *Supporting bilingual and minority teachers: How administrators, teachers, and policy makers can help new teachers succeed.* Retrieved February 16, 2009, from www.nwrel.org/request/may01/bilingual.html.
An article that gives help to schools on how they can better support, encourage, and retain bilingual and minority teachers.

Short, D. (2000). *Training others to use the ESL standards: A professional development manual.* Alexandria, VA: Teachers of English to Speakers of Other Languages.
This book contains tools that will prepare ESL specialists to incorporate ESL standards in their programs.

Snow, M. (Ed.). (2000). *Implementing the ESL standards for pre-K–12 students through teacher education.* Alexandria, VA: TESOL Publications.
Each chapter contains tasks designed to assist teachers in the implementation process.

Tarone, E. and Tedick, D. (2000). *Conversations with mainstream teachers: What can we tell them about second language learning and teaching?* Retrieved February 16, 2009, from http://carla.acad.umn.edu/esl/minnetesol2000.html.
Answers frequently asked questions such as: Why do we need English as a second language or bilingual education?

# Internet Resources for ELLs

In addition to the resources presented here, note that each of the chapters in Part 3 also lists useful resources that may be utilized by students.

## Online Dictionaries

The following is a collection of free-access dictionaries on the World Wide Web.

Alpha Dictionary: www.alphadictionary.com/index.shtml
Cambridge Dictionaries Online: http://dictionary.cambridge.org
Dictionary.com: http://dictionary.reference.com
Die.net Online Dictionary: http://dict.die.net
Encarta World Dictionary: http://encarta.msn.com/encnet/features/dictionary/dictionaryhome.
    aspx
Lexicool: www.lexicool.com
Merriam-Webster Dictionary: www.m-w.com/dictionary.htm
Omniglot: www.omniglot.com/links/dictionaries.htm
One Look Dictionary Search: www.onelook.com
Oxford Dictionaries: www.askoxford.com/dictionaries
Word2Word: www.word2word.com/dictionary.html
Your Dictionary: www.yourdictionary.com

## Dictionaries

Cambridge Learner Dictionaries: www.cambridge.org/elt/dictionaries/cld.htm

This collection includes beginners and advanced learners' dictionaries. Pronouncing dictionaries and grammar resources are supplemented with CDs to aid comprehension. The *English Grammar in Use* is a self-paced study and reference guide for intermediate and above language learners.

Hill, J. and Lewis, M. (Eds.). (1997). *The LTP Dictionary of Selected Collocations.* Sydney: Language Teaching Publications.

Designed for intermediate and advanced learners; frequently used collocations are grouped by nouns, adjectives, verbs, and adverbs.

Kauffman, D. and Apple, G. (2000). *Oxford Picture Dictionary for the Content Areas.* New York: Oxford University Press.

Color illustrations are used to define over 1,500 vocabulary words from the subjects of social studies, science, and math. Although it is intended primarily for elementary and middle school students, this resource can nonetheless be very useful to recent arrivals. Ancillary materials include a teacher's book, student workbook, wall charts, overhead transparencies, and sound recordings.

Lea, D. (2002). *Oxford Collocations Dictionary for Learners of English.* New York: Oxford University Press.

This unique dictionary provides over 170,000 common word combinations to help students speak and write English more naturally and fluently.

Longman Learner Dictionaries: www.longman.com/ae/dictionaries

This collection offers dictionaries for beginning, intermediate, and advanced language learners. Basic picture dictionaries, pronunciation dictionaries, and bilingual dictionaries are all included in this series. Additionally, the *Longman American Idioms Dictionary* helps students understand common American expressions.

*Longman Dictionary of American English.* (2004). Boston, MA: Pearson Education.

Intermediate-level dictionary including full-color pictures and interactive CD-ROM.

## Online Translation Services

AltaVista Babel Fish: http://world.altavista.com/
Applied Language Solutions: www.appliedlanguage.com/free_translation.shtml
Google Language Tools: www.google.com/language_tools?hl=en
Im Translator: http://freetranslation.imtranslator.com/lowres.asp
Omniglot: www.omniglot.com/links/translation.htm
World Lingo: www.worldlingo.com/en/products_services/worldlingo_translator.html

## Internet Sites: English Language Support

DiscoverySchool.com: http://school.discovery.com/students
Study tools and learning adventures help students with homework and class work.
EFL/ESOL/ESL Songs and Activities: www.songsforteaching.com/esleflesol.htm
Lyrics and sound clips are offered for a variety of songs that help students learn vocabulary for things such as colors, shapes, and food, among many other topics.
English Forum: www.englishforum.com/00/students/
Online study resources, interactive English language exercises, online dictionaries, and other tools. Full texts of popular novels are also included.
English Online (E. L. Easton): http://eleaston.com/english.html

In addition to language instruction and support, this site offers quizzes, tests, and links to many social studies topics.

ESL Connect: www.eslconnect.com/links.html

Student visitors to this gateway site can access links to Homework Help, Crosswords and Puzzles, and other activities that support English language learning.

ESL: English as a Second Language: www.eslgo.com/quizzes.html

Tests students' knowledge of subject–verb agreement, prepositions, punctuation, and vocabulary.

ESL Independent Study Lab: www.lclark.edu/~krauss/toppicks/toppicks.html

The ESL Center, housed at Lewis and Clark College in Portland, Oregon, contains speaking and listening exercises and activities that promote learning English as a second language.

ESL Partyland: www.eslpartyland.com

Billed as "the cool way to learn English," this website allows users to enter depending on whether they are a teacher or a student. Students can access interactive quizzes, discussion forums, a chat room, and interactive lessons on a variety of topics.

eViews: English Listening Exercises: www.eviews.net

Although there is a fee associated with this site, there is a free trial available. The listening exercises are designed for intermediate to advanced English students. English is recorded at normal speed and includes comprehension checks.

Grammar and ESL Exercises: http://owl.english.purdue.edu/owl/resource/611/01

Hosted by Purdue University, this site offers the ELL interactive exercises, printable (offline) exercises, and concise explanations of grammar and punctuation rules.

Grammar Safari: www.iei.uiuc.edu/student_grammarsafari.html

This site provides "grammar safari" activities wherein students "hunt" and "collect" common, specific words as they are used in documents accessible on the internet.

Intensive English Institute: Internet English Resources: www.iei.uiuc.edu/student_internet_res. html

Listening resources, oral communication resources, and a movie guide for ELLs are just a few of the helpful links provided on this site.

Interesting Things for ESL/EFL Students: www.manythings.org

This website is for people studying English as a second language (ESL) or English as a foreign language (EFL). There are quizzes, word games, word puzzles, proverbs, slang expressions, anagrams, a random-sentence generator, and other study materials.

Internet Treasure Hunts for ESL Students: http://iteslj.org/th/

Links to scavenger hunts on the internet that develop language skills.

iTools: www.itools.com/

Language tools, translation services, and researching resources.

Learn English: www.learnenglish.de

Online games, tests, quizzes, and pronunciation guides assist students learning English.

Longman English Language Teaching: www.longman.com

In addition to free access to the *Longman Dictionary of Contemporary English Online*, the ELT Teens Resource Library includes online activities, support materials, and free resources for teenage learners of English.

OWL (Online Writing Lab): http://owl.english.purdue.edu/handouts/esl/eslstudent.html

Help with idioms, grammar, spelling, and vocabulary. Links to quizzes, tests, and interactive sites.

Randall's ESL Cyber Listening Lab: www.esl-lab.com

> Listening lab that allows students to practice listening skills, develop a natural accent, and understand slang.

Resources for English as a Second Language: www.usingenglish.com/

> The English Language Reference section provides a glossary of grammar terms, English idioms, and irregular verbs.

Self-Study Quizzes for ESL Students: http://a4esl.org/q/h

> These self-paced quizzes allow ELLs to test their understanding of language features such as vocabulary, homonyms, grammar, and idioms.

To Learn English: www.tolearnenglish.com/

> A site designed to help the language learner including placement tests, lessons and exercises, and a club.

## Audio-Visual Materials

Childs, Charlsie. (2003). *Improve your American English accent: Overcoming major obstacles to understanding*. New York: McGraw-Hill.

> Audio CD.

Collis, Harry. (2007). *101 American English idioms and CD*. New York: McGraw-Hill.

> Book and CD.

Dale, Paulette and Poms, Lillian. (2004). *English pronunciation made simple*. White Plains, NY: Pearson ESL.

> Book and two CDs.

Gilbert, Judy. (2004). *Clear speech from the start: Basic pronunciation and listening comprehension in North American English*. London: Cambridge University Press.

> Student's book with audio CD.

Gillett, Amy. (2004). *Speak English like an American*. Ann Arbor, MI: Language Success Press.

> Book and audio CD set.

Yates, Jean. (2005). *Pronounce it perfectly in English*. Hauppauge, NY: Barron's.

> Sound recording (four CDs).

# Glossary

**Additive bilingualism:** Theory that the acquisition of a second language does not interfere in the learning of the native language; second language can be acquired either simultaneously or after native language development.

**Affective filter:** Created by affective variables such as levels of motivation, self-esteem, and anxiety that can block language acquisition or learning if the variables make language users too self-conscious or too embarrassed to take risks during communicative exchanges.

**Basic Interpersonal Communication Skills (BICS):** In effect, language skills needed for everyday personal and social communication.

**Bilingual education:** Although most instruction is in English, concepts are explained in students' primary language and a sheltered English approach is used for academic subjects.

**Cognitive/Academic Language Proficiency (CALP):** Language skills needed for cognitive/academic tasks in the mainstream classroom.

**Comprehensible input:** Language presented at the student's level of comprehension. Input is made comprehensible through the use of visuals, context, and other cues.

**Developmental bilingual education:** Instruction is provided in the student's native language for an extended time period while simultaneously learning English resulting in bilingualism; often used synonymously with **late-exit bilingual education**.

**Dual-language programs:** Instruction occurs in both the native language and English to develop strong skills and proficiency in both. Also known as **two-way immersion**.

**Early-exit bilingual education:** Transition to English as quickly as possible, often using sheltered instructional strategies; some content instruction in the native language is provided; transition to mainstream in 2–3 years.

**English language learner (ELL):** Student whose limited proficiency in English affects his or her academic achievement in school. Also known as limited English proficient student.

**English as a new language (ENL):** Used by the National Board for Professional Teaching Standards in place of English as a second language (see below).

**English as a second language (ESL):** The learning of English by speakers of other languages; often used synonymously with ESOL (see below).

**English to speakers of other languages (ESOL):** The learning of English by speakers of other languages; often used synonymously with ESL (see above).

**Heritage learner:** Student who is exposed to a language other than English at home. Heritage learners usually have varying degrees of knowledge of the home language.

**Immersion:** Instructional approach wherein 100 percent of the instructional time is spent communicating through the target language; in comparison with submersion, the class is composed mostly of speakers of the target language with only a few nonnative speakers.

**Immersion language instruction:** Instruction—including academic content—in the student's *nonnative* language. Students are mainstreamed into regular, English-only classrooms with no special support.

**Language levels:** This book uses the four language levels: level 1—preproduction; level 2—early production; level 3—speech emergent; and level 4—intermediate fluency.

**Language minority (LM) student:** A student whose primary home language is not English. LM students may have limited English proficiency or may be fluent in English.

**Late-exit bilingual education:** In contrast to **early-exit bilingual education**, transition to mainstream occurs in 4–6 years; significant amount of instruction in native language while gradually increasing instruction in English.

**Limited English proficiency (LEP):** Students whose limited proficiency in English affects their academic achievement in school. Also known as **English language learners (ELLs)**.

**Mainstreaming:** Practice of integrating ELLs into regular classrooms.

**Maintenance bilingual education:** Instruction is delivered in both native language and target language; often used synonymously with **late-exit bilingual education**.

**Pull-out:** Students are pulled out of their regular, English-only classrooms for special instruction to develop English language skills.

**Self-contained:** ELL classrooms located in "regular" schools but separate from regular education classrooms; ELLs are provided with special instruction apart from their peers.

**Sheltered English instruction:** Using comprehensible content and strategies to teach grade-level subject matter in English while simultaneously also developing English language skills. Also known as **Specially Designed Academic Instruction in English**.

**Sheltered immersion:** Instructional approach that promotes English language development while providing comprehensible grade-level content.

**Silent period:** Common, varying period of time during which a new language learner listens to, but does not speak in, the new language—also known as preproduction stage or level 1.

**Specially Designed Academic Instruction in English (SDAIE):** Using comprehensible content and strategies to teach grade-level subject matter in English while simultaneously also developing English language skills.

**Structured immersion:** Students' proficiency levels in English are taken into account so subject matter is comprehensible.

**Submersion:** Instructional approach wherein the class is composed entirely of students learning a target language; 100 percent of the instructional time is spent communicating through the target language.

**Subtractive bilingualism:** When the acquisition of a second language interferes with the maintenance of the native language, effectively replacing the first language.

**Total physical response (TPR):** Instructional approach integrating both verbal and physical communication (and often movement) so that students can internalize and eventually "code break" a new language; especially effective with beginning language students, vocabulary instruction, and students who are primarily kinesthetic learners.

**Transitional bilingual education:** Language acquisition theory emphasizing fluency in learner's native language first, before acquiring fluency in second language.

**Two-way immersion:** Instruction occurs in both the native language and English to develop strong skills and proficiency in both. Also known as **dual-language programs**.

# Notes

## 1.1 Orientation

1 Proposition 227 was part of a referendum in California to abolish bilingual education for ELLs in favor of more instruction in English. The *No Child Left Behind* legislation is a federal initiative to oversee teacher performance and student improvement in literacy and numeracy through such accountability measures as standardized testing in schools.

## 1.7 Not All Parents are the Same: Home–School Communication

1 Two research studies from the Center for Research on Education, Diversity & Excellence (CREDE) have recently been published through the Center for Applied Linguistics. The two books, arising out of a four-year and a three-year study, respectively, center on the solidification of home–school ELL communication. The first, entitled *Creating Access: Language and Academic Programs for Secondary School Newcomers*, describes the ins and outs of an effective education model—newcomer programs for immigrant students—and is designed to help district personnel create a newcomer program or enhance an existing program. The second book, called *Family Literacy Nights: Building the Circle of Supporters within and beyond School for Middle School English Language Learners*, discusses a project to improve students' education through a home–school collaboration called "Family Literacy Nights." The program brought parents of linguistically and culturally diverse students together with teachers and students, resulting in greater parental involvement and improved student learning. This report offers practitioners strategies for implementing similar programs.

# References

## Series Introduction

Ladson-Billings, G. (2001). *Crossing over to Canaan: The journey of new teachers in diverse classrooms*. San Francisco: Jossey-Bass.

## Introduction

August, D. and Shanahan, T. (Eds.) (2006). *Developing literacy in second language learners: Report of the National Literacy Panel on Language-minority children and youth*. Mahwah, NJ: Erlbaum.

Cummins, J. (2000). *Language, power and pedagogy: Bilingual children in the crossfire*. Clevedon, UK: Multilingual Matters.

Kindler, A. (2002). *Survey of the states' limited English proficient students and available educational programs and services: 2000–2001 summary report*. Washington, DC: National Clearinghouse for English Language Acquisition.

Lee, J., Grigg, W., and Donahue, P. (2007). *The nation's report card: Reading 2007 (NCES 2007–496)*. National Center for Education Statistics, Institute of Education Sciences, U.S. Department of Education, Washington, D.C.

National Assessment of Educational Progress. (2005). *The nation's report card*. Retrieved February 16, 2009, from http://nationsreportcard.gov/reading_math_grade12_2005/s0211.asp?subtab_id=Tab_id=tab1#chart>http://nationsreportcard.gov/reading_math_grade12_2005/s0211.asp?subtab_id=Tab_id=tab1#chart>

Rance-Roney, J. (2008). Creating intentional communities to support English language learners in the classroom. *English Journal*, 97 (5): 17–22.

## Part 1

Baca, L. and Cervantes, H. (2004). *The bilingual special education interface.* Columbus, OH: Merrill.

Bailey, A. L., Butler, F. A., Borrego, M., LaFramenta, C., and Ong, C. (2002). Towards a characterization of academic language. *Language Testing Update,* 31: 45–52.

Baker, C. (2001). *Foundations of bilingual education and bilingualism* (third edition). Clevedon: Multilingual Matters.

Bassoff, T. C. (2004). Three steps toward a strong home–school connection. *Essential Teacher,* 1 (4). Retrieved July 17, 2007, from www.tesol.org/s_tesol/sec_document.asp?CID=659&DID=2586.

Boscolo, P. and Mason, L. (2001). Writing to learn, writing to transfer. In P. Tynjälä, L. Mason, and K. Lonka (Eds.), *Writing as a learning tool: Integrating theory and practice.* Dordrecht, the Netherlands: Kluwer Academic Publishers, pp. 83–104.

Brinton, D. (2003). Content-based instruction. In D. Nunan (Ed.), *Practical English language teaching.* New York: McGraw-Hill, pp. 199–224.

Carrasquillo, A. L. and Rodriguez, V. (2002). *Language minority students in the mainstream classroom* (second edition). Boston: Multilingual Matters.

Clark, D. (1999). *Learning domains or Bloom's taxonomy.* Retrieved August 3, 2007, from www.nwlink. com/~donclark/hrd/bloom.html.

Coady, M., Hamann, E. T., Harrington, M., Pacheco, M., Pho, S., and Yedlin, J. (2003). *Claiming opportunities: A handbook for improving education for English language learners through comprehensive school reform.* Providence, RI: Education Alliance at Brown University.

Collier, V. P. (1995). Acquiring a second language for school. *Directions in Language and Education,* 1 (4). Washington, DC: National Clearinghouse for Bilingual Education.

Collier, V. and Thomas, W. (1997). *School effectiveness for language minority students.* Washington, DC: National Clearinghouse for Bilingual Education. Retrieved December 2, 2006, from www.ncela.gwu/pubs/resource/effectiveness/index.htm.

Consent Decree. (1990). Retrieved January 17, 2007, from www.firn.edu/doe/aala/lulac.htm.

Crawford, J. (2004). *Educating English learners: Language diversity in the classroom* (fifth edition). Los Angeles: Bilingual Educational Services.

Cummins, J. (1979). Cognitive/academic language proficiency, linguistic interdependence, the optimum age question and some other matters. *Working Papers on Bilingualism,* 19: 121–129.

Cummins, J. (1980). The cross-lingual dimensions of language proficiency: Implications for bilingual education and the optimal age issue. *TESOL Quarterly,* 14 (2): 175–187.

Cummins, J. (1986). Empowering minority students: A framework for intervention. *Harvard Educational Review,* 56 (1): 18–36.

Cummins, J. (1992). Bilingual education and English immersion: The Ramírez report in theoretical perspective. *Bilingual Research Journal,* 16: 91–104.

Cummins, J. (2001). *Negotiating identities: Education for empowerment in a diverse society.* Los Angeles: California Association for Bilingual Education.

Dalton, J. and Smith, D. (1986). *Extending children's special abilities – strategies for primary classrooms.* Retrieved February 19, 2007, from www.teachers.ash.org.au/researchskills/dalton.htm.

Diaz-Rico, L. and Weed, K. Z. (2006). *The crosscultural, language and academic development handbook* (third edition). Boston: Pearson Education.

Echeverria, J. and McDonough, R. (1993). *Instructional conversations in special education settings: Issues and accommodations.* Educational Practice Report 7. National Center for Research on Cultural Diversity and Second Language Learning. Retrieved May 10, 2007, from www.ncela.gwu.edu/pubs/ncrcdsll/epr7.htm.

Ellis, R. (2005). *Instructed second language acquisition: A literature review.* Report to the Ministry of Education, New Zealand. Retrieved January 18, 2007, from www.educationcounts.edcentre.govt.nz/publications/downloads/instructed-second-language.pdf.

Gay, G. (2000). *Culturally responsive teaching: Theory, research, and practice.* New York: Teachers College Press.

Genesee, F. (Ed.) (1999). *Program alternatives for linguistically diverse students.* Santa Cruz, CA: Center for Research on Education, Diversity and Excellence. Retrieved January 8, 2007, from www.cal.org/crede/pubs/edpractice/Epr1.pdf.

Gold, N. (2006). *Successful bilingual schools: Six effective programs in California*. San Diego: San Diego County Office of Education.

Gollnick, D. M. and Chinn, P. C. (2002). *Multicultural education in a pluralistic society* (sixth edition). New York: Merrill.

Hakuta, K., Butler, Y. G., and Witt, D. (2000). *How long does it take English learners to attain proficiency?* Santa Barbara: University of California Linguistic Research Institute Policy Report (2000–2001).

Hoover, J. J. and Collier, C. (1989). Methods and materials for bilingual education. In M. Baca and H. T. Cervantes (Eds.), *The bilingual special interface*. Columbus, OH: Merrill, pp. 231–255.

Kern, R. (2000). *Literacy and language teaching*. Oxford: Oxford University Press.

Kindler, A. (2002). *Survey of the states' limited English proficient students and available educational programs and services: 2000–2001 summary report*. Washington, DC: National Clearinghouse for English Language Acquisition.

Krashen, S. (1981). *Principles and practice in second language acquisition*. English Language Teaching series. London: Prentice-Hall International.

Long, M. (1996). The role of the linguistic environment in second language acquisition. In W. Ritchie and T. Bhatia (Eds.), *Handbook of second language acquisition*. San Diego: Academic Press, pp. 413–468.

Long, M. H. (2006). *Problems in SLA*. Mahwah, NJ: Lawrence Erlbaum Associates.

Lyster, R. (1998). Recasts, repetition and ambiguity in L2 classroom discourse. *Studies in Second Language Acquisition*, 20: 51–81.

Lyster, R. (2001). Negotiation of form, recasts, and explicit correction in relation to error types and learner repair in immersion classrooms. *Language Learning*, 51 (Suppl. 1): 265–301.

Lyster, R. (2004). Differential effects of prompts and recasts in form-focused instruction. *Studies in Second Language Acquisition*, 26: 399–432.

Lyster, R. (2007). *Learning and teaching languages through content: A counterbalanced approach*. Amsterdam: John Benjamins.

Lyster, R. and Ranta, L. (1997). Corrective feedback and learner uptake: Negotiation of form in communicative classrooms. *Studies in Second Language Acquisition*, 19: 37–66.

Lyster, R. and Mori, H. (2006). Interactional feedback and instructional counterbalance. *Studies in Second Language Acquisition*, 28: 321–341.

Meltzer, J. (2001). *The adolescent literacy support framework*. Providence, RI: Northeast and Islands Regional Educational Laboratory at Brown University. Retrieved August 11, 2004, from http://knowledgeloom.org/adlit.

Meltzer, J. and Hamann, E. T. (2005). *Meeting the literacy development needs of adolescent English language learners through content-area learning. Part Two: Focus on classroom teaching strategies*. Providence, RI: Education Alliance at Brown University.

Oberg, K. (1954). *The social economy of the Tlingit Indians of Alaska*. Unpublished doctoral dissertation. University of Chicago.

Ortiz, A. (1984). Language and curriculum development for exceptional bilingual children. In Chinn, C. P. (Ed.), *Education of culturally and linguistically different exceptional children*. Reston, VA: Council for Exceptional Children–ERIC Clearinghouse on Handicapped and Gifted Children, pp. 77–100.

Ovando, C. and Collier, V. (1998). *Bilingual and ESL classrooms: Teaching in multicultural contexts*. Boston: McGraw-Hill.

Pienemann, M. (1988). Determining the influence of instruction on L2 speech processing. *AILA Review*, 5: 40–72.

Pienemann, M. (1989). Is language teachable? Psycholinguistic experiments and hypotheses. *Applied Linguistics*, 10 (1): 52–79.

Pienemann, M. (2007). Processability theory. In B. van Patten and J. Williams (Eds.), *Theories in second language acquisition: An introduction*. Mahwah, NJ: Lawrence Erlbaum Associates, pp. 137–154.

Ragan, A. (2005). Teaching the academic language of textbooks: A preliminary framework for performing a textual analysis. *The ELL Outlook*. Retrieved 13 August, 2007, from www.coursecrafters.com/ELL-Outlook/2005/nov_dec/ELLOutlookITIArticle1.htm.

Richards, H. V., Brown, A. F., and Forde, T. B. (2004). *Addressing diversity in schools: Culturally responsive pedagogy*. Tempe, AZ: National Center for Culturally Responsive Educational Systems. Retrieved 27 July, 2007, from www.nccrest.org/Briefs/Diversity_Brief.pdf.

Ruiz, N. T. (1989). An optimal learning environment for Rosemary. *Exceptional Children*, 56 (2): 130–144.

Ruiz, N. T. (1995a). The social construction of ability and disability: I. Profile types of Latino children identified as language learning disabled. *Journal of Learning Disabilities*, 28 (8): 476–490.

Ruiz, N. T. (1995b). The social construction of ability and disability: II. Optimal and at-risk lessons in a bilingual special education classroom. *Journal of Learning Disabilities*, 28 (8): 491–502.

Scarcella, R. (2003). *Academic English: A conceptual framework*. Technical Report 2003-1. Irvine, CA: University of California Linguistic Minority Research Institute. Retrieved July 2, 2007, from www.ncela.gwu.edu/res-about/literacy/2_academic.htm.

Skehan, P. (1998). *A cognitive approach to language learning*. Oxford: Oxford University Press.

Swain, M. (1995). Three functions of output in second language learning. In G. Cook and B. Seidlhofer (Eds.), *Principle and practice in applied linguistics*. Oxford: Oxford University Press, pp. 125–144.

U.S. Census Bureau (2005). *Statistical abstract of the United States*. Retrieved February 24, 2008, from www.census.gov/prod/www/statistical-absract.html.

Valdez, G. (2000). Nonnative English speakers: Language bigotry in English mainstream classes. *Associations of Departments of English Bulletin*, 124 (Winter): 12–17.

de Valenzuela, J. S. and Niccolai, S. L. (2004). Language development in culturally and linguistically diverse students with special education needs. In L. Baca and H. Cervantes (Eds.), *The bilingual special education interface* (fourth edition). Upper Saddle River, NJ: Merrill, pp. 125–161.

Zamel, V. and Spack, R. (1998). *Negotiating academic literacies: Teaching and learning across language and cultures*. Mahwah, NJ: Lawrence Erlbaum.

Zehler, A. (1994). *Working with English language learners: Strategies for elementary and middle school teachers*. NCBE Program Information Guide, No. 19. Retrieved May 25, 2007, from www.ncela.gwu.edu/pubs/pigs/pig19.htm.

## Part 2

Anaya, R. (1972). *Bless me, Ultima*. New York: Warner Books.

Anstrom, K. and DiCerbo, P. (1998). *Preparing secondary education teachers to work with English language learners: English language arts*. Washington, DC: Center for the Study of Language and Education.

August, D. and Pease-Alvarez, L. (1996). *Attributes of effective programs and classrooms serving English language learners*. Santa Cruz, CA: National Center for Research on Cultural Diversity and Second Language Learning.

Brisk, M. E. (1998). *The transforming power of critical autobiographies*. Paper presented at the Annual Meeting of the Teachers of English to Speakers of Other Languages. Seattle, Washington, March 17–21.

Carroll, P. S., Blake, F., Camalo, R. A., and Messer, S. (1996). When acceptance isn't enough: Helping ESL students become successful writers. *English Journal*, 85 (8): 25–33.

Cruz, M. (2004). Can English language learners acquire academic English? *English Journal*, 93 (4): 14–17.

Ernst-Slavit, G., Moore, M., and Maloney, C. (2002). Changing lives: Teaching English and literature to ESL students. *Journal of Adolescent and Adult Literacy*, 46 (2): 116–128.

Freeman, Y. and Freeman, D. (2004). Connecting students to culturally relevant texts. *Talking Points*, 15 (2): 7–11.

Goldenberg, C. (1992). Instructional conversations: Promoting comprehension through discussion. *Reading Teacher*, 46 (4): 316–326.

Goldenberg, C. (2008). Teaching English language learners: What the research does—and does not—say. *American Educator*, 32 (1): 8–22.

Groenke, S. L., Scherff, L., and Rodriguez, R. J. (2008). ELL and the English/language arts. *English Leadership Quarterly*, 30 (3): 1.

Kooy, M. and Chiu, A. (1998). Language, literature, and learning in the ESL classroom. *English Journal*, 88 (2): 78–84.

Meltzer, J. and Hamann, E. T. (2005). *Meeting the literacy development needs of adolescent English language learners through content-area learning part one: Focus on motivation and engagement*. Providence, RI: Education Alliance at Brown. Retrieved February 16, 2009, from www.alliance.brown.edu/pubs/adlit/adell_litdv1.pdf.

National Council of Teachers of English and International Reading Association (1996). *Standards for the English language arts*. Retrieved February 11, 2009, from www.ncte.org/standards.

National Council of Teachers of English (2005). *Position paper on supporting linguistically and culturally diverse learners in English education*. Retrieved February 16, 2009, from www.ncte.org/cee/positions/diverselearnersinee.

National Council of Teachers of English, ELL Task Force (2006). *Position paper on the role of English teachers in educating English language learners (ELLs)*. Retrieved February 11, 2009, from www.ncte.org/edpolicy/ell/about/124545.htm.

Olsen, L. (1997). *Made in America: Immigrant students in our public schools*. New York: New Press.

Olson, C. B. and Land, R. (2007). A cognitive strategies approach to reading and writing instruction for English language learners in secondary school. *Research in the Teaching of English*, 41 (3): 269–303.

Rubin, R. and Patterson, L. (2002). Revaluing: Coming to know who we are and what we can do. *Voices from the Middle*, 10 (1): 21–26.

Rubinstein-Avila, E. (2003). Facing reality: English language learners in middle school classes. *English Education*, 35 (2): 122–136.

Saunders, W. M. and Goldenberg, C. (1999). *The effects of instructional conversations and literature logs on the story comprehension and thematic understanding of English proficient and limited English proficient students*. Long Beach, CA: California State University.

Wolfe, P. (2004). The owl cried: Reading abstract literary concepts with ESL students. *Journal of Adolescent and Adult Literacy*, 47 (5): 402–413.

Young, M. W. (1996). English (as a second) language arts teachers: The key to mainstreamed ESL student success. *English Journal*, 85 (8): 17–24.

## Part 3

Achebe, C. (1995). *Things fall apart*. New York: Anchor Books.

Adler, M. (1984). *The Paideia program*. New York: Macmillan.

Alexie, S. (2007). *The absolutely true diary of a part-time Indian*. New York: Little, Brown.

American Council on the Teaching of Foreign Languages (1999). *ACTFL proficiency guidelines—Speaking*. Retrieved December 24, 2008, from www.actfl.org/i4a/pages/index.cfm?pageid=3325.

Anaya, R. (1972). *Bless me, Ultima*. New York: Warner Books.

Anonymous (2007). *Sir Gawain and the green knight: A new verse translation*. (S. Armitage, Trans.). New York: W. W. Norton.

Andrews, R., Torgerson, C., Beverton, S., Locke, T., Low, G., Robinson, A., and Zhu, D. (2004). The effect of grammar teaching (syntax) in English on 5 to 16 year olds' accuracy and quality in written composition: Review summary. University of York, UK. Retrieved on November 9, 2009, from www.york.ac.uk/depts/educ/research/ResearchPaperSeries/EnglishGrammar(Syntax).pdf.

Andrews, R., Torgerson, C., Beverton, S., Freeman, A., Locke, T., Low, G., Robinson, A., and Zhu, D. (2006). The effect of grammar teaching on writing development. *British Educational Research Journal*, 32 (1): 39–55.

Angelou, M. (1994). *Phenomenal woman: Four poems celebrating women*. New York: Random House Publishing Group.

Anstrom, K. and DiCerbo, P. (1998). *Preparing secondary education teachers to work with English language learners: English language arts*. Washington, DC: Center for the Study of Language and Education.

Bean, J. C., Chappell, V. A., and Gillam, A. M. (2005). *Reading rhetorically: A reader for writers*. New York: Pearson/Longman.

Beck, I. L., McKeown, M. G., Hamilton, R. L., and Kusan, L. (1998). *Questioning the author: An approach to enhancing student engagement with text*. Newark, DE: International Reading Association.

Beck, I. L., McKeown, M. G., Hamilton, R. L., and Kusan, L. (2002). *Bring words to life: Robust vocabulary instruction*. New York: Guilford Press.

Beers, K. (2003). *When kids can't read: What teachers can do*. Portsmouth, NH: Heinemann.

Billmeyer, R. and Barton, M. L. (1998). *Teaching reading in the content areas: If not me, then who?* Aurora, CO: MCREL.

Billings, L. and Fitzgerald, J. (2003). Dialogic discussion and the Paideia seminar. *American Educational Research Journal*, 39 (4): 907–941.

Burke, J. (2008). *The English teacher's companion* (third edition). Portsmouth, NH: Heinemann.

Calderon, M. (2007). *Teaching reading to English language learners, grades 6–12*. Thousand Oaks, CA: Corwin Press.

Calkins, L. M. (2001). *The art of teaching reading*. New York: Longman.

Carroll, P. S. and Hasson, D. J. (2004). Helping ELLs look at stories through literary lenses. *Voices in the Middle*, 11 (4): 20–26.

Chopin, K. (1992). *The awakening*. New York: Bantam Books.

Cisneros, S. (2005). *The house on Mango Street*. New York: Random House.

Cohen, E. G. (1986). *Designing groupwork: Strategies for the heterogeneous classroom* (second edition). New York: Teachers College Press.

Conference on College Composition and Communication (1988). *The national language policy position statement*. Urbana, IL: National Council of Teachers of English. Retrieved February 16, 2009, from www.ncte.org/cccc/resources/positions/123796.htm.

Corwin, M. (2001). *And still we rise: The trials and triumphs of twelve gifted inner-city students*. New York: HarperCollins.

Cruz, M. (2004). Can English language learners acquire academic English? *English Journal*, 93 (4): 14–17.

Curtis, C. P. (1999). *Bud, not buddy*. New York: Yearling.

Dickens, C. (2007). *A tale of two cities*. New York: Signet Classic.

Daniels, H. (2002). *Literature circles: Voice and choice in book clubs and reading groups*. Portland, ME: Stenhouse.

Diaz-Rico, L. T. and Weed, K. Z. (2006). *The crosscultural, language, and academic handbook: A complete K–12 reference guide* (third edition). Boston: Allyn & Bacon.

Draper, S. (2001). *Romiette and Julio*. New York: Simon & Schuster.

Echevarria, J., Vogt, M. E., and Short, D. J. (2004). *Making content comprehensible for English language learners: The SIOP model* (second edition). Boston: Allyn & Bacon.

Ernst-Slavit, G., Moore, M., and Maloney, C. (2002). Changing lives: Teaching English and literature to ESL students. *Journal of Adolescent and Adult Literacy*, 46 (2): 116–128.

Ferris, D. R. (1999). One size does not fit all: Response and revision issues for immigrant student writers. In L. Harklau, K. M. Losey, and M. Siegel (Eds.), *Generation 1.5 meets college composition: Issues in the teaching of writing to U.S.-educated learners of ESL*. Mahwah, NJ: Lawrence Erlbaum Associates, pp. 143–157.

Ferris, D. and Hedgcock, J. S. (2005). *Teaching ESL composition: Purpose, process, and practice* (second edition). Mahwah, NJ: Lawrence Erlbaum Associates.

Ferris, D. and Roberts, B. (2006). Error feedback in L2 writing classes: How explicit does it need to be? In P. K. Matsuda, M. Cox, J. Jordan, and C. Ortmeier-Hooper (Eds.), *Second-language writing in the composition classroom: A critical sourcebook*. Boston: Bedford/St. Martin's Press, pp. 380–402.

Fitzgerald, F. S. (2004). *The great Gatsby*. New York: Simon & Schuster.

Fisher, D., Rothenberg, C., and Frey, N. (2007). *English language learners in the English classroom*. Urbana, IL: National Council of Teachers of English.

Flinn, A. (2002). *Breathing underwater*. New York: HarperCollins.

Florida Department of Education (2008). *Bureau of Student Achievement through Language Acquisition: Statistics*. Retrieved January 20, 2009, from: www.fldoe.org/aala/omsstat.asp.

Freeman, D. and Freeman, Y. (2000). Meeting the needs of English language learners. *Talking Points*, 12 (1): 2–7.

Freeman, Y. S. and Freeman, D. E. (1998). *ESL/EFL teaching: Principles for success*. Portsmouth, NH: Heinemann.

Freytag, G. (1900). *Technique of the drama: An exposition of dramatic composition and art* (E.J. MacEwan, Trans.). Chicago, IL: Scott, Foresman and Company. (Original work published 1863.)

Frodesen, J. (2001). Grammar in writing. In M. Celce-Murcia (Ed.), *Teaching English as a second or foreign language* (third edition). Boston: Heinle & Heinle, pp. 233–248.

Gass, S. M. and Selinker, L. (2001). *Second language acquisition: An introductory course* (second edition). Mahwah, NJ: Erlbaum.

Gersten, R. and Baker, S. (2000). What we know about effective instructional practices for English language learners. *Exceptional Children*, 66 (4): 454–470.

Goodman, K. (1986). *What's whole in whole language?* Portsmouth, NH: Heineman Educational Books.

Graham, C. (1978). *Jazz chants*. New York: Oxford University Press.

Graham, C. (1993). *Grammarchants: More jazz chants*. New York: Oxford University Press.

Graves, M. F. and Prenn, M. C. (1986). Costs and benefits of various methods of teaching vocabulary. *Journal of Reading*, 29 (7): 596–602.

Graves, M. F. and Watts-Taffe, S. M. (2002). The place of word consciousness in a research-based vocabulary program. In A. Farstrup and S. J. Samuels (Eds.), *What research has to say about reading instruction* (third edition). Newark, DE: International Reading Association, pp. 140–165.

Haussamen, B., Benjamin, A., Kolln, M., and Wheeler, R. S. (2003). *Grammar alive! A guide for teachers*. Urbana, IL: NCTE.

Hedgcock, J. (2005). Taking stock of research and pedagogy in L2 writing. In E. Hinkel (Ed.), *Handbook of research in second language teaching and learning*. Mahwah, NJ: Lawrence Erlbaum Associates, pp. 597–613.

Herz, S. K. and Gallo, D. R. (2005). *From Hinton to Hamlet: Building bridges between young adult literature and the classics* (second edition). Westport, CT: Greenwood Publishing Group.

Hesse, K. (1997). *Out of the dust*. New York: Scholastic.

Horwitz, E. K. (2008). *Becoming a language teacher: A practical guide to second language learning and teaching*. Boston: Pearson.

Hurston, Z. N. (2006). *Their eyes were watching God*. New York: HarperCollins.

Irvin, J. L., Buehl, D. R., and Klemp, R. M. (2007) *Reading and the high school student: Strategies to enhance literacy*. Boston: Pearson.

Kappell, D. (2009). *Magnetic poetry in the classroom*. Minneapolis, MN: Magnetic Poetry. Retrieved February 16, 2009, from www.magpo.com/educat/teach1.html.

Kaywell, J. (Ed.). (1993–2000). *Adolescent literature as a complement to the classics*. (Vols. 1–4). Norwood, MA: Christopher-Gordon Publishers.

Kooy, M. and Chiu, A. (1998). Language, literature, and learning in the ESL classroom. *English Journal*, 88 (2): 78–84.

Kottler, E., Kottler, J., and Street, C. (2008). *English language learners in your classroom*. Thousand Oaks, CA: Corwin Press.

Krashen, S. (1981a). *Principles and practice in second language acquisition*. English Language Teaching Series. London: Prentice Hall International.

Krashen, S. (1981b). *Second language acquisition and second language learning*. Oxford: Pergamon Press.

Krashen, S. (2003). *Explorations in language acquisition*. Portsmouth, NH: Heinemann.

Langer, J. (1995). *Envisioning literature: Literary understanding and literature instruction*. New York: Teachers College Press.

Lee, H. (1960). *To kill a mockingbird*. New York: Warner Books.

McCauley, J. K. and McCauley, D. S. (1992). Using choral reading to promote language learning for ESL students. *Reading Teacher*, 45 (7): 526–533.

Mundy, J. and Hadaway, N. L. (1999). Children's information picture books visit a secondary ESL classroom. *Journal of Adolescent and Adult Literacy*, 42 (6): 464–475.

Myers, W. D. (2006). *Street love*. New York: HarperCollins.

National Council of Teachers of English and International Reading Association (1996). *Standards for the English language arts*. Retrieved February 11, 2009, from www.ncte.org/standards.

National Council of Teachers of English and International Reading Association (1998). *Rationales for challenged books: Prepared by NCTE in Partnership with IRA*. [CD]. Urbana, IL: NCTE.

National Council of Teachers of English Language Learner Task Force (2006). *NCTE position paper on the role of English teachers in educating English language learners (ELLs)*. Retrieved February 11, 2009, from www.ncte.org/about/over/positions/category/div/124545.html.

Olson, C. B. and Land, R. (2007). A cognitive strategies approach to reading and writing instruction for English language learners in secondary school. *Research in the Teaching of English*, 41 (3): 269–303.

Panofsky, C., Pacheco, M., Smith, S., Santos, S., Fogelman, C., Harrington, M., and Kenney, E. (2005).

*Approaches to writing instruction for adolescent English language learners: A discussion of recent research and practice literature in relation to nationwide standards on writing.* Providence, RI: Brown University.

Parabakht, T. S. and Wesche, M. B. (1997). Vocabulary enhancement activities and reading for meaning in second language vocabulary instruction. In J. Coady and T. Huckins (Eds.), *Second language vocabulary acquisition.* Cambridge, UK: Cambridge University Press, pp. 174—200.

Pennington, M.C. (2003). The impact of the computer in second language writing. In B. Kroll (Ed.), *Exploring the dynamics of second language writing.* New York: Cambridge University Press, pp. 287–310.

Peregoy, S. F. and Boyle, F. B. (2001). *Reading, writing, and learning in ESL: A resource book for teachers* (third edition). New York: Longman.

Pienemann, M. (1989). Is language teachable? Psycholinguistic experiments and hypothesis. *Applied Linguistics,* 10 (1): 52–79.

Pienemann, M. (2007) Processability theory. In B. van Patten and J. Williams (Eds.), *Theories in second language acquisition: An introduction.* Mahwah, NJ: Erlbaum, pp. 137–154.

Pritchard, R. J. and Honeycutt, R. L. (2007). Best practices in implementing a process approach to teaching writing. In J. Fitzgerald, S. Graham, and C. A. MacArthur (Eds.), *Best practices in writing instruction.* New York: Guilford Press, pp. 28–49.

Pullum, G. (1999). African American vernacular English is not standard English with mistakes. In R. S. Wheeler (Ed.), *The workings of language: From prescription to perspectives.* Westport, CT: Praeger, pp. 59–66.

Richard-Amato, P. A. (1996). *Making it happen: Interaction in the second language classroom.* New York: Longman.

Richard-Amato, P. A. (2003). *Making it happen.* White Plains, NY: Pearson Education.

Roberts, T. A. and Billings, L. (1999). *The Paideia classroom: Teaching for understanding.* Larchmont, NY: Eye on Education.

Rodby, J. (1999). Contingent literacy: The social construction of writing for nonnative English-speaking college freshmen. In L. Harklau, K. Losey, and M. Siegal (Eds.), *Generation 1.5 meets college composition.* Mahwah, NJ: Lawrence Erlbaum Associates, pp. 45–60.

Rodriguez, R. (1982). *Hunger of memory.* Boston: Bantam Books.

Rumbaut, R. G. and Ima, K. (1988). *The adaptation of Southeast Asian refuge youth: A comparative study. Final Report of the Office of Resettlement.* San Diego, CA: San Diego State University, Department of Sociology. (ERIC Document Reproduction Service No. ED299372).

Rumberger, R. and Gándara, P. (2000). The schooling of English learners. In E. Burr, G. Hayward, B. Fuller, and M. Kirst (Eds.), *Crucial issues in California education.* Berkeley, CA: Policy Analysis for California Education (PACE).

Ryan, P. M. (2002). *Esperanza rising.* New York: Scholastic.

Samway, K. D. (2006). *When English language learners write: Connecting research to practice, K–8.* Portsmouth, NH: Heinemann.

Sasser, L. (1992). Teaching literature to language minority students. In P. A. Richard-Amato and M. A. Snow (Eds.), *The multicultural classroom: Readings for content-area teachers.* White Plains, NY: Longman.

Scarcella, R. (2003). *Academic English: A conceptual framework.* Santa Barbara, CA: University of California Linguistic Minority Research Institute.

Scarcella, R. C. and Rumberger, R. W. (2000). Academic English key to long term success in school. *University of California Linguistic Minority Research Institute Newsletter,* 9: 1–2. Retrieved February 16, 2009, from http://lmri.ucsb.edu/publications/newsletters/v9n4.pdf.

Selinker, L. (1972). Interlanguage. *International Review of Applied Linguistics,* 10 (3): 201–231.

Shakespeare, W. (1977a). *Julius Caesar.* In A. Harbage (Ed.), *William Shakespeare: The complete works* (ninth edition). New York: Viking.

Shakespeare, W. (1977b). *Romeo and Juliet.* In A. Harbage (Ed.), *William Shakespeare: The complete works* (ninth edition). New York: Viking.

Shakespeare, W. (1977c). *The Merchant of Venice.* In A. Harbage (Ed.), *William Shakespeare: The complete works* (ninth edition). New York: Viking.

Silva, T. and Brice, C. (2004). Research in teaching writing. *Annual Review of Applied Linguistics,* 24: 70–106.

Smagorinsky, P. (2008). *Teaching English by design: How to create and carry out instructional units.* Portsmouth, NH: Heinemann.

Smith, M. and Wilhelm, J. (2002). *Reading don't fix no Chevys: The role of literacy in the lives of young men.* Portsmouth, NH: Heinemann.

Spandel, V. and Stiggins, R. J. (1990). *Creating writers: Linking assessment and writing instruction.* New York: Longman.

Steinbeck, J. (2002). *The grapes of wrath.* New York: Penguin Group (USA).

Strong, W. (1996). *Writer's Toolbox: A sentence-combining workshop.* New York: McGraw-Hill.

Taylor, M. D. (1976). *Roll of thunder, hear my cry.* New York: Puffin Books.

Terrell, T. D. (1991). The role of grammar instruction: A communicative approach. *Modern Language Journal*, 75 (1): 52–63.

Tovani, C. (2000). *I read it, but I don't get it.* Portland, ME: Stenhouse.

Uscategui, M. (2008). *What you say, and how you say it: Examining word choice and voice in writing.* Paper presented at the meeting of the Tampa Bay Area Writing Project, Tampa, FL, September.

VandeWeghe, M. (2007). What about vocabulary instruction? *English Journal*, 97 (1): 101–104.

Walker, L. (1996). *Readers theatre in the middle school and junior high classroom.* Colorado Springs, CO: Meriwether Publishing.

Wallace, C. (2007). Vocabulary: The key to teaching English language learners to read. *Reading Improvement*, 44 (4): 189–193.

Weaver, C. (2008). *Grammar to enrich and enhance writing.* Portsmouth, NH: Heinemann.

Wise, R. (Producer), Robbins, J. and Wise, R. (Directors). (1961). *West Side Story.* [Motion picture]. United States: United Artists Films.

# Index

2038

# eBooks

eBooks – at www.eBookstore.tandf.co.uk

## A library at your fingertips!

eBooks are electronic versions of printed books. You can store them on your PC/laptop or browse them online.

They have advantages for anyone needing rapid access to a wide variety of published, copyright information.

eBooks can help your research by enabling you to bookmark chapters, annotate text and use instant searches to find specific words or phrases. Several eBook files would fit on even a small laptop or PDA.

**NEW:** Save money by eSubscribing: cheap, online access to any eBook for as long as you need it.

### Annual subscription packages

We now offer special low-cost bulk subscriptions to packages of eBooks in certain subject areas. These are available to libraries or to individuals.

For more information please contact webmaster.ebooks@tandf.co.uk

We're continually developing the eBook concept, so keep up to date by visiting the website.

## www.eBookstore.tandf.co.uk